WALL STREET CAPITALISM

The Theory of the Bondholding Class

WALL STREET CAPITALISM

The Theory of the Bondholding Class

E RAY CANTERBERY

Florida State University

World Scientific
Singapore • New Jersey • London • Hong Kong

Published by

World Scientific Publishing Co. Pte. Ltd.

P O Box 128, Farrer Road, Singapore 912805

USA office: Suite 1B, 1060 Main Street, River Edge, NJ 07661

UK office: 57 Shelton Street, Covent Garden, London WC2H 9HE

British Library Cataloguing-in-Publication Data
A catalogue record for this book is available from the British Library.

WALL STREET CAPITALISM

ISBN 981-02-3850-9
ISBN 981-02-3851-7 (pbk)

Printed in Singapore by FuIsland Offset Printing

Contents

Preface

"Acknowledgments" seems too weak an expression, bringing to mind a wave of the hand merely to acknowledge someone's presence. Embarking on modern maturity, this author, at least, is moved not to say more, but to put it differently. "Appreciations" might be a better heading for this section. I have been blessed with close proximity not only with many of the giants in the fields of economics and finance, but with their uncommon readership, friendship, and generous support. In expressing my appreciations, my focus on this volume doubtless will leave some out or inadequately thanked. None of my readers and cheerleaders, of course, are responsible for anything that might have come out wrong.

For as long as I have been an economist, John Kenneth Galbraith has faithfully read my manuscripts and has been a source of inspiration and encouragement. Our friendship, as I recall, dates to a 1965 meeting in an oasis of the American desert, the Camelback Inn in Phoenix. I remember sipping, appropriately, water, along with some decent scotch. I was working on a book manuscript published as *Economics on a New Frontier*, an economic history of the Kennedy–Johnson years; Galbraith had served as John F. Kennedy's ambassador to India. Though Galbraith probably could have had any post he wanted, as he has noted, Kennedy was pleased to have him in his administration but at a suitable distance such as in India. From that distance, he nonetheless sent many cables to the White House pushing his own positions on domestic economic policies, as well as urging Kennedy to stay out of Vietnam. Consistently, Galbraith has counseled me to be steadfast in my own progressive positions. In this volume—another that he has eloquently championed—I believe that I have kept the faith.

Little more need be said of John Kenneth Galbraith: it has been written in detail elsewhere. His stature as a leader in the Democratic Party, as one of the most influential economists of the twentieth century, as a supporter of many good causes, and as a distinguished man of letters is assured. I personally appreciate most his sardonic wit, sense of fun, and unerring diplomacy.

The late Hyman Minsky, a mutual friend, was a member of my PhD dissertation committee at Washington University. When he summarized in one sentence the precise meaning of some 200 pages on my theory of foreign exchange, I knew that I was in the presence of genius. Oddly, I read nothing by Hy except and until someone placed his *John Maynard Keynes* in my hands sometime during the mid-1980s, a book that is more Minsky than Keynes. I somehow already knew all about his "financial fragility hypothesis," our communications being seemingly telepathic, my own concerns on the issue paralleling his. We were under some of the same influences, such as our mutual friends, Sidney Weintraub and Joan Robinson, as well as Paul Davidson. The legendary Abba Lerner, another friend, was frequently disputing all four in my presence, Abba being reluctant to accept Keynes's playful descriptions of uncertainty in financial markets. Among the uncertain things, much about financial fragility instructs the present volume and I appreciate having had Hy's bear-like presence for so long; the reader will have to judge the degree to which I am under his influence.

Robert Solow and James Tobin also were important economic advisers in the Kennedy Administration, and went on to win Nobel

Prizes in economics. Kennedy's Council of Economic Advisers was arguably the best ever with Tobin as one of its three members and Solow on its staff. With his quick wit and disarming grace, Solow rightly ranks not only among the best, but among the best-liked of American economists. Still, I have struggled to take seriously his advice that not all economists have a sense of humor, especially since he does not take it seriously either. From its inception as a proposal and an incomplete manuscript, Bob has backed this project. We shared the common goals of educating Bill Clinton on the importance of infrastructure investment and the pitfalls awaiting those obsessed with balanced federal budgets at any cost. As I relate in this volume, Clinton chose or was pushed politically along a different path in his economic program. Its consequences for continuing income and wealth inequalities, not to mention financial instability, already can be documented. At this writing, the worst of the unwinding of debt positions is yet to come. All economists can appreciate Bob Solow's continued and seemingly effortless scholarship on the central economic issues of the day.

James Tobin, like me, has some strain of Minsky in him. Perhaps that is why he, too, was a strong and early supporter of this volume. Galbraith, Solow, and Tobin appeared equally astounded at the rise to popularity of Reaganomics. Early in the Reagan years, in *Challenge: The Magazine of Economic Affairs*, Tobin wrote a courageous but devastatingly accurate and persuasive critique of Reagan's deadly combination of supply-side economics and harsh monetarism. His calibrations on the effects of monetarism turn out to correct, virtually to the decimal point. In this volume I take his argument a step further to show how the historic Reagan–Bush deficits funded by massive bond sales led to the rise of what I call the bondholding class and to still more mischief.

More recently, in the face of rising financial instability, Tobin has proposed a tax on speculative foreign exchange and stock transactions. It is a tax strongly opposed by Robert Rubin, Clinton's second U.S. Treasury Secretary, and by that long-time

defender of free markets, Alan Greenspan, head of the Federal
Reserve System. Herein, I recommend the deployment of the
Tobin Tax not only to foreign exchange speculation but to all
domestic financial speculation. In a departure, I recommend a
higher initial tax, graduated by time to maturity of the financial
instrument. Jim Tobin may find this new version a bit "too
taxing." Still, I greatly appreciate having a shared verdict on
Reaganomics; moreover, with his pioneering proposal of the Tobin
Tax, I feel confident in taking it to the next level.

Everyone appreciates George P. Brockway, even those who
disagree with him, for he disagrees so amicably. He, too, brings
a sense of fun to economics. He read more than one draft of my
manuscript, making some strong recommendations in the early
going. His advice greatly improved the outcome. Among other
things, he directed me to a book by Treval C. Powers that lends
empirical support for my view of the national effects of personal
savings on economic growth. (Moreover, his final chapter has a
take on inflation similar to that of Sid Weintraub.) Ideas from
George's own *The End of Economic Man* populate my chapters on
recommended policies. Not only is his great humanity apparent in
his presence, Brockway's writings elevate economic civility to
elegant heights while bringing uncommon common sense to a
sometimes dismal science. Like Ken Galbraith, George never ends
a letter or a discussion without urging me never to despair, never
to relent to a convenient but misguided conventional wisdom. I
truly appreciate that.

Robert Heilbroner, deservedly one of the most widely read
economists ever, seemed to harbor few doubts about the direction
of this project from its inception. His support has been unrelenting.
Being unsure about the title, I had several alternatives on the cover
page, until it fell into the hands of Heilbroner. "I vote for 'Wall
Street Capitalism'," he said. That was good enough for me. Like
many others, my interest in economics was first aroused by the
vision of economics conveyed so stylishly in his classic *The Worldly*

Philosophers. He has since written many other important books, often warning of the consequences of runaway capitalism. Bob Heilbroner ranks among the great public intellectuals of the final half of the twentieth century, and his social conscience is as great as his heart. Surely, all of us can appreciate his dedication to a panoramic view of capitalism.

H. Peter Gray and John Q. Adams have enticed me back to numerous national economic association meetings and projects. Uniquely, Peter and I served as presidents of both the Eastern Economic Association (EEA) and the International Trade and Finance Association. John (then, too, Tobin and Solow) has served as president of the EEA; he also has been president of the Association For Evolutionary Economics. James Gapinski asked me to contribute chapters to two of his edited volumes; those ideas on savings and the "Casino Effect" reappear in lighter prose in Part IV. Even when I was tempted to take economics a bit too seriously, they have reminded me of how important it is to be eclectic and have fun. Though many would claim that I need no such nudging, I do need the reassurance. Likewise, Max Caskie has given wonderful editing advice on several chapters (while Elizabeth Newberry was skilfully doing the graphics), and eliminated some bad puns. They have urged me to take on various responsibilities that have been exceedingly gratifying. More important, they have shown an appreciation for a wit that seems to retain its edge even when dealing with some pretty dull points. I appreciate their perceptiveness.

These individuals are national treasures. It is not the presently massive net worth of the financial wealth-holders that protects and sustains capitalism. The contemporary obsession with bond prices or stock indices as the proper measures of America's well-being is misplaced; these financial illusions will be unmasked. Then, The Bond Market no longer will be an American icon. The critics of financial excesses better serve sustained prosperity and will gain their rightful places in the pantheon of capitalism.

Introduction

The White House now seems incidental to the future of the American economy. This is our inevitable conclusion once we understand that Wall Street considers money to be more important than politics, that money is controlled by the heads of the Federal Reserve and the U.S. Treasury, and that these people have been handpicked by Wall Street since at least 1979. This is why the first financial reaction to the historic impeachment of President William Jefferson Clinton in 1998 was a strong upward leap in the Standard and Poor's 500 Index—up 22 percent for that year *through* Impeachment Day. Wall Street's quarter-century of control has important implications not only for ordinary Americans but for the global economy.

Look in your rearview mirror and you will see Wall Street gaining on you. At the end of 1998, Alan Sloan, *Newsweek*'s respected Wall Street editor, told us:

> These days, the markets are looking not to the President, but to Greenspan [Chairman of the Federal Reserve Board], Treasury Secretary Robert Rubin and Rubin's No. 2, Larry Summers [Rubin's successor]. Clinton, shminton. If Greenspan, Rubin and Summers left office at the same time, that's what the markets would consider a *real* crisis of state.[1]

Notably, Rubin and Greenspan helped President Clinton orchestrate the smoothest march to Secretary Summers in American

1

cabinet history. After an intra-day recess in the Dow, Wall Street, the only critic anyone seems to care about anymore, accepted Summers' booking with a market ovation, soon to be followed with campaign contributions to Al Gore. Still farther back, we can make out some wonderfully comforting remarks from Alan Greenspan: "The current economic performance ... is as impressive as any I have witnesse.... It is possible we have moved beyond history."[2]

The "end of history" refers to the unquestioned and presumably permanent dominance of U.S. free-market capitalism in the world community. Apparently Greenspan believed that the end of history would be a happy ending for the American story of the twentieth century, already dubbed by Theodore Roosevelt "the American Century." Though this conjectured "happy ending" was a long time coming—roughly a quarter-century—some measures of U.S. economic performance had seemly turned favorable by early 1998. Unemployment and inflation had not been lower since the early 1970s. The federal budget had gone from deep deficits to a surplus. Moreover, the contrasts with other economic powers were stark: Japan was inching toward a 1930s-style depression, the Asian tigers had lost their roar, and Russia was rusting. Even if the U.S. were standing still—amidst a global economy in decline—the American economy still would look pretty good.

Why, then, do ordinary Americans, those who work for a living (when employed), feel such disquietude? For one thing, having been told every day that we live in a global economy, Americans are wondering how they can stay afloat when other major economies sink. For another thing, in the past twenty-five years workers have seen no improvement in their overall living standards. Moreover, their insecurity remains high because workers have been downgraded to temporary or part-time jobs offering few benefits—such as the health insurance that more than forty million Americans don't have. Meanwhile, income and wealth inequalities *have* "moved beyond history."

What could Alan Greenspan possibly have been thinking? It is important to know not only because the head of the Federal Reserve is the most powerful individual affecting jobs, incomes, and wealth in the global economy, but because the Federal Reserve head is a central figure in the story that I want to tell. Verily, many will say that he is the villain of the piece. Like others who have headed the American central bank, chairman Greenspan began his reign with a deep aversion to goods inflation. His self-appointed mission was not only to declare the end of history but the end of this type of inflation. Somehow, one suspects that, in his mind, they were one and the same.

The Great Inflation Anomaly

Goods inflation—and the Federal Reserve has generally been right about this—is closely connected to wages inflation. When the price of labor (the wage rate) goes up, that is bad news, according to recent Federal Reserve heads, and requires quick and brutal punishment. The retribution is unemployment. The *threat* of unemployment has been held—like the suspended blade of a guillotine—over the throats of workers for the past quarter-century. Literally, for those who need to work, losing their jobs is much like losing their lives. Even temporary employment is better than the guillotine; temporary work, too, serves the central bank's anti-inflation aspirations because of the job insecurity it breeds for all workers.

Those benefitting from Federal Reserve policies are on Wall Street. Beginning during the late 1970s, a sustained threat of unemployment and depressed wages, not to mention rising inequality, bred the greatest bull market in securities in American history. However, this confluence of interests of Wall Street, the Federal Reserve System, and the U.S. Treasury has created not only a class rich beyond ordinary imagination, but also a great anomaly. Whereas rising prices for ordinary goods or wages signal inflation and must be restrained by whatever measures may be required, rising prices of financial assets are *considered good news*! No threats are voiced; no obligatory punishment is meted out. Let the bull be; let the bull run! Even a finance official raising a finger in mild dissent is reckoned dangerous: the rites of laissez faire have been extended to bulls. Wages cannot be allowed to keep abreast of productivity, much less outrun it, but financial asset prices racing faster than their fundamental or underlying values not only go unchallenged, but are celebrated.

They should be challenged. Little good can come to a whole society from irrepressibly bullish asset prices outrunning their true economic values. When generally sustained, as they were for nearly two decades in the U.S., this discrepancy between illusion and reality is a speculative bubble. A bubble, it is called, for its tendency to burst. Such a bubble formed over Tokyo during the 1980s. When it burst, Japan slid into deep recession, and its recovery seemed destined for sometime during the twenty-first century. At the end of the twentieth century, Japan's banking system was teetering on the brink of collapse. Though economists are not in complete accord regarding the role of the Great Crash of 1929 in the Great Depression, it was certainly not a good portent of things to come. Bond markets closing and stock markets crashing can destroy a financial system on the way to throwing an entire economy into a tailspin. Since that time when securities became important in the American experience, never has so much volatility visited U.S. and global financial markets.

An old-fashioned anomaly is not necessarily a bad thing. An aberration or two should have an honored place in every society: an aberrant notion serving one's own purpose without damage to another's is not particularly evil. However, the anomaly of high employment and rising wages being bad for society while spiraling financial asset prices and extravagant profits on Wall Street are good, is not an anomaly of this genre. There is more at stake than volatility and rising risks. While about 5 percent of American households were becoming extraordinarily rich from financial asset inflation during the last quarter of the twentieth century, the other 95 percent of households were becoming worse off. Moreover, the two outcomes were linked; those few becoming increasingly wealthy did so at the expense of the rest.

A New and Strange Indicator of American Well-being

Because of this distressing anomaly—goods inflation being bad and financial asset inflation being good—bullishness in financial markets has become the most respectable indicator of American economic well-being. The bondholding class, as we may call it—a small number of people trading in pieces of engraved paper—has taken over. A job for everyone who wants one and growth in middle-class wages have become bad omens for them. Interest rates, bond prices, stock prices, and a plethora of financial derivatives, expanding seemingly apace with the universe, are now more important to the economy than the mundane facts of salaries and wages or full employment. Despite its damage to working Americans, "the bond market" has displaced the late Joe DiMaggio as the great American icon. A few players in the financial markets have gained unimaginable wealth, influence, and political power at the expense of ordinary families.

The bondholding class evolved and continues to thrive in an environment shaped for its own convenience. Its few families own not only virtually all bonds held by households, but most of the value of stocks and other marketable assets. The bondholding class is an elite of super- or supra-rich families, its small population strengthened by some investment bankers and security dealers on Wall Street, most trading on their own accounts. This new American leisure class consists of families whose yearly incomes begin at around $190,000 and go up into the tens of millions of dollars (in 1992 dollars). The families number only about 1.1 million or about 500,000 adults, but their *average* wealth is at least $7.9 million. The support group for the bondholders comprises a small number of professionals on Wall Street, the U.S. Treasury, and the Federal Reserve System—often affectionately called simply "the Fed" or pejoratively "the Reserve." (The New York area, including New Jersey, employed only about 190,000 people in the securities industry by the end of 1996, rising to 340,000 in early 1998.) The bondholding class even has its own editorial page—that of the *Wall Street Journal*.

The Unique Power of the Bondholders

Since the media's fixation is on the Dow Jones Index, why are the few bondholders so powerful? "Class" certainly does not automatically translate into power. After all, the underclass *lacks* power, and the working class did not have much going its way during the final quarter of the twentieth century. The bondholders not only have "class" but *power*, for several reasons.

First, far more wealth is made in bonds than most people are aware and, equally important, the interest payments on government bonds are not only known in advance (unlike stock dividends) but are guaranteed (unlike stock dividends). The most recent data show that the median value of bond holdings among families with incomes of $100,000 or more is nearly *twice* the median value of their stock holdings. (The median is such that half of these families held more and half held less than $58,000 in bonds and $30,000 in stocks.) If we discount the total returns to stocks for risk (by about, say, 3 percent), the average yearly total returns to stocks and bonds during the 1980s and the 1990s were about equal. The last time this relation held was during the Jazz Age.

Second, during the past quarter-century, increased volatility in the bond market made bonds more like stocks and thus good substitutes; wealth holders looking for capital gains could now ply either market, a game not played since the 1920s. Now, the market players move into bonds *or* stocks, depending upon expectations and market conditions. Today, however, bond wealth is more concentrated at the top than stock wealth. Overall, only slightly more than 4 percent of American families own any marketable bonds whatsoever. Yet, the market in U.S. government bonds is the largest financial market in the world with a daily trading volume exceeding $500 billion, or more than $100 trillion yearly. About 95 percent of the market is in the U.S., mostly on Wall Street. Worse, the unprecedented volatility in bond prices due to the activities of the bondholding class has led to an explosion in speculative derivatives, contributing to worldwide financial fragility.

Third, since shareholders time their sales with increases in bond yields, bond market conditions can cause frighteningly abrupt downward movements in the stock market. Contrary to popular opinion, bonds are nowadays held only briefly. The average holding period for a U.S. Treasury bond or note is just one month, or 359 months short of the maturity of the bellwether Treasury. The average holding period for a Treasury bill is three weeks, a week short of the shortest-lived T-bill. The tight connection between the bond and stock markets gives the bondholding class still more power—power over the fate of stock prices.

Fourth, since monetary policy has been the dominant public policy instrument for a quarter century, and since the bondholders decide the destiny of bond *and* stockholders, the Federal Reserve has conducted monetary policy with a view toward keeping the bondholders happy. Because of the bondholders primal fear of inflation, monetary policy has had a strong anti-inflationary, anti-growth, and anti-employment bias. The tango between the bondholding class and the monetary and fiscal authorities not only set the pace for American economic policy for the last decades of the twentieth century, but continues. It not only endures, it dominates the global dance floor.

Odd as it may seem, these nodes of power of the bondholding class seem invisible to the world at large. Even people highly

knowledgeable of the exercise of governing power have been slow
to understand the prodigious power of the bondholders. Not until
1993 did James Carville, then an important political adviser to
President-elect Bill Clinton, confide, "I used to think if there was
reincarnation, I wanted to come back as the President or the Pope
or a .400 baseball hitter, but now I want to come back as the
bond market. You can intimidate everybody." When President-elect
Clinton's key economic advisers told him that he would have to
go along with Greenspan's guardianship of the bondholders, the
President, one of America's most informed economic policy wonks,
first responded: "You mean to tell me that the success of the
[economic] program and my reelection hinges on the Federal
Reserve and a bunch of fucking bond traders?"[3] As Clinton was
made to realize, when he stepped into the White House, he
became the tenant of Alan Greenspan.

How Ordinary People are Hurt

The few wealthy families often have only as much power as money
can buy. The bondholding class, however, has far more power
than its massive net worth confers, which brings us to the power
most damaging to ordinary people. The American bondholders
have redefined progress to benefit mostly themselves. In turn, since
Wall Street depends on the rich for its profits, it has revamped
its indicators of economic well-being, as it defines the "good
economy." Most Wall Street economists say slow, steady growth
with low inflation is better for the economy than sharp booms and
busts. As Wayne Angell, once a Fed governor and later, Chief
Economist at Bear Stearns, a bond underwriting company, put it,
"We do best—and grow most—when the permanent goal is zero
inflation."[4]

What these pundits really mean is that slow growth and zero
inflation are good for *Wall Street*. Once content to end booms
with busts, the Federal Reserve has now compromised by providing

perpetual economic sloth. The head of the Fed conjures up images of frightened *Burgers* pushing wheelbarrows of Deutschmarks toward their grocer during the German hyperinflation of the 1920s. Under these influences, the talking head tells us that the American economy can grow no faster than 2.3 percent yearly and probably no faster than 2 percent, for the unemployment rate cannot remain below about 6 percent for long without igniting ruinous inflation. As early as summer 1997, President Clinton, too, was celebrating slow growth during his incumbency as the "good economy." Good for whom, we might ask? The answer starkly reveals what is at stake for the many on behalf of the few.

A self-serving myth on Wall Street tells us that wealth has been democratized during the past quarter century by widespread participation in booming financial markets. In truth, between 1983 and 1995 the top fifth of American households *gained* about 11 percent to reach an *average* net *financial* wealth value of $730,000. The second fifth *lost* 4.3 percent, the third fifth *lost* 7.8 percent, and the bottom 40 percent *lost* an astounding 68.3 percent, ending up with a *negative* net financial net worth or –$10,600. If we climb back to the top, we find the top 1 percent *gained* nearly 20 percent during this time, enough to elevate the *average* value of their financial wealth to $7.4 million. If they continued to receive their proportionate share of the new wealth created by the bond and stock markets during the next three years, their *average* financial holdings would then reach $10.0 million in 1998.

Did the thunderous financial markets between 1995 and 1999 make up for these losses among working Americans? If the bottom 80 percent of households retained their 1995 share of net financial wealth (rather than continuing to lose wealth), the average addition to their financial health would have been about $1,500. This would be sufficient to bring the bottom 40 percent up to *minus* $9,100. That is, the gains for each of the top million-plus households would be about $2.6 million, while the gains for each of about 89 million families would have been, at best, $1,500. In truth, rising debt has outweighed any bond or stock gains for most families. By 1997, the middle fifth of households—those living the American Dream—had *less net worth* than they had in 1989, after adjusting for inflation.[5]

While the bondholding class was getting richer, ordinary people had a reversal of their former good fortunes. The slower economic growth imposed by the Federal Reserve combined with other forces put downward pressures on wages and employment even as it made corporate CEOs richer through the financial markets. For these reasons, among others, we need to confront head-on this anomaly whereby economic growth and the middle class are sacrificed on the altar of The Bond Market.

In the past, the American economy has grown faster—much faster—without reckless inflation. From 1960 to 1973, for example, real gross domestic product (GDP) growth averaged 4.2 percent a year. Moreover, by spring 1999 the unemployment rate had gone down to 4.2 percent *without any signs* of significant goods inflation. Faster economic growth solves many social problems while easing others. If attitudes and policies were changed so as to increase the yearly rate of growth of the U.S. GDP by only one percentage point, in 2021 the *real* economy would be almost $3.1 trillion larger than what we now can expect. This $3.1 trillion would be shared by everyone, not merely the bondholding class.

A sustained growth pace of 4 percent a year would expand the economy by almost $5 trillion in the same time. The extra $124 to $200 billion achieved annually from faster growth dwarfs the yearly cuts of $7 to $8 billion in the welfare overhaul bill passed in 1995. A cumulative $124 billion yearly would roughly equal the estimated peak amount in the Social Security Trust Fund in 2019, or $2.9 trillion. Most important, an economy growing 1 percent faster would provide better-paying *full-time* employment for every job-seeker. When we did experience some solid growth during 1996–99, the federal budget moved to surplus and, though the gains were in pennies, wage rates rose modestly. By spring 1999, however, global deflation was writing an end to the prospect that ordinary people would share in the explosion in financial wealth.

The Federal Reserve can at least make the claim, whether it is true or not, that it "single-handedly achieved price stability,"—but only in commodities. It remains, at the time of writing, nonetheless vigilant, expecting commodity inflation at any moment. Brisk consumer spending pushed up workers' total wages and benefits an inflation-adjusted 1.8 percent in 1998, the only meaningful increase in five years. Growth in consumer spending at twice the speed of growth in incomes accounted for the year's improvement, an obviously unsustainable pattern. During 1998 consumers had spent 99.5 per cent of their total income. Not only were they borrowing to buy, they were borrowing (often on home equity lines) to place bets on Wall Street. Contrary to his views regarding financial asset inflation, Alan Greenspan was quick to tell lawmakers— as if they needed to be told—that the possible emergence of wage pressure is one of the central bank's principal concerns.

In this, paradoxes abound for the future conduct of monetary policy. Economic growth is now connected, unlike at any time since the Roaring Twenties, to bond and stock prices. Any move by the Federal Reserve to preserve or limit growth will be magnified by the financial markets' reactions. With consumers' confidence tied to the performance of the stock market, a crash would be withering. Though the Fed claimed that its easing of monetary policy in fall 1998 was meant to moderate the effects of global financial turbulence on American financial markets liquidity, its effects were to prop up equity prices and even inflate an Internet stock speculative bubble within the cosmic financial bubble. Worse, a false sense of confidence among consumers was restored.

What Is at Stake and What Can be Done About It

If we are to know what to do regarding the reversal of fortunes for wage earners, we truly need an understanding of the economy to counter the *ideology of the bondholding class*, as I call it. Only then will we discover that the wealth of the bondholders plays a role in the economy very different from that claimed by Wall Street. Rather than providing for real investment in the real economy that will trickle down to real workers, the bondholding class diverts funds away from constructive economic roles and toward wasteful speculation. In effect, perpetual prosperity on Wall Street requires the *evaporation* of personal savings, or what I call the *Angels' Share* of savings.

The citizen willing to read beyond what has become sacred ground, will find a series of significant reform proposals to embrace. The impenetrable veil of money masking true knowledge of money's potentially more humane role in society, once lifted, reveals a way to have interest and principal without bondage. Thereafter, a reform of the Federal Reserve System will free both monetary and fiscal policy to do what they only rarely achieved—foster strong and real economic growth that benefits more than just people at the top.

Much is at stake. The energy force of traditional capitalism seeps out when Wall Street capitalism dominates the society. Capitalism thrives among puddles of inequality sprinkling down from productivity differentials, but it cannot survive amidst a sea of inequality spawned by bondholders. Limits to sustainable inequality exist. When a dominant new leisure class gains power through unearned income—financial capital gains and interest—speculative bubbles float where real production once ruled. When great amounts of money are made from money—not from production—real investments in factories, machines, tools, and people suffer and so do middle class incomes, employment, and wealth.

NOTES

1. Alan Sloan, "The Real Bottom Line," *Newsweek*, December 28, 1998/ January 4, 1999, p. 56.
2. In his remarks before the Joint Economic Committee of Congress, June 10, 1998.
3. Quoted by Bob Woodward, *The Agenda: Inside the Clinton White House* (New York: Simon & Schuster, 1994), p. 84.
4. Wayne Angell, "Virtue and Inflation," *Wall Street Journal*, June 24, 1994, p. A10.
5. The sources for these data are detailed in Chapter 11.

I.

THE BOND MARKET: A NEW AMERICAN ICON

ONE

Goldilocks and the Good News Bears

"There's no use trying," she said: "one *can't* believe impossible things."
"I daresay you haven't had much practice," said the Queen, "When I was
your age, I always did it for half-an-hour a day. Why, sometimes I've believed
as many as six impossible things before breakfast."
  Lewis Carroll, *Alice's Adventures in Wonderland* [1872]

This chapter begins and ends with a fable; in between, we begin
to engage the reality of our economic situation. In 1999, despite
that the U.S. was alone among industrialized nations in running
a budget surplus, Wall Street promoted, and the media generally
accepted, the dubious assertion that all of America's problems had
ended the day the budget was balanced. The media's approbation
of this clearly confirms the bondholders' ability to delimit good
public policy by defining what constitutes good news for Americans.

First, the Good News From the Financial Pages

Two eras in twentieth century America, the Jazz Age and the Great
Bull Market of the 1980s–90s, were defined not only by an
extraordinary exuberance in the financial markets but also by two
other characteristics, unique to these times. First, during most of
both eras, financial asset prices were judged the most important
measures of economic well-being. (Prior to the 1920s, stocks were

17

of little importance to almost everyone.) Second, bond and stock prices moved upward in tandem.

In the 1980s, prices of U.S. bonds began an unmistakable ascent along with the Dow. Even the exceptional but abrupt interruptions in this overall upward trend were instructive. On those rare occasions when the twins did go their separate ways, repercussions were dramatic. Rising bond prices and falling stock prices preceded the crash of 1987, the mini-crash of 1989, and a series of mini-crashes beginning during the summer of 1997. Otherwise, the trend was unmistakable.

Not only did these patterns distinguish "good news" from "bad news" on Wall Street, they dominated the thoughts of citizens and public officials during the last decades of the twentieth century. To understand what Wall Street means by "good news," consider some of the highs and lows in the financial markets. Though the bond and stock markets remained highly volatile throughout 1995–98, lurching down with each rumor of an improving real economy and up with well-received "bad news," the Dow gained 26 percent during 1995 and another 33.5 percent during 1996, the best two-year showing for the barometer in twenty years. The bull continued to roar in 1997; the Dow cracked the 7,000 barrier by Valentine's Day, up 9 percent for the year and rising at an annual rate of 67 percent. On April 29, the U.S. Labor Department reported that Americans' wages and benefits rose a timid 0.6 percent in the first quarter: the bond market soared and the Dow bounded 179.01 points. On May 3, following an announcement by the Clinton administration and congressional Republican leaders of an agreement to balance the budget by 2002, the Dow rose 94.72 points.

The bond market, however, struggled during that week to absorb a flood of new Treasury securities, pulled back amid signals from Alan Greenspan that while inflation had been mild, consumer pricing pressures remained a worry. Thereupon, on May 7, the Dow plunged 139.67 points. Then, after a series of new highs came the "bad news" on May 16 that housing construction had jumped an unexpected 2.6 percent in April and that consumers' confidence was surprisingly strong. The Dow shed its nearly 140 points.

Persistently "good news" came none too soon for these *good news bears.* "The market believes the economy is slowing, and in the meanwhile profits will be good and any increase in interest rates will be modest," glowed A. Marshall Acuff, market strategist at Smith Barney, Harris Upham & Co. "Wall Street isn't too concerned about the economy," he added.[1] Bond prices rose and the Dow shot up, gaining 135.64 and settling at another record high of 7,711.47. Another piece of "good news" was a third straight month of decline in retail sales. The financial markets were looking so good that Ralph Lauren offered shares of stock instead of his famed Polo shirts. The shares opened $6 higher than their offering price. Continued weakness in retail sales (despite bullishness in Polo shirts) and negligible wage growth were sufficient "to bolster the case that the Fed will keep rates steady through their July meeting," said James Solloway, Research Director at Argus Research.[2] In contrast, a six-year *runaway inflation in financial asset prices* was to be greatly admired.

By now, amid signs that workers were beginning to receive modest wage gains for the first time in nearly a quarter century, Wall Street was looking beyond U.S. borders for "good news" and hoped to find it in the troubles besetting Japan, Malaysia, South Korea, Indonesia, Thailand, and the Philippines. The Asian economies, burdened with industrial overcapacity, ominous real estate bubbles, and failing banks, were beginning to have an adverse effect on U.S. manufacturing growth, and some economists were forecasting a substantial reduction in the rate of U.S. GDP growth, which in turn would ease the perceived pressures in the labor markets for employment and higher wages. For Wall Street, this would be "good news."

Some temporary setbacks were to be expected along the way. For instance, when the Hong Kong stock market crashed on October 27, 1997, it triggered a global financial jolt that included a record breaking 550-point one-day drop in the Dow. That, of course, was bad news. Moreover, the Asian crisis was taking its time to slow immoderate consumption. Falling import prices kept people buying, and inflation, rising at an annual rate of only 0.9 percent during the first months of the year, was close to price stability—even though the nation's unemployment rate, at 4.2 percent in May 1998, was the lowest measured since 1970.

By early spring 1999, the Dow had reached a new record as it cracked 9,700 for the first time. A now rapidly-growing economy ignited fears that the Fed would have to raise interest rates. However, the unemployment rate edged up slightly to 4.4 percent in February and the Asian crisis and a slowdown in Europe were finally biting the American economy. "This is a sign that the economy is truly not overheating," said Brian G. Belski, chief investment strategist at George K. Baum & Co., in Kansas City. The "good news" had come none too soon. The inflation-sensitive bond market soared. Larry Watchel, a market analyst at Prudential Securities said, "I'm sure at sometime next week the Dow will be sweeping up toward 10,000."[3]

Now we know. A good news day in the editorial offices of the *Wall Street Journal* and for the Federal Reserve generally is made by rising *financial asset* prices—and, associated with this, rising unemployment. The reasons for celebrating bad news for workers are several, most notably the perceived connection between rising employment and rising inflation. The slightest swell in the federal budget is also decried as "bad news" because budget deficits are thought to be inflationary. The bondholder, of course, hates inflation and so do bankers, central or otherwise. Wonderfully, too, those whose incomes are exclusively or mainly from capital gains, bond interest payments, and stock dividends are immune to the calamity of employment.

And, Now, the Bad News About Why "Good News" is Bearish

"Good news" on Wall Street was not always bad news for working stiffs. During the quarter century following World War II, members of Congress, presidents, and even heads of the Federal Reserve believed that everyone wanting a well-paying full-time job should have it. But concern for workers has gradually eroded; keeping the financial markets happy is the first priority in Washington today. Formerly separated by a cultural distance unbridgeable even by shuttle flights, Wall Street and Pennsylvania Avenue are now as one.

There was a time when most professionals on Wall Street despised the federal government because it redistributed wealth from the rich to the poor—or so they professed. Today, although the Street claims that the government still has "too many regulations on financial institutions and markets," it otherwise has no quarrel with the government. Besides, Wall Street holds a scimitar over the White House and the Federal Reserve: if fighting that dreaded inflation is not given proper priority over ordinary jobs, the Street will crash its own financial markets, a threat infused with greater and greater calamity as the speculative bubble gains girth.

This shift in concern away from the masses and toward a financial elite is so dramatic that we would expect some populist leader to have noticed it and marshaled the troops. However, increasing income and wealth inequalities are presently near-invisible in American politics. Judging from the media and the level of political attention, most Americans are intensely concerned with assuring the continued appreciation in bond and stock market prices and running federal budget surpluses.

Surely this is piffling. What players in the financial markets *think* about federal deficits and the national debt does affect bond and stock prices, but even so, such a broad obsession with *financial asset inflation* seems illogical.

After all, why *should* most people care? Fully 96 percent of all U.S. families hold *no* bonds directly. Some 60 percent of households do not own *any* bonds *or* stocks, and of the 40 percent that do (either directly or indirectly), most own very little in these assets. For example, those in the bottom 40 percent of household wealth holders own an average of only $1,600 in stocks, held mainly (indirectly) in pension and mutual funds. When real estate is factored out, that bottom 40 percent has more debt than assets. (By historical principles, this group should be pulling for cheap money, not fighting it.) *Half* of all stock held by U.S. families is held by the best-off 5 percent. A tiny sliver, or the best-off 1 percent of the wealth holders, hold about *half* the value of *all* financial assets.[4] Bond wealth is even more concentrated. Of the total assets held by the top 1 percent, two-thirds are held in bonds (including open-market paper and notes). In stark contrast, the *bottom 90 percent* of Americans hold only a tenth of their wealth in bonds.

Worse, the cosmic clustering in financial wealth that has occurred since the early 1980s shows no sign of curtailment. Doubtless, the two million or so readers of the *Wall Street Journal* are probably *very* concerned about any real or imaginary effects of public policy on securities prices, but the typical wage earner has little reason to read the *Journal*.

Besides, the Gallup Poll asked flat-out in early 1991, "Which is more important, creating jobs or reducing the deficit?" Jobs won by more than two to one. Despite being told repeatedly by pundits, Federal Reserve chairs, Treasury heads, and presidents alike why balancing the federal budget is essential to save the Republic from hyperinflation, 65 percent of respondents opted for creating jobs and only 28 percent for reducing the federal deficit. Those who must work for a living apparently do not welcome being unemployed.

Although most people are much more concerned about having good jobs than about financial asset inflation, political rhetoric has diverted public attention away from years of stagnant wages and job insecurity toward the *dire consequences* of federal budget deficits and the advantages of surpluses. In truth, the main concern on Pennsylvania Avenue, with Congress on the hill and the White House below it, is *not* with budget deficits: the central worry is the effect of the deficits and national debt on the mental and financial health of the Street where the bondholding class trades. Wall Street and the *Wall Street Journal* tell us that deficits *always* cause inflation. Thus, federal deficits are bad news because inflation is bad news, and inflation truly *is* bad news for the few members of the bondholding class. (Of course, we might suspect that Wall Street's true motive is to reduce the size of government by diminishing its revenues and restricting its spending.)

Mostly Bad News "Trickled Down" to Ordinary People

Undeniably, the circumstances have improved enormously for those we might describe as the *rich* (top 10 percent), *very rich* (top 5 percent), *super-rich* (top 1 percent), and *supra-rich* (top half of 1 percent). Moreover, the latter are truly *riche* rich; after smoothing peaks (such as billionaire stock-picker Warren Buffet) and high valleys (the CEOs of medium-sized firms), their *average* pre-tax income in 1992 was $575,900. Averages, of course, can conceal a great deal—even some good deals. In 1975, Alden W. Clausen, then head of the Bank of America, earned $348,018, enough to pay 53 other bank employees, from tellers to loan officers. In 1995, Richard M. Rosenberg, then Chairman and Chief Executive Officer of the same bank, earned $4,541,666 and some cents, enough to pay 116 *more* bank employees—that is, 169 such salaries—even though the bank was downsizing (laying off workers) at that time.

The incomes of the supra-rich grew by about 63 percent during the 1980s to claim *more than half* the total income growth among all families. Thus a true believer in the trickle-down mythology of the bondholding class would expect the 1990s to favor the lesser breeds with a decent shower of dollars if not a Niagara-sized cascade. It hasn't happened. The compensation of General Electric's CEO went from $500,000 in 1975 to $5.25 million in 1995; over the same period, the average earnings of more than 73 million blue-collar and white-collar workers—shipping clerks, nurses, truck drivers—failed to keep pace with the inflation rate, falling to $20,559, down $3,529 from their inflation-adjusted dollars of 1975. The bottom 60 percent of families—nearly a super-majority even by congressional standards—has suffered a *decline* in real incomes. Bad news, not wealth, has trickled down.

Similarly, the poverty rate, no matter how it might be adjusted for this or that, reversed its downward trend in 1979 and had risen by more than two and a half percentage points of the U.S. population by 1997. Some 35.6 million Americans were "officially" poor in 1997. On top of this, not only have the poor become more numerous, they have also become poorer. Conditions grew even worse during the 1990s.[5] In 1997 dire poverty meant a pre-tax income of $9,674 for a family of four, roughly equal to two *monthly* mortgage payments on a $500,000 home. Whereas in 1979 about a third of the poor were "direly poor," with incomes only half or less of the "official" poverty level, by 1997 more than two-fifths of the poor were direly poor.

Some of the very rich became super-rich and many of the very poor became direly poor. The twentieth century's fifty-year trend toward greater economic equality has been, in its last two decades, cruelly reversed.

The Bondholders Look to the Pope of Wall Street

The U.S. government turned with a vengeance from tax finance to debt finance in the 1980s and the early 1990s, and American corporations that were mainly concerned with equity finance shifted primarily into debt finance. Accordingly, bonds began to dominate.

The bond market—once thought dull, because it once was—became a forum of great excitement. Today's few bondholders watch every quiver of every economic indicator for a sign of what may happen to the price of their bonds. These concerns alone are sufficient to keep the *Wall Street Journal* in business, its daily circulation being roughly equal to the number of major bondholding families plus members of their support group on Wall Street and along Pennsylvania Avenue.

When wearing their stockholders' hats, the wealth holders appear to look to the bond market for direction. The truth is, they look *beyond* the bond market to the *Wall Street Journal* and the Federal Reserve chair to find out what might happen next in the bond market. There are precedents; the medieval faith, thought to have been in God, more often than not was in land; the bondholding faith, thought to be in bonds, more often than not was in Alan Greenspan. Bondholders look to the Fed chair, the Pope of Wall Street, for hints of subtle shifts in the interest rates influenced directly by the Reserve. Tension is palpable on Wall Street when Alan Greenspan (or his successor) prepares to speak. It is, in many ways, a medieval spectacle.

The fears of bondholders and bankers are not to be taken lightly. Had they lived in medieval times, the bishop's prayers might have been for them, not for the peasants. The bondholders' common anxiety does not concern the security of their own employment, nor the insecurity of the employment of others. Their anxiety is manifestly about inflation in the prices of ordinary goods and services—of Fords, denims, a steak dinner, and a beer—because goods inflation causes bond prices to fall. Sometimes, when their hands tremble as they hold the bond price page of the day's *Wall Street Journal,* they tremble for good reason.

Their lives have become dreadfully complex. It is not simply inflation they fear. They fear *what the Federal Reserve will do in its attempt to slow the inflation*. They fear that it will take action to raise a key interest rate in its pious devotion to price stability.

Even Alan Greenspan's tortured rhetoric often signaled inflation just around the corner. The connected markets will pass this higher interest rate and inflation anxiety along to all rates in the spectrum of maturities, including the interest rate on long-term bonds. Since the price of a bond moves in the direction opposite to its interest rate, a rising interest rate means a falling bond price and, far worse, a capital loss for the bondholder. In recent years any *hint* of interest rate hikes by the Pope of Wall Street causes a stampede of bears from the bond market.

However, the concerns of the typical family are not so much with the fears of the holders of securities, but with what those fears portend for the family itself. In the white marbled palace of the Federal Reserve Board, what was once inflation anxiety has become psychosis. In his anxiety, Alan Greenspan developed a very unhealthy distaste for economic growth, the growth in the nation's real gross domestic product. A wary public has learned, often at the feet of Greenspan, that rampant inflation necessarily accompanies rapid economic growth, only to sabotage it. Of all sectors of the public, the bondholders most deeply dread the association of inflation and economic growth. The bondholding class has come to fear positive economic growth because of the higher interest rates and capital losses that will darken its path. Few seem to have noticed Alan Greenspan's contradictory stance—namely, the nation can have rapid economic growth *only* if the growth is *slow*!

Whereas the Fed can fool some of the people some of the time, it can no longer fool all of the bondholders at any time. They comprise an advance guard, watching the news. They are ever so alert. Almost anything—a few more autos sold, a modest dip in applications for unemployment compensation, an uptick in the price of gold, an upward ripple in the wholesale price index, a wave in the consumer price index pool, or a vaguely discernable swelling in the index of consumer confidence—can spread a contagion of fear. The slightest hint of improving economic conditions can send the bond holders into a panic bond sell-off!

Always vigilant for bondholder anguish, Alan Greenspan seemed to sense these concerns in his congressional testimony in July 1993:

> The process of easing monetary policy ... had to be closely controlled and generally gradual, because of the constraint imposed by the marketplace's acute sensitivity to inflation.... At the end of the 1970s, investors became painfully aware that they had underestimated the economy's potential for inflation. As a result, monetary policy in recent years has had to remain alert to the possibility that an ill-timed easing could be undone by a flare-up of inflation expectations ...[6]

Soon thereafter, Greenspan began a long round of interest rate hikes.

In February 1994 Fed chairman Alan Greenspan began increasing a key interest rate—out of fear of inflation. Yet it was not impending inflation, but inflation expected *as much as two years later*. After the first interest rate increase, the Dow dropped nearly 100 points in one day, a remarkable decline at the time. By all accounts from the financial experts, the market fell because the interest rate hike of a quarter percentage point was *insufficient to slow the economy*. Thus, the stock market fell because the market players *expected* still more interest rate increases and a slower economy to follow. The Federal Reserve raised the same key interest rate a total of *seven times* by July 1995.

It is easy, therefore, to illustrate how ordinary people are hurt by the perverse fact that good news for them is bad news on Wall Street. In the fullness of time, Greenspan accomplished his mission; signs during the spring and summer of 1995 pointed to an economy on the road to slow growth or sloth. Already, job growth was declining as the economy slowed from a gazelle's gait to a turtle's crawl. Wall Street bond dealers and stock traders broke open the champagne, adding effervescence to the speculative bubble that began to encircle the financial markets. Declaring "temporary victory over [goods] inflation," Greenspan lowered the key interest rate, but only by a quarter percentage point.

The bond and stock markets moved in tandem. While Greenspan was fretting over inflation in commodity prices and upward "pressures" on wages, his policies—aimed at pleasing the bondholding class—assured a sustained bull market in financial assets. The expectation and, later, full realization of lower interest rates on bonds not only gave bondholders tremendous capital gains but gave stock market players an extra trillion dollars in a few months. In mid-September 1995 the Dow cracked the 4,800 barrier (in retrospect, a seemingly modest roadblock) as the bond market rallied on still more weak economic news. Not only had much of the new wealth come directly from the bond market, the price of bonds also became the leading indicator for movements in stocks.

The Great Speculative Bubble of the 1980s and 1990s

Sufficient irony abides in Wall Street's success to fill an F. Scott Fitzgerald novel. Much more asset price inflation followed in the later nineties, as financial asset markets continued to roar. The overall dollar value of the stock market reached an unprecedented 100 percent of the yearly gross domestic product by early 1997 (the previous high being 81 percent of GDP in August 1929). Yet, the financial tempest of the next two years would blow away this immodest record even as the winds of politics blew away President Clinton's political enemies.

By marshaling Wall Street's *bond market strategy*, as I will call it, Greenspan created not just any bull market, but the Great Bull Market of the twentieth century. As early as December 1996 and his famous "irrational exuberance" speech, however, Greenspan realized that he had overdone it; he had created hyperinflation in financial assets. He had used so much leavening in the cake he baked for Wall Street that it threatened eventually to explode, with massive loss of dough. Greenspan did not want to be responsible for the greatest stock market crash in history. If blame was to be avoided, he might find his excuses in the subsequent events.

As a matter of fact, Greenspan was in a great quandary by the end of 1997. Labor markets, by the Reserve's standards, were becoming unbearably tight, and inflation had to be just around the corner. However, if Greenspan raised the federal funds rate, something he was apparently born to do, it might trigger that record-breaking stock market crash. Well, if you can't be good, be lucky. The Asian currency meltdown, the collapse of the Russian economy, and the implosion of a gigantic hedge fund, Long-Term Capital Management, gave Greenspan not only breathing space but also reason to lower the federal funds rate, not once, but three times. Doing for Wall Street what he was unwilling to do for ordinary hard-working Americans, Greenspan created a rally in the American financial markets at the end of a year in which the average daily swing for the Dow Industrials rose to 2.7 percent or as much as 243 points *daily*.

The Fable of the Bears

As we have seen, the standard for stellar economic performance is no longer a low unemployment rate but, rather, rising prices in the securities markets. Only the rise in prices of commodities, ordinary manufactured goods, or capital goods strikes fear deep in the heart of the bondholding class. They have absolutely no fear of inflation in bond and stock prices! From this definition of the good economy came, sometime in 1995, the idea of the *Goldilocks economy*, an economy based not on myth, but on a mildly twisted, though beloved, fairytale:

> *Once upon a time there were three bears: Papa Bear, Mama Bear, and Baby Bear. Papa Bear had a large bond portfolio, Mama Bear held a great amount of stocks, and Baby Bear was*

studying to be a central banker. Baby Bear was reading a comic book on the conduct of monetary policy published by the New York Federal Reserve Bank.[7]

"I think the economy is too hot," said Papa Bear. "Auto sales went up at an annual rate of 8 percent last month, whereas the expected increase was only 2 percent; the data were published in the Wall Street Journal *this morning."*

"Well, I think you are mistaken," said Mama Bear. "Auto sales may have gone up but, when I logged onto the computer, lumber prices were way down. I believe the economy is too cold. I'm going to sell all my stocks!"

"Based on what I just learned from the New York Fed's comic book," spoke up Baby Bear, "I think you're both wrong. When strong sales in one part of the economy are offset by weak prices in lumber, the Fed chair calls those 'mixed signals;' when he senses a lack of direction of the economy up or down, he follows a neutral monetary policy, leaving interest rates where they are. I think the economy is just right!*"*

As we all know, Goldilocks, a bond broker, was simpatico with Baby Bear's temperature reading.

"I suggest you take Baby Bear's temperature as the correct reading for the economy," advised Goldilocks, as she teased her blond curls. "The economy is just right."

"Sell me more bonds," thundered Papa Bear.

"Sell me more stocks," whispered Mama Bear.

And the Good News Bears all lived richly ever after.

But what about the rest of the animal kingdom? The economic conditions were ideal for the financial markets, but the job and income prospects were tepid for those working for a living.

In the greatest economic perversion of capitalism since the 1920s, rentier incomes from financial assets have been moving generally counter to the incomes of working people. The rich put their accumulated personal savings into play in financial markets where the Federal Reserve guarantees returns to be higher than in the production economy in which slow growth or "sloth" is the order of the day. This upside-down, Alice-in-Wonderland capitalism is continuing to widen the already great chasm between the haves and the have-nots.

The world of capitalism has not always revolved around the use of personal savings for speculative gains; nor has public policy always favored slow economic growth and minimal wages for workers. Yet these unhistoric principles, now firmly embedded in our economy, have for the majority succeeded in transforming the American Dream into a nightmare. To better understand the proper role of bonds in American society, we next consider their uses during the 1950s and 1960s. In this nostalgic turn, we learn just how much the financial world has changed.

NOTES

1. The quotation is from an Associated Press release written by John Hendren, May 12, 1997.
2. The quotation is from a New York Associated Press release on June 13, 1997.
3. The quotations are from a New York Associated Press release by Rachel Beck on March 6, 1999.
4. This discussion is based on data from the *1995 Survey of Consumer Finances* by the Federal Reserve System. See "Family Finances in the U.S.: Recent Evidence from the Survey of Consumer Finances," *Federal Reserve Bulletin*, January 1997, pp. 1–24. The $1,600 figure is based on projections through 1997. That is, the Great Bull Market in stocks did not make ordinary Americans better off, after taking into account the erosion in wages and benefits.
5. Most of these income data can be derived from U.S. Bureau of the Census reports. Census data have been combined with other data to present a complete statistical picture of the income and wealth distributions among families and individuals in: Lawrence Mishel, Jared Bernstein, and John Schmitt, *The State of Working America: 1998–99* (Ithaca, NY/London: Cornell University Press, 1999). For detailed tables and charts, see especially Mishel, *et al's* Chapter 1 on family

income, Chapter 3 on wages, Chapter 5 on wealth, and Chapter 6 on poverty. *The State of Working America* is a regular report by the Economic Policy Institute; it is widely considered to be the best source of information on the well-being of American workers.

6. This is a portion of testimony presented by Greenspan before the Committee on Banking, Finance, and Urban Affairs of the U.S. House of Representatives on July 20, 1993.

7. *The Story of Monetary Policy* (New York: Federal Reserve Bank of New York, 1996). This *is* a comic book published by the New York Fed, but not the only one.

———◦◆◦———

TWO

The Widows of Chevy Chase Country Club

"What you doing, Nick?"
"I'm a bond man."
"Who with?"
I told him.
"Never heard of them," he [Tom Buchanan] remarked decisively.
"You will," I answered shortly. "You will if you stay in the East."
F. Scott Fitzgerald, *The Great Gatsby* [1925]

Bonds always have been important to a small minority of Americans. Historically, bonds have provided fixed, assured income for lenders, while retail markets in bonds have provided ready liquidity or cash for both lenders and borrowers. Half a century ago, even the word "bond" evoked images of little, elderly, and more often than not, Republican widows in tennis shoes; trading in bonds was their racket. In action, slow as it often was, they had little need to keep their eyes on the ball.

Typical of these bondholders were the widows of Chevy Chase Country Club in Bethesda, Maryland. Close enough to the U.S. Treasury to visit the source, these sprightly conservative women put their money in bonds, not out of greed, but out of the warm comfort from a safe instrument and its slow yet steady income stream, and out of the assurance that their late, beloved, and long-departed husbands were smiling their approval from Heaven.

33

All was right and in its place in the universe of bonds. Even retail brokers in New York, reputedly trained in fast bucks, were nevertheless content with miserly commissions in exchange for the solitude.

It is hard to say who has changed the most, the lenders or the borrowers. No grieving widow from the fifties or sixties would recognize today's bond market. No investment broker on the expressway to his next fortune would want to be a bond dealer on memory lane. Even the definition of a bond seems oxymoronic today. After all, a bond is supposed to be a "security" representing a debt on the part of the issuer (the borrower) and a loan on the part of the owner (the lender).

Coupon bonds, then, as now, paid a specified amount of interest to the owner every six months, but the term of ownership has been drastically shortened. Then, bondholders held a bond until maturity, when its principal or face value was repaid by the borrower—be it American Motors, the federal government, or the lusty city of Chicago. Nowadays, few would consider such a strategy; the modern bondholder is comforted only by the prospect of reselling the bond next week for a hefty capital gain. Modern maturity is just an AARP publication. Today, the bond market is for speculators.

Recognizing how far the bond market has strayed from its original social purpose helps us to appreciate what is at stake. Not only does this historical shift increase financial fragility, it provides a reason for the relatively new historical bias against strong economic growth and full employment.

Why Rich People Buy Bonds and Stocks, Or Is It Obvious?

Why do people, the widows of Chevy Chase or others for that matter, purchase assets in the first place? Why do they buy bonds, stocks, boats, or houses? The reason, clearly, is they can afford to. Anyone with substantial wealth can buy a variety of assets, and most do. Moreover, they can buy a greater value of assets as their wealth grows. But even for the rich, a bond or a share of common stock is a luxury, for the rich can get along quite well without either. Stocks and bonds are bought with spare cash, therefore they tend to wind up in the hands of the people with the most cash to spare. We should thus not be surprised to find that Bill Gates or Warren Buffet hold more financial securities than a plumber or even a professor of economics.

This reality has not dispelled the persistent myth that bonds and stocks are widely held in great amounts. The *Wall Street Journal* shouts the fact that 37 to 40 percent of American families own stock directly or indirectly and calls it a great achievement of liberty and capitalism. Mostly, however, this is token ownership. As to bonds, they are held by few households. What the *Journal* fails to even whisper is that the 1 percent of families at the top of the wealth pyramid hold nearly half of all financial wealth while the bottom 80 percent hold only about one-sixteenth.

The rich are no longer as conservative in finance as the widows of Chevy Chase. Since the rich can buy what they please, considerations other than mere preservation of capital help them to decide what assets to hold and in what amounts. High on the list of every well-off family is the asset's expected rate of return. If a General Motors bond, for example, has a return of 15 percent half of the time and 5 percent the other half of the time, its expected return (or average return) is 10 percent.[1] If the expected total return on that bond goes up compared to the expected total return on, say, Procter & Gamble common stock, then the bond becomes more attractive, and the amounts purchased will rise. As noted before, for the first time since the 1920s, the returns on both bonds and stocks have been high and not greatly different during the 1980s and 1990s. The parallel patterns for these three decades are dramatized in Figure 2.1. The patterns of returns in all other decades are disparate.

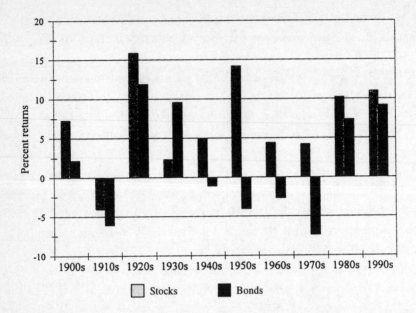

Figure 2.1 Inflation-adjusted Total Returns on Bonds and Stock, 1900–1996

Source: The method for the calculations is derived from Doug Henwood, *Wall Street* (London/New York: Verso, 1997), p. 327. Henwood's results are reported for the earlier decades.

NOTE: Total returns are computed from index numbers representing cumulative real total returns (that is, interest and dividends are reinvested). For stocks, the index number equals the sum of dividend yields plus capital gains, adjusted by inflation measured by the consumer price index (CPI). For bonds, the index equals average interest payments plus capital gains adjusted by the change in the CPI. The data have not been adjusted for the lower risk associated with bonds; had they been, the real returns on bonds would nearly equal those on stocks for the 1980s and 1990s.

The newly perceived opportunity for choice and substitution makes most bondholders, holders of more diverse financial instruments than simply bonds. Therefore, members of the bondholding class, despite their affinities for bonds, hold other assets—and especially stocks—when the expected rates of return impel them in that direction. Owners of large portfolios frequently switch back and forth between stocks and bonds, being hyper-alert to the prospect of capital gains by moving deftly among markets. For them, capital gains taxes, too, are important. But that has always been true, as a matter of faith.

How the "Trickle Down" Myth Was Cultivated, Even at Eisenhower's Chevy Chase

Any self-respecting golfing member of the Chevy Chase C.C. knew about "capital gains" and capital gains taxes during the fifties or sixties. The widows left such odious details to their accountants, but the men had read about the grave importance of low or zero capital gains taxes in Republican campaign literature.

As the Republican party wanted everyone to know, the true concern of the typical Chevy Chase handicapper was far from selfish. Beneficial as capital gains tax cuts might be for the bondholder, any gain was infinitesimal compared with the benefits to redound to the blue collar worker on Detroit's assembly lines. A new issue of bonds from General Motors would enjoy a ready sale if the bond buyers knew that a premature and profitable sale of the bonds would not increase their taxes. In turn, new plants would be built, new equipment and tools installed, and more workers would be hired at $2.50 an hour.

As parables are told and retold they begin to take a shape more flattering to the storyteller. The men in the stately old clubhouse began to favor zero or low capital gains taxes to benefit the working class. The "trickle-down" benefits could be directly seen in the enhanced tips for the caddies upon each reduction or evasion of capital gains taxation. If there were doubts, they could be eased by a nice chat with President Dwight D. Eisenhower (a member during the 1950s) or, later, C. Douglas Dillon, another member and the U.S. Secretary of Treasury issuing bonds during the Kennedy administration. Members often bragged about the tips on the bond market that "Ike" gave them.

"Ike" himself was not rich, and being among the wealthy few did not guarantee being among the few playing Chevy Chase. Though President John F. Kennedy was denied membership in the Club apparently because his money, unlike the Club's wine, was too new to trickle down, there is much to be said, nonetheless, for a pristine golf course, untrampled by a membership so small. The same widows, timid in the bond market, were assertive in the protection of their turf. As the story is told, an invited player, hitting an iron to a green within sight of the clubhouse, not only displaced a sizable piece of turf, but thoughtlessly neglected to replace the divot. Within seconds two golf carts loaded with much of the membership, their hair and scarves flying in the wind, came charging up the fairway, looking much like the Kemper cavalry. "One more unreplaced divot," the surrounded foursome was told, "and you'll never set foot on *our* course again!" As was the turf, the players were put properly in their place.

Most of these club members, too, were giving little thought to capital gains from bonds but were simply enjoying a few rounds of golf and the fixed income from coupon payments. The name "coupon payment" comes from the now-outmoded practice of clipping a coupon off the bond and sending it to the bond issuer, who, in exchange, sent the interest payment back to the bondholder. In truth, most Chevy Chase members were, when not chipping, clipping.

In those charming days, if truth be told, the concern with capital gains taxes came more reliably from buying and selling rapidly appreciating real estate. Still, that capital gains taxation was as much a source of anxiety as a four-foot putt, and the "trickle-down" parable was still invoked. Those haggard men, though exhausted after 18-hole matches, nonetheless found the time over cocktails in the clubhouse to lament the plight of construction workers unemployed because of the oppressive taxes extorted from the Club's membership.

New Bond Issues: They Still Raise Cash for Private Firms and Governments

The fundamental things apply, even as time goes by. A bond holder, even if living in Casablanca, still can expect to be paid interest and, eventually, the principal amount or face value of the bond. Short-term bonds mature in one to five years, intermediate-term bonds in five to ten years, and long-term bonds in as much as thirty or more years. Still, for interest rate quotations, the 30-year U.S. Treasury bond is often called the "bellwether bond."

Today, as in yesteryear, bonds appear in two kinds of markets. Securities are first issued in something called the *primary market*, where their primary gilded colors are unfurled and the buyer is likely to buy a $1,000 corporate bond or a $10,000 U.S. government bond. Procter & Gamble, for example, might issue $50 million of 9 percent bonds due in the year 2020, in order to upgrade its technology or to build new warehouses. The only cash P&G will see is the net proceeds from this initial sale, and P&G does not have to pay off the debt until the year 2020 (unless it chooses to exercise a recall provision to repay earlier).

The primary bond market is innocence personified, much like a young Ingrid Bergman before she went to Italy. A truly conservative CEO rightly considers his company's issuance of new bonds to be a moral, capitalistic act. After all, the debt is backed by the value of their new, advanced factory and equipment. Corporate debt pleases economists too, who once even saw virtue in a timely and modest amount of federal government borrowing.

The Resale of Bonds and the Social Usefulness of Liquidity

The other bond market is the *secondary market* (actually, the "secondhand" market). In it, trade goes on minute-by-minute in outstanding securities, which have been bought at least once and are now being resold. Ownership of these "previously owned securities" changes from Fred to Rose in exchange for cash. Just as the *resale* of a 1992 Ford Taurus yields no direct revenue to the Ford Motor Company, the *resale* of a P&G or U.S. government long-term bond provides no funds for Procter & Gamble, or for Uncle Sam. The ownership of the wealth represented by the car or the bond has simply shifted from one person or institution to another. Unlike most cars, however, a bond does not necessarily depreciate, and the seller may enjoy a profit from say, the resale of a 10-year P&G bond before its maturity date. But while P&G and the U.S. Treasury have no stake in subsequent resales, they are still committed to make interest payments on the bonds; that is, the servicing costs of the bonds continue as time goes by for the bond (until its maturity).

Not so very long ago, the secondary market for bonds was like a long forgotten Rose—an afterthought. And so it still might be, had the market continued to be dominated by Republican (or Democrat) widows, who tended to hold onto their bonds for dear life. Of course, even then a bondholder facing a medical crisis might urgently need cash. In such a crisis, it was convenient for Aunt Grace to be able to resell a few of her bonds. In this sense, the secondary market served a useful social purpose and still does, by providing liquidity.

Watching the Resale of Bonds Has Become Exciting

In the good old days at Chevy Chase the resale market was used almost exclusively for liquidation during family emergencies. In contrast, more recent activity in the secondary bond market rejects family values in favor of the one-night stand. Bond traders buy "long-term bonds" to hold for only a few seconds, minutes, hours, days, weeks or months. Some even prostitute themselves at the altar of greed; sometimes the "John" or bond dealer makes most of the profits. Whereas virginal new issues used to attract a great deal of attention, today, wise bond traders watch every jiggle or even more importantly every *expected* jiggle in the secondary market. They love to speculate in "previously owned" bonds.

Authentically conservative business values continue to play their roles in new issues, since the primary bond market usually retains a direct and true connection to business acumen, responsible action, and social benefits. But while the primary bond market is a source of new funds for business enterprise, the secondary market loses its true social purpose once it is used to perform harmful acts beyond the provision of liquidity or ready sale for those who truly *need* to turn their bonds into cash. The same can be said for stocks. They are no longer bought for their measly dividends; even retirees are seeking capital gains. When secondary markets take on lives of their own, as they have, they become speculative and are little different from the activities at high-stake gaming tables at the Mirage in Las Vegas or at the Trump Castle Casino Resort in Atlantic City.

This sea change in the securities markets, with the secondary market in bonds joining the turnover in stocks as a source of great day-to-day profits, has gone unrecognized by small investors. The Beardstown Ladies Investment Club, comprising some daring senior women, has stayed ahead of the red or blue tennis-shoe crowd by buying only stocks for presumably higher returns rather than bonds for their interest income. Still, the Club's audited returns turned out to be only 9.1 percent yearly rather than what it mistakenly thought was 23.8 percent. Besides, the big players have not turned to bonds for their interest. Just as the divorced Donald Trump still claimed to have good company—since he had himself—the bondholder's interest payments continue as ever. But interest is chump change next to the potential capital gains.

More importantly, the expanding role of the resale market in bonds has led to enhanced conditions for such potential capital gains. When the participants are looking for quick trades, the secondary market dominates; quick trades, especially in large amounts, lead to bond price volatility. Sharp up-and-down movements in bond prices, in turn, provide opportunities for greater capital gains *and* losses. Speculators love volatile markets and volatile markets love speculators.

The total return on very short-term bonds is roughly the coupon rate or, in the case of short-term Treasury-bills, the initial yield to maturity. This comforting, even reliable relationship was once the standard and was true for long-term bonds selling at prices below their face values. For example, the coupon rate on a $1,000 bond increment paying a coupon amount of $100 per year for ten years and repaying the face value amount of $1,000 at the maturity date is a seemingly handsome 10 percent ($100/$1,000). However, if the bond is bought for $900 (i.e., below its par value of $1,000), the yield to maturity rises to 11.75 percent. At a price of $800, the yield to maturity rises still more to 13.81 percent (according to a bond table). In the Chevy Chase era of stable bond prices, members had little reason to sell such an admirably yielding long-term bond. The bond deserved the *nom de plume*, "fixed-income security."

Except for T-bills and very short-term bonds, however, price volatility has led to great instability in yields to maturity. Beginning in the early 1980s, price movements—up *and* down—of 20 percent within a year, with corresponding variations in returns, have become commonplace for bonds more than ten years from maturity. "Of course," the wary citizen says, "you are writing about junk bonds! I invest my money in 'gilt-edged' securities like long-term U.S. Treasury bonds because they always provide a safe return." The good citizen is correct if he holds the bonds and never has to sell them prior to their maturities. If you are an 80-year-old retiree holding bonds maturing in thirty years, you should live so long! But if you are forced by financial circumstances to sell at a time when interest rates are rising (bond prices falling), you could incur a loss or, at best, only a small gain.

The resale bond market has become exciting. We can immediately see how greatly things have changed by looking at bond yields

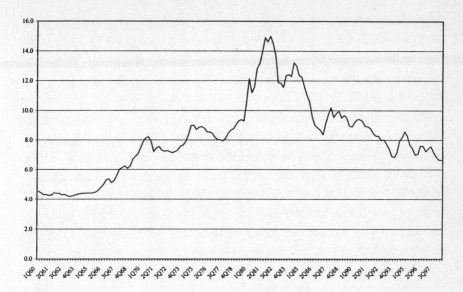

Figure 2.2 Index of Corporate Aaa Bond Yields, First Quarter 1960–Second Quarter 1998

Source: Moody's Investor Service
NOTE: These are average yields on selected private corporate Aaa bonds, seasonally adjusted.

over a long period. Figure 2.2 illustrates a popular selection of corporate bond yields. Long-term federal government bond yields follow a virtually identical pattern. Complete calm left the bond market during the late sixties as the war in Vietnam heated up. The two run-ups in yields during the seventies were related to the OPEC scare and the energy crises. After this, in the eighties, the yields simply went crazy—peaking in 1981 as bond prices collapsed— and have never recovered their traditional stability.

The volatility in individual returns is even greater than that displayed by average yields. Consider, for example, the prices and one-year returns on a U.S. Treasury bond with a coupon rate of $11\frac{1}{4}$ percent maturing in the year 2015. The price of this long-term bond was a little more than $1,540 in 1993. Falling to slightly above $1,320 in 1994, its year-to-year return was a dreadfully negative −7.0 percent. The next year, however, the price leaped to about $1,600 and the total gain to the bondholder was 29.6 percent.[2]

These zigzags in bond prices are important to speculators who are making money on whether prices rise or fall. Those burdened by carrying large portfolios simply switched into stocks in 1994 and back into bonds in 1995. The typical American family, however, can afford bonds only by buying into a mutual bond fund instead of holding a specific bond such as the 2015 Treasury bond. The mutual fund has performed poorly because a fund committed to bonds cannot simply sell all its bonds when bond prices are falling. The mutual fund holder, even those in stocks, has no control over when the fund's securities are bought or sold and can incur heavy losses.

Officials at corporations, the U.S. Treasury, and municipalities could once go for months without checking on bond prices in the secondary or resale markets. Now, they and Federal Reserve officials often receive hourly updates. Any economist who has been present when a major investment bank scandal hits the wires at the Federal Reserve Board of Governors can sense the excitement running from one governor to another. They race around the aisles of their white marble palace in Washington, D.C., talking with animation rarely seen in central bankers, whirling in and out of the chair's sanctuary and vice chair's chapel, seeking absolution. The governors know that U.S. Treasury bond prices will take a dive.

Secondary market prices are watched anxiously because new bond issues must offer buyers yields competitive with the yields available on existing bonds. If ten-year U.S. Treasuries are yielding 8 percent in the secondary market, *new issues* of ten-year Treasuries cannot be offered at yields *below* 8 percent. Any yield lower than 8 percent will cause potential buyers to shun the new issue as a thing defiled. In these circumstances, the best corporate bonds will have to offer yields *above* 8 percent.

Higher interest rates ripple through the economy. The higher the interest payments on a new issue, the more the new issue will cost the Ford Motor Company, the U.S. Treasury, or the city of Miami. This servicing cost of debt must be paid out of corporate profits or, for governments, out of general revenue. Servicing costs alone can bankrupt corporations and municipalities; in fact, in recent history, they have.

Speculators Invade the Old World of Bonds

The world of bonds really has changed. The buyers, once hardcore financial conservatives, the trustees for widows and orphans, are now speculators. The bond dealers now populate a world as fast-moving and exciting as that of stockbrokers. Underhand dealing is, of course, not unknown. The bond market now resembles not so much a marketplace as a giant casino. The U.S. Treasury, once a player with slow reflexes, must now move about the casino with the deftness of a Spanish bolero dancer. The slow dance at Chevy Chase C.C. is over; the winsome widows in tennis shoes have been displaced by sharp speculators doing the fandango in $1,500 Armani suits, silk Adam Smith ties, and black mirror-shine shoes—the "beautiful people." But, if the casino ever closes, it won't be a pretty sight.

NOTES

1. In general, the expected return is the sum of each possible realized total return weighted (multiplied) by the probability of its happening, or $R^e = \sum \rho_i R_i$, where R^e is the expected total return, ρ_i is the probability of realizing R_i, and R_i is the realization of the total return. In our General Motors bond example, $R^e = (.5)(15\%) + (.5)(5\%) = 10\%$.

2. The bond page of the *Wall Street Journal* quotes bond prices per $100 of face value, including fractions (ignored in the prices stated in the text). For instance, the price of the U.S. Treasury $11\frac{1}{4}$s of 2015 was reported as $154\frac{6}{32}$ at the end of 1993 and $132\frac{3}{32}$ at the end of 1987.

THREE

The Sacred College of Bonds and Money

Doubtless the widows of Chevy Chase had great respect for the Federal Reserve System, an old and venerable institution headquartered not far from the genesis of government bonds, the U.S. Treasury. The Fed buys and sells bonds, not to make capital gains, though that happens, but to influence the nation's money supply and interest rates. The widows would not have understood how the Fed controls money by buying and selling bonds, nor do most Americans even today. After all, the Federal Reserve cultivates mystery to serve its institutional purposes. Since heads of the Federal Reserve play leading roles in our story of the bondholding class, it is important to understand not only what the Federal Reserve does, but why it can pretty much have its own way, or, at least, the way of its chairman.

Alan Greenspan, for example, has enjoyed the power of a medieval pope while the Federal Reserve System itself has an independence akin to that of the Vatican. During the Middle Ages, the Church had worldly as well as religious powers, although it was engaged in long and bitter struggles with Roman governments. The Reserve, the scarcely secular ruler of bonds and money, avoids such struggles, serving as a fourth and unequal branch of government in the political Holy See. In this way, the powers of the President of the United States and the congressional majority are greatly constrained. Not only were Bill Clinton's domestic economic policies defined by Alan Greenspan, but Greenspan also turned Wall Street into a quasi-Papal State. In turn, Clinton and his investment-banker advisers remained subservient to the Reserve. Paul Volcker, Greenspan's predecessor, helped to create the bondholding class, but it was Greenspan who sustained and nurtured it.

Occasionally, a President of the United States will exert his own independence, as did Truman with his seizure of the steel industry during the Korean hostilities, Kennedy with his attack on steel prices in the spring of 1962, Johnson with his dumping of surplus government aluminum to prevent private price increases, Nixon with Watergate, Reagan with the Iran–Contra operations, and Clinton with Monica Lewinsky. However, stern consequences usually quickly follow. A stock market crash followed Kennedy's actions; impeachment, Nixon and Clinton's; and scandals, Reagan's. Still, Clinton came much closer to having his way with Monica Lewinsky than with Alan Greenspan.

For, in vivid contrast, the Pope of Wall Street never has to tarnish his carefully cultivated dignity with mea culpas, not only because the effects of the Reserve's policies are diffused and not entirely obvious but because—like the popes of the Middle Ages—he is infallible. Moreover, just as the Reserve can effectively prevent financial panics as a lender of last resort, any hint that the bond or stock market might crash or even go into a swoon if the Chairman of the Federal Reserve does not have his way with the economy, is taken seriously in the political Holy See.

The Reserve's mission, *unlike* that of the Vatican, has never been allied with the interests of working class people or the poor during the past quarter century. For the working class the conduct of monetary policy is religion without the sacraments. The members of the Reserve's board and its Reserve bank presidents have generally served the financial community, its laity. No conspiracy exists; the Federal Reserve no longer is *expected* to serve any other constituency. Nevertheless, any comparison between an authority that can at any moment prevent credit from flowing sufficiently to lubricate the industrial machine and a President who can only temporarily seize an industry or squeeze an intern is invidious. The former is the more seditious because it can subtly and mysteriously impede the expansion of the *entire* economy, including employment, while the latter, with the entire world watching, can hold control for only a few moments in historical time.

The Federal Reserve System: From Populist Origins to Financial Elitism

Odd as it might seem today, populist sentiment forged the Federal Reserve Act of 1913 that established the Federal Reserve System. The seven members of the Federal Reserve Board, the ruling body of the Federal Reserve System, were to be appointed for 14-year terms, a compromise with the *lifelong* appointments of Supreme Court Judges. The purpose for the Fed was the same as for the Supremes; purification would come through "independence" from the unwashed politicos. The President, elected for a four-year term by commoners, can probably appoint one or two new members, but not a controlling majority, nor members of the President's choosing. An incoming President would be stuck with the current chairman of the Board. These two sacred edicts still stand.

Unlike other central banks in the industrialized world, the Reserve was not established as a *centralized* public bank. The Reserve, by a conception often considered immaculate by its Wall Street laity, would be owned privately by bankers. The Federal Reserve became that great oxymoron of public policy, a *quasi-*public institution.

Purity, as ever, is in the eye of the beholder. The passage of the Federal Reserve Act of 1913 required political compromise. The representatives and senators of Congress in each state wanted a piece of the action. As a result, not one but twelve Federal Reserve banks were established in twelve Federal Reserve districts. Moreover, not two but twenty-four branch Federal Reserve banks were built, two in each district. This geographic diversity was meant to do for finance what the establishment of states had done for states' rights—diffuse the Reserve's power. The unintended consequence has been the opposite. The failure of the System to act as lender of last resort to a collapsing banking system during the early 1930s led to reform legislation in 1935 that centralized power and budget-setting in the Federal Reserve Board and the Federal Open Market Committee (FOMC).

The purposes of the 1913 Act, as expressed by its founders, were "to give the country an elastic currency, to provide facilities for discounting commercial paper, and to improve the supervision of banking." By "elastic currency" they meant a money and credit supply responsive to the needs of a growing nation, a money supply independent of the vagaries of gold and silver mining. To "discount commercial paper" each of the twelve Reserve Banks had, and still has, a discount window, a window of opportunity for the private banks. The Fed bought the short-term debt notes that banks took when they lent to business places and to farmers. Since the cash received by the private banks was less than the face value of the notes, the discount rate provided interest to the Reserve Banks. Today, in contrast, it is mainly U.S. Treasury bills, the government's short-term debt instruments, that are discounted for advances from the discount window.

At the beginning, there were no mandates to end inflation (as they knew it), and even less so for maximizing employment. In short, the Federal Reserve and its twelve banks behaved very much like a private bank, leap-frogging the "quasi" feature. If business was bad and private bankers could find no takers for loans, the Federal Reserve banks refused to lend money to the private bankers. When the bankers were naughty, instead of going to confession, they went to the discount window. In truth, currency was no more "elastic" than steel balls dropped from the leaning tower of Pisa.

The Accidental Discovery of Money Management Via U.S. Treasury Bonds

The present-day way of monetary policy-making was discovered unwittingly in the 1920s. The making of profits was never far from the minds of the Reserve Bank presidents. After all, they were "semi-private" bankers, oxymorons of a different stripe. Since a U.S. Treasury security was a safe parking place for funds, the Reserve Banks began buying and selling government securities for their own portfolios. In turn, the securities provided a modest return that helped to pay for services and salaries at the Reserve Banks. Few bankers or economists understood the potentially far-reaching consequences of these little purchases and sales, though they were expanding and contracting the money in circulation.

If the St. Louis Fed bought $1 million in U.S. Treasury bonds, private bank lending would multiply that $1 million by perhaps tenfold. This happened because the private seller of the bonds would deposit the proceeds from the sale in a truly private commercial bank. After setting aside reserves for this deposit, the private bank could lend out the balance, say $900,000. In turn, the banks receiving the $900,000 as spent proceeds of the loan could lend $810,000 more, and so it went. That initial purchase would expand the supply of money. Usually, a cresting of interest rates followed in the money supply wake. If the St. Louis Fed or any other Reserve Bank dramatically sold bonds, the money supply would shrink. Normally, interest rates would rise like coastal rivers at high tides.

Since eleven of the presidents of the twelve Reserve Banks did not understand the powerful effects of their actions in the bond market, their buying and selling actions created confusion and sometimes chaos. One Reserve Bank might be selling bonds while a second was buying bonds. Benjamin Strong, the wise and aptly strong president of the New York Federal Reserve Bank during the Jazz Age, was the odd man in: he understood the effect of these "open market operations" on the money supply and interest rates. He persuaded the other Reserve Banks to at least coordinate their operations.

Since Strong understood these things, the New York Fed began to handle sales and purchases for all the Reserve banks to prevent market disruptions. To decide when to buy or when to fold, the twelve Reserve Banks formed an Open Market Investment Committee in April 1923. Since these open market operations were too small at the time to be important, the Federal Reserve Board approved of the new committee and unwittingly ceded a powerful financial lever to its banks, only later to be reclaimed. Today, of course, the FOMC, comprising the seven Governors, the president of the New York Federal Reserve, and four of the remaining Reserve presidents on a rotating basis, directs open market operations. When a vote of the FOMC membership is taken, it is by Sacred Ballot. It, not the Board alone, is the *Sacred College of Bonds and Money*.

The Omnipotence of the Fed's "Independence"

Since the studiously "nonpolitical" Fed today is in the anomalous position of having powers that affect, directly and indirectly, the entire business community and every worker in the land, yet without any clearly defined responsibilities to the American people, it is appropriate to question such a degree of independence, which rivals that of a medieval Vatican. How has the Federal Reserve achieved and maintained its resplendent autonomy? More importantly, how has the Reserve been able to maintain its power and immortality, despite intelligent and forceful criticism?

Although the original purpose of the Fed was to give the country "an elastic currency," more recently, the instructions (under the Humphrey–Hawkins Act) are that it shall "promote effectively the goals of maximum employment, stable prices, and moderate long-term interest rates." This admirable declaration has, nonetheless, had little effect on the Reserve's behavior. Like purity, whatever is "maximum" has always been a matter of opinion.

Since the early 1950s, the Reserve has crusaded compulsively against inflation, the bondholders' mortal enemy. To inflate goods prices is mortal sin. Though he kept redefining "maximum employment," Alan Greenspan often suggested that counteracting inflation was the only way to moderate long-term interest rates, and achieve maximum employment and steady economic growth. No matter how it was stated or qualified, Greenspan was first and foremost the self-declared opponent of inflation. No remission from fighting inflation was possible. If, however, the financial markets were threatened, as they were by the end of August 1998, concern with goods inflation could be set aside to maintain financial asset inflation. As it turns out, Greenspan had been a long-time ally of the bondholders.

As noted, the Reserve claims that it can succeed in its self-appointed task only if left alone, protected from the common people and their elected representatives. Yet, just as there was once a second pope in Avignon, the spirited independence of the Fed was once ceded to the U.S. Treasury during the Second World War to ensure a receptive market for Treasury issues and to reduce the debt costs of the conflict. The Treasury–Fed accord of 1951 withdrew this financing responsibility, and by 1956 President Eisenhower was speaking in a manner that delighted private financiers: "The Federal Reserve is set up as a separate agency of Government. It is not under the authority of the President, and I ... believe it would be a mistake to make it responsible to the political head of state." The General who had led the invasion of Normandy had just surrendered the White House to the Sacred College of Bonds and Money.

The basic premise behind this independence is so obvious—or so embarrassing—that it is seldom mentioned: the public is either too ignorant or too immoral to be trusted with money management. Having exorcized the evil of bedeviled voters, the Sacred College is spiritually beyond the influence of the carping citizen. A Federal Reserve head can exert his power over the economy without taking into account the various special interest groups—or, the truth is, the public.

The Acknowledged Influence of Investment Bankers

Even so, the Fed's independence is less than pure: the devout laity in the private financial community greatly influence the Sacred College. Indeed, although the Fed was created to supervise the American banking system, we might suppose that the relationship was just the reverse, given the solicitude with which Fed officials consider the views of bankers—investment *and* commercial bankers—today.

American capitalism has always shown a genius for producing specialists whenever anything—of value or not—is to be sold. Investment bankers are the specialists employed to help corporations and governments peddle new bond issues. Most large broker-dealers with household names such as Merrill Lynch and Smith Barney have large investment banking operations as a natural extension of their brokerage business in the financial resale markets. The other large investment bankers have remained secretive, largely unknown to the public. When knowledgeable financiers speak of Salomon Brothers, J.P. Morgan, Morgan Stanley and Goldman Sachs, they talk respectfully in hushed tones. These firms know everything about government regulations related to securities issues and the proper paperwork required for a public sale. Not only do they have the experience to help borrowers set the terms of a debt issue, they have that great capitalist tool, "contacts with potential buyers."

Investment bankers, going all the way back to Pierpont Morgan, do not, of course, place new bond issues as a charitable act. They fully expect to make a profit. Despite this potential, investment banking has never been free of risk. Since most borrowers reach agreements in which the investment banker guarantees a successful sale (to those contacts), by that they *underwrite* the issue. At the same time, the underwriter assumes the issuer's risk of being unable to sell the entire issue. If, God forbid, something goes wrong in the financial markets, the underwriter must absorb any resulting losses. Investment bankers do not like this to happen because the underwriter's profit from the bond issue comes from the difference between the price the investment banker pays for the bonds and the price at which they sell the bonds to investors. This difference—highly regarded by the underwriter—is the spread or differential. The bankers have considerable control over this spread because buyers usually cannot afford to open more than one account and thereby cross-check offering prices.

Still, any untoward event that disrupts a bond sale is a nightmare for the underwriter. Even after the initial sale, the underwriter normally holds a goodly value of the bonds on its own account. Suddenly, a currency crisis might break out, as it did during August 1998 in Russia, causing interest rates to shoot up ("spike" is the word often used). Since the interest payments or coupon rate had already been set, the Russian bonds' selling price plunged, raising the calibrated yield. (Lowering the selling price of the bonds not only increased the cost of borrowing, it reduced the funds received, be it by the government or by Russian firms.) Worse, from the underwriters' perspective, the spread (and *their* profit) on new issues narrowed. Worse still, they knew that any new issue would not be fully subscribed or sold. As a result of the Russian crisis, Salomon (now Salomon Smith Barney Holdings) quickly experienced $60 million in related bond losses.

Traditionally, the most powerful firms on Wall Street have been the major investment banking houses, the largest and most prestigious being Salomon, Morgan Stanley, Merrill Lynch Capital Markets, First Boston, and Goldman Sachs. The country's largest corporations, state and local governments, and even the U.S. Treasury, come to these firms for money in return for their new issues of bonds and stocks. In the comparatively slow year of 1979, Salomon raised $17 billion for private corporations from the sale of bonds and notes and some $1 billion from new stock issues, not to mention another $17 billion from state and local government bonds. Since 1979, when financial industry profits and salaries were "only" 28.4 percent of gross business investment, the industry has been doing much better. The industry's share of gross business investment had risen to an average of 43 percent during the early 1990s. The lower the level of real investment, the greater the rewards from financial activities.

Being highly specialized and prized, investment bankers are among the few. Entering the 1980s and the genesis of the bondholding class, the top five brokers managed 65 percent of the new bond and stock issues for corporations. The ten top firms managed 87 percent.[1] When ventures are too large for one bank, the investment banking houses often combine their resources, though nominally they are competitors. It is a far better thing to cooperate than to forego profits.

From an already small population of dominant investment and commercial bankers, the Federal Reserve Bank of New York selects a still smaller group of securities dealers and commercial banks as *primary* dealers and brokers in its securities. In any particular year the Reserve designates about fourteen bank dealers, a dozen registered dealers, and eighteen or twenty unregistered dealers. These private dealers are, in turn, brokers for large private customers, such as commercial banks, insurance companies, large finance companies, and wealthy clients. These *exclusive* private dealers are the "primary dealers" in the U.S. government securities market.

The designated dealers comprise a Who's Who of Wall Street and are the major players in the government bond market. Continental Illinois National Bank and Trust Company of Chicago was a bank dealer until it declared bankruptcy in 1984 and was bailed out for $1.7 billion by the Federal Deposit and Insurance Corporation. Other bank dealers include Chase Manhattan

Government Securities, Inc., Morgan Guaranty Trust Company of New York, and Irving Securities, Inc. Registered dealers include Goldman, Sachs & Co., Bear, Stearns & Co., Inc., and Salomon Brothers, Inc. Unregistered dealers include Merrill Lynch Government Securities, Inc., and Drexel Burnham Lambert Government Securities, Inc. These investment banks, with office suites adorned with fine old antiques, precious artwork and silver tea services, until recently had no public presence in the retail brokerage business. Once highly specialized as wholesale underwriters of securities, however, they remain devoted to bonds. Clinton's second Secretary of Treasury, Robert Rubin, once a lender as head of Goldman Sachs, then went to his old firm as a borrower.

The Federal Reserve and the U.S. Treasury's close friendship with the bond dealers and brokers on Wall Street continues to this day even though underwriting, once the primary source of the great profits, has been outrun by the bulls in the rapidly expanding resale market of the 1990s. Even the staid investment banks are changing as consolidation on Wall Street is putting the investment banks under the same umbrella as the giant retail brokers. The investment banks have been lured into the retail end of the industry as major players have poured money into the secondary securities markets. Even Morgan Stanley has merged with Dean Witter Discover. Not long thereafter, speaking of umbrellas, Travelers Group (Smith Barney's parent company) bought Salomon. The merged company, Salomon Smith Barney Holdings, is the third biggest securities firm on Wall Street, behind the Morgan Stanley combination. Salomon had to rebuild its reputation as an investment powerhouse after a Treasury bond bid-rigging scandal in 1991.

Secrets at the Reserve

Few Americans know that private commercial bankers own shares in the Federal Reserve banks, nor that a small coterie of private

investment bankers have intimate ties to the Federal Open Market
Committee. As in the Vatican during its battles with Holy Roman
emperors, secrecy is power and much of monetary policy is a
private affair conducted behind closed doors. Afterward, even when
the doors are open, very little is revealed. Though Federal Reserve
operations are highly technical, they are not impenetrable. Since
the mystique of money is a useful tool, however, the Reserve has
long attempted to cultivate public ignorance.

Members of Congress are understandably intimidated by the
flood of statements and arguments advanced by the 500 economists,
the monks employed by the Reserve. Public statements on current
or future policy are inconsistent or vague. Statements on past
policy normally blame any economic adversity on forces beyond
the Reserve's control, though the Reserve's head is eager to accept
credit for any good news. Again, infallibility comes to mind. The
technical goals, prepared for public consumption, always vacillate.
At one time, the Reserve head's testimony before Congress will
show "a need to maintain the existing degree of pressure on [bank]
reserve positions." At another time, he will declare: "We should
sustain moderate growth in M2 and M3 money supplies over
coming months." Moreover, when the head of the Sacred College
speaks, it is *ex cathedra*.

For example, Greenspan had much to say about the money
supply but frequently changed his definition since the Reserve
publishes M1, M2, and M3. These money supplies become larger
though less liquid as they approach M3, which includes even
institutional time deposits. Though Greenspan gave Congress
money supply "targets" twice yearly, they were sufficiently wide to
be nearly meaningless. Besides, when the Reserve failed to hit even
a broad target, Greenspan then redefined it. To the Congress and
to the White House, Alan Greenspan himself was a moving target.

What Greenspan or any Federal Reserve head *intends* to do is,
as always, a secret—except for vague promises to Congress to
maintain a rate of expansion between x and y percent in a "key

version" of the money supply over the balance of the year. Beginning informally in 1994 and formally in February 1995, the Fed adopted the practice of announcing policy changes immediately following the FOMC meetings. However, not everyone understands the announcements and much second-guessing takes place.

To this day many financial firms employ economists as "Fed watchers"—much like the mysterious "watchers" in "The Highlander" television series—to track the activity of the Trading Desk, the FOMC, and the economy. They include forecasters such as Wayne Angell at Bear Stearns, William Brown at J.P. Morgan, Irvin L. Kellner at Chase Regional Bank, and Maury Harris at PaineWebber. Informational activities of the Fed watchers help speed changes in expectations and the pace at which the bond and stock markets move. As in "The Highlander," heads roll if financial executives make grave mistakes. Overall, the Fed watchers have added to financial market volatility between the meetings of the FOMC.

Consider a sample of what not only the Fed watchers, but the New York Reserve trading desk, must decipher. Part of the directive of the September 26, 1995 meeting of the Sacred College goes like this: "In the implementation of policy for the immediate future, the Committee [FOMC] seeks to maintain the existing degree of pressure on [private bank] reserve positions. In the context of the Committee's long-run objective for price stability and sustainable economic growth, and giving careful consideration to economic, financial, and monetary developments, slightly greater reserve restraint or slightly less reserve restraint would be acceptable in the inter-meeting period. The contemplated reserve conditions are expected to be consistent with modest growth in M2 and M3 over coming months."[2]

What do these sacred and solemn utterings mean? We are not sure of the Fed's priorities: perhaps the Fed is concerned about maintaining price stability at this time rather than sustainable economic growth. Or, perhaps the Fed is seeking price stability to achieve—in its opinion—"sustainable" economic growth. The Fed watchers will tell us that the phrase "slightly greater reserve restraint or slightly less reserve restraint" is a symmetrical directive, usually meaning the Sacred College believes no immediate need exists to adjust policy and the direction of the next policy move is just as likely to be easing as tightening. That is, the directive implies that the direction of the next policy move is equally likely to be up or down, a random walk. Such a directive gives us little to go on between FOMC Meetings.

Although the Fed is actually targeting the fed funds rate rather than a money supply growth rate, it does not mention interest rates anywhere in the directive, yet it mentions the money supply "monitoring ranges" several times. Nevertheless, the Fed watcher can "guess" that current plans call for a stable fed funds rate. The Congress is paying attention only to the targeted growth rates in the various money supplies though the Fed had told them on July 19, 1995 that "... considerable uncertainty remains about the future relationship of money and debt to the fundamental objectives of monetary policy; the Committee will thus continue to rely primarily on a wide range of other information in determining the stance of policy."[3] Like the proverbial drunk searching for his keys, the Congress is looking only under the light it knows, the money supply lamp-post.

The Federal Reserve Maintains Its Sovereignty Through Its Bond holdings

How does the System, a much better keeper of secrets than the Vatican of medieval times, retain its sovereignty? I must quickly add: the Fed's independence is circumscribed by the possible threat of being altered by a new congressional act. Thus far, however, the Reserve's isolation—much like Pope Pious IX's (and his three immediate successors') withdrawal into the Vatican and refusal to acknowledge the government in Rome—has forestalled public outrage and pressures for reform. Most importantly, not only is the Reserve protected by Wall Street, it is handsomely self-financing. The System "earns" interest and capital gains (and losses) on its vast government securities dealings. It can't lose: when capital gains are down, interest payments are up, and when interest payments are down, capital gains are up. Like the great clerical landowners at the end of the Middle Ages, the Reserve is a rentier.

The Reserve pays its own formidable expenses out of its own formidable earnings. Not only do these resources insulate the System from congressional budgetary threats, they provide funds sufficient to build new, multi-billion dollar regional banks. Today, these new banks are to finance what the cathedrals of the Middle Ages were to the abbots, bishops and other prelates. What is not set aside for building monuments to bonds and money is used for high-salaried bank officers, economists, and others. Whatever is left over after "expenses" reverts to the Treasury and, *yes*, helps to reduce deficits or increase surpluses and pay interest to bondholders.

The total income of the twelve Reserve Banks in 1995 was $25.4 billion—or about half the entire GDP of Ireland—with expenses of more than $2 billion. Of these expenses, $968 million went into salaries and other personnel expenses. Some $23.4 billion was paid to the U.S. Treasury as interest on Federal Reserve Notes and $283.1 million was retained as "surplus." Among the individual banks, the New York Fed was by far the most expensive to operate. Its salaries were $163.9 million for 4,109 employees with $228,500 going to the president of the bank, making him a one-percenter.[4] The budget for the Board of Governors is separate from those of the Reserve Banks. In 1995, the total operating expenses of the Board were $167.1 million with $100.4 million going into salaries.

Unsurprisingly, the Federal Reserve System is the largest employer of economists in the world, half of whom are at the Board. Spread around American universities, these economists would fill twenty or more academic departments in major research universities. With so many economist-monks, we might suppose that the Reserve *would* be infallible. Certainly the devotion of the monks is inspirational. When this confidential fraternity of economists joins the Reserve, it has been called "taking the veil."

Taking the Veil, but Lifting It

The communication skills of Alan Greenspan and other Fed head's communication skills are not what made them popes on Wall Street as well as in the political Holy See. We cannot, therefore, trust their *ex cathedra* statements as truths that will set the middle class free. The Reserve has a well-funded public relations apparatus unrivaled by any organization—public, private, or international. For example, if legislation opposed by Greenspan came before the Senate Banking Committee, he might visit half the members of the Committee, then he would contact the boards of directors at the Reserves' member banks. These board members are the leaders of American business. These people would then call their members of Congress, who in turn would begin to waver in their support of the legislation. If this pressure proved inadequate, Greenspan might then contact foreign central banks, who one way or another could let it be known that the legislation wasn't a good idea. If that failed, the finance ministers of G-7 (now G-8) countries might call the White House. Eventually, the President may get calls from the French president, the British prime minister, and other heads of state. Suddenly, everyone that the members of the Senate Banking Committee thought was favoring the new laws would be questioning the judgment of the Committee.

At last, Alan Greenspan would testify before the Committee. He spoke, like Paul Volcker before him, with that impenetrable veil over ordinary English. For example, when this committee asked Greenspan about the advice of a Merrill Lynch broker who received nearly $100 million in commissions from Orange County before it collapsed in a spasm of bankruptcy, Greenspan said that both brokers and their customers should be "unburdened by any perceived need to take into consideration the interest of their counterparties." The senators, unable to follow Greenspan and thinking it the failure of their own knowledge, have long since grown numb and uninterested. They are unable to translate Greenspanspeak. "The greed of the profit-seeker is the unexcelled protector of the consumer," is what he meant. In turn, the senators are unable to perceive how, as we will see, Greenspan's series of interest rate hikes in 1994 contributed to the Orange County bonds disaster.

We next establish why it is important to understand what the head of the Federal Reserve does—in order to lift the veil. If we ignore what the chair says and simply watch the effects of what he does, the veil is lifted. We discover over the next few chapters, therefore, how the chair of the Federal Reserve System embraced Wall Street's view of the world and thereby unleashed forces culminating in the creation of the bondholder class, to the great distress of ordinary Americans.

NOTES

1. The other five brokerages making up the top ten were Blyth Eastman Dillon; Lehman Brothers Kuhn Loeb; Kidder, Peabody; Dillon Read; and Prudential-Bache Securities.
2. "Minutes of the Federal Open Market Committee," *Federal Reserve Bulletin*, January 1996, p. 47.
3. "Monetary Policy Report to the Congress," *Federal Reserve Bulletin*, August 1995, pp. 758–59.
4. Board of Governors of the Federal Reserve System, *82nd Annual Report* (Washington, D.C.: Board of Governors of the Federal Reserve System, 1995), pp. 294–95.

II.

WALL STREET FACILITATES THE TAKEOVER BY THE BONDHOLDERS

FOUR

━━◆◆◆━━

Money and Wall Street's Bonding:
A Love Story

English landowners did not sit down one day and exclaim, "I say, wouldn't it be lovely if we were to become, as it were, a landed aristocracy!" The English landed aristocracy, whose power peaked during the 18th century, evolved over centuries as an outgrowth of feudalism. A landed aristocracy *seems* like part of a grand plan, in retrospect, only because historians explained the evolutionary process *after*, not before it happened.

Similarly, Wall Street laid no plans for a bondholding class, nor did the political right, Ronald Reagan, nor, for that matter, the Clinton Administration. Still, the heads of the Federal Reserve and U.S. Treasury have always had soft hearts for bondholders and hard heads for workers. With rare exceptions, the head of the Federal Reserve and the Secretary of the Treasury have risen from Wall Street. Serendipity, however, does not absolve any of these players of complicity nor common intent to benefit the richest citizens. All these players believed that the rich should be better rewarded and enjoy lower tax rates, including lower taxes on financial capital gains.

Wall Street brokers and investment bankers, to be sure, were not disinterested. Their commissions and profits depend more on the rich than on the poor. If poverty were more profitable, of course, this would not be the case. The poor, nonetheless, were seldom absent from Wall Street's ideology. Wall Street claimed that great tax cuts for the rich, especially taxes on capital gains, would bring the homeless off the streets and streaming into factories.

Still, the bondholding class arose only after bonds became sexy, and that took an exceptional confluence of events. It required the inflation of the 1970s, the rise of a mystical something called "monetarism," the massive and ironic federal budget deficits during the Reagan–Bush years, and the prominent role of junk bonds in corporate takeovers. Since Wall Street participated mightily in all of these events, the Wall Street players in New York and those assigned to Washington, D.C. were among the villains. The new era of financial innovation led by junk bonds was as much a forerunner to the bondholding class as feudalism was to the landed aristocracy. Bonds were to become as much a source of political power as was land in feudal times, but much faster.

This and the next two chapters trace the emergence of the bondholding class over the past quarter century as these influences converged. At the climax, a deluge of bonds, supplied by federal deficits in the public sector and by junk bond king Michael Milken in the private sector, was poured out, to be lapped up by the grateful beneficiaries of massive tax cuts. Not only does the rise of the bondholding class define the financial and economic history of the final quarter of the twentieth century, it continues to present a formidable barrier to prosperity for common folks.

The Ideology of the Bondholding Class

Ideas that are otherwise perfectly good often become self-regarding ideologies. Adam Smith, writing during the rise of the merchant class, logically justified the use of the market. Though he never said that the market should be deployed in every nook and cranny of society, the merchants seized on the notion that it *should*. Out of self-interest, the merchants created a bastardized version of laissez faire whereby whatever the merchants did (including price-fixing and monopolization) was *good*; if workers attempted to do the same thing (forming guilds or unions) in *their* self-interest, *that* was very bad. By *that*, the merchants meant bad for the merchants. The merchants quickly discovered the social benefits of unemployment and poverty, not for themselves but for those seeking employment.

In this regard, as in others, ideology always has been two-edged. It is insufficient to say that what you (merchants) do is always beneficial; too many cases occur in which that is obviously not the case. Therefore, it is not simply important, it is imperative that a lower economic or social class is denigrated. The complete laissez faire ideology had to explain not only why many were jobless and poor, but why this poverty was necessary. To the merchants the explanation was obvious: the jobless poor were lazy and immoral. More poverty would eventually spur them to prosper. They had yet to evolve sufficiently to become merchants. Even today, new classes require an ideology disguised as scientific judgment, the bondholding class being no exception.

The ideology decreeing evolutionary fitness to the bondholding class emanated from Wall Street. It consists of four main ideas, only the first of which resides in the land of the truth. First, inflation is bad for bondholders (it is also bad for stockholders, but only because it is initially bad for bondholders). Second, the sole cause of inflation is an excessively fast growth rate in the money supply. Third, while the Reagan deficits were vital to victory in the Cold War and inflationary only if fed by rapid growth in the money supply, subsequent deficits were not only inflationary but evil because they expanded the public sector at the expense of private enterprise. Fourth, and finally, household savings, the main source of real investment and essential capital accumulation in the economy, will "trickle down" from the rich to the working class and the poor, assuring full employment in the fullness of time.

In the refinement of what became the bondholders' ideology, Wall Street had considerable support from the gifted pen of George

Gilder and his book *Wealth and Poverty*. Gilder, the adopted son of banker David Rockefeller, left no doubts regarding the true sources of economic growth. "Material progress," he wrote, "is ineluctably elitist: it makes the rich richer and increases their numbers, exalting the few extraordinary men who can produce wealth over the democratic masses who consume it..."[1] Families like the Rockefeller's and DuPont's could be trusted to put their money to good productive use; blue-collar workers could be trusted only to squander their pay checks during weekends made for Michilob or perhaps a cheaper beer. "The current poor," wrote Gilder, "white even more than black, are refusing to work hard."[2]

During inflation the failure of enough people to volunteer for the Reserve's army of the unemployed was an irritant on Wall Street. Gilder converted such angst into conservative faith: federal budget deficits were due to excessive payments made to mothers with dependent children and the working poor. In a damnation of welfare worthy of Charles Dickens' Scrooge, Gilder concluded that welfare motivates the poor to choose leisure over work. "In order to succeed," he wrote, "the poor need most of all the spur of their poverty."[3] In contrast to the poor, the needed spur for the rich was *more* wealth. Since only the rich have enough savings to be able to devote them to capital formation, their reduced tax rates would stimulate economic growth.

The excess income of the poor, the witless leisure class, makes them lazy whereas *the rich do not have enough wealth* to keep them from sloth. Though bountiful unemployment was a good thing, it was no longer sufficient. The unemployed would have to be taken off welfare, putting more downward pressures on wages, even as they raised the true unemployment rate.

If a Wall Street ideology is to serve the bondholding class, then it must become a policy program. From the ideology comes what we may call the *bond market strategy*. It is of three parts. First, since Wall Street has the most reliable understanding of inflation, the heads of the Federal Reserve System and U.S. Treasury should be selected by, from, and for Wall Street. Second, since household savings create real investment, the rich, who save more than the poor or the middle class, should have low income taxes and modest or zero capital gains taxes. Third, since the (post-Reagan) federal budget deficits were causing inflation and crowding out private investment, it is imperative to balance, at the least, the federal budget yearly—if necessary, by amending the Constitution. Federal surpluses would be even better.

Inasmuch as Wall Street has shifted its stance on federal deficits twice in the post-Reagan era, the justification for its original, pre-Reagan, position should be made clear. In those days, inflation was supposed to be routed by reining in the growth of the money supply, leaving as the primary enemy, Big Government. According to a 1979 editorial in the *Wall Street Journal,* "A tax cut would reduce the size of government relative to the private sector. It would be an inroad on the power that has been concentrated in Washington,..." Moreover, "if the tax proponents [the supply-siders] are right and the economy booms, there would no longer be a sluggish economy as one excuse for expanding government."[4] Since Reagan's massive tax cuts went to Wall Street's clients, Wall Street did not complain about federal deficits growing like topsy during the Reagan years.

The facts, of course, do not correspond with this ideology. The cumulative yearly federal deficits equal the tax breaks and federal interest payments to the very rich, the top 5 percent. Reagan's deficits benefitted mostly the rich because they could afford the bonds. Neither mothers on welfare nor a spendthrift working class can be blamed for the deficits or today's huge federal debt. Yet, since the bondholders, not to mention, in turn, Paul Volcker and Alan Greenspan at the Reserve, argued that deficits cause inflation, it would be inconvenient to blame the deficits on those holding interest-earning bonds. The notion that reckless welfare recipients with no fears of inflation were the guilty parties better served the *ideology of the bondholding class.* Even as late as the 1997 Balanced

Budget Act the victims were blamed for the deficits, a less than poetic denouement.

Of course, in suggesting that government is too big and needs cutting down to size, the editors of the *Wall Street Journal* probably thought they were just doing their duty, following in the hallowed footsteps of that first prophet of western capitalism, Adam Smith (1723–90), and resisting the infernal blandishments of that false prophet, John Maynard Keynes (1883–1946).

Two Contrary Views of Economic Reality: Adam Smith and John Maynard Keynes

The great contest in U.S. economic policy springs from the ideas attributed to these two intellectual giants. To Smith—the inspiration for classical economics—is attributed the importance of *laissez faire*, by which the only proper role for government in the economy is to make the city streets safe for businessmen. With the *invisible hand* at work in markets, capitalism is as self-regulating as the planetary system. In this utopia no business cycle and no unemployment (except that which was voluntary) could occur. To Keynes is attributed the contrary notion—that great fluctuations in output and employment are consequences of capitalism's excesses. Government alone is capable of smoothing the economic cycle and maintaining or restoring full employment. I will explore these for a little space.

In freshman economics we are taught that Adam Smith instructed the world about the way markets magically self-adjust to the betterment of all. The magic ascended to higher planes. Smith not only imbued capital accumulation with high morality, as it is "increased by parsimony and diminished by prodigality," but believed that all savings become real capital investment. As he put it, "what is annually saved is as regularly consumed as what is annually spent, and nearly in the same time too; but it is consumed by a different set of people."[5] Later, in 1803 the idea was popularized by a French journalist, J.B. Say, and became known as Say's law, whereby personal savings bringing about an equal value of real business investment prevented "general gluts" or economy-wide surpluses. In good time a bastardized version of Say's law, "supply creates its own demand," got embedded in Wall Street ideology and eventually in the second part of the *bond market strategy*. However, Smith's grand vision was how to get the engine of growth started, a natural for his times at the leading edge of the industrial revolution.

Later, David Ricardo (1772–1823), once a stockbroker and member of the British Parliament, explained inflation as a purely monetary phenomenon. The money supply, no matter how great or how small, could not influence the "real" economy of plant, equipment, natural resources, and labor. Inflation, however, was different: the sole cause of generally and persistently rising prices was a rising supply of money. Money was a veil hiding those real forces. In lifting that veil, Ricardo was a forerunner of monetarism (embedded in the Wall Street ideology and the first part of the *bond market strategy*). Ricardo, too, embraced Say's law, making it a fairly unassailable doctrine up until the 1930s.

In sharp contrast, the most popular American interpretations of Keynesianism not only oppose monetarism but reject the idea that everything in the economy comes from parsimonious savings. Even the notion of using government policy to steer the economic ship of state is heresy to the classicals. To Keynes, however, unless a policy affects the total demand for goods and services in some way, it has no effect at all. Indeed, the Keynesian counterpart of Say's law would read "demand creates its own supply." Still, Keynes did not dispute Smith's idea that businesses depend upon *other* people's savings as sources of funds for real investment.[6] Keynes nonetheless broke the direct link between savings and investment envisioned by Smith and Say. Since, as Keynes put it, households with net savings are different from entrepreneurs building factories, and what households plan to save has no direct connection to what the entrepreneurs plan to invest.

Indeed, things are vice versa: when households consume more, they have *fewer* savings, and capitalists have a reason to spend more in building and outfitting industrial plants. The throughly capitalistic act of buying capital goods adds to employment and incomes. Then, higher than expected personal savings come from the rising employment and income created by the expansion of private industry. However, because of the uncertainty of profitable returns to entrepreneurial activity, Keynes believed that modern corporations could not always be counted on to invest enough to assure full employment for labor. Though we cannot be sure that the investment will be there for us, when it is, it enhances savings. In the savings–investment lacunae, corporate investment creates saving(s)! (Whether saving is singular or plural and real or nominal will be explained later.) Moreover, Keynes dismisses the classical idea that money is simply a veil over the "real" economy. Instead, the supply of money helps to decide interest rates that, in turn, influence business investment.

During times of extraordinarily low confidence, uncertainty regarding entrepreneurial returns and bond prices (and hence interest rates) is lethal, leading to a collapse in business investment and final total demand. Keynes called final total demand, *effective demand,* the demand materializing not only in the sale of capital goods, but in the sale of clothing, autos, houses, and battleships. Keynes, writing his *General Theory of Employment, Interest, and Money* during the Great Depression of the 1930s, attributed those frightening conditions to a collapse in business investment and *inadequate* effective demand. Moreover, wrote Keynes, a rudderless economic ship of state may sink without sensible government budgetary policies. When Keynes was writing his *General Theory,* of course, free enterprise capitalism appeared not simply to be sinking, but going to the bottom of the turbulent economic seas.[7]

How have these contrary views attributed to Smith and Keynes affected national economic policies? By the early 1980s a popular but flawed understanding of what Adam Smith meant was diminished to the wearing of the Adam Smith necktie (filled with little cameos of Smith's profile) out of devotion only to free markets and to remarkably limited government.[8]

Smith, a lecturer on moral philosophy at Glasgow, would have rejected both out of four-in-hand. Still, according to the wearers of the Adam Smith necktie, government is the problem; the market is *the solution*. During the early years of Reagan's presidency, the supply-siders believed tax cuts to be the route to diminished government. In this way the supply-siders rejected the Keynesians and the inherent instability they attribute to capitalism.

We need not be true believers of one side or the other to understand what happened. In Chapter 12, in fact, I will contend that on an important, even crucial, matter affecting the bondholding class as well as ordinary people, Smith and Keynes were both wrong-headed.

Milton Friedman Gives Wall Street an Idea

Bondholders not only came face-to-face with inflation during the 1970s, but quickly surmised that the policies of the American Keynesians were ill-adapted to the new inflationary environment. Nonetheless it wasn't until the end of the decade that the war against inflation began to be fought on David Ricardo's turf by slowing the growth of the supply of money. Nearing the end of the twentieth century, an era of global commodities *deflation*, the economist-monks and the Federal Reserve were still fighting the long-vanquished inflation of the 1970s.

The 1970s reality contrasts sharply with the money part of the Wall Street ideology. In truth, the inflation had little to do with the supply of money. The spark igniting the 1970s inflation came from the mismanagement of the Vietnam War in the late 1960s. This inflationary brush fire was fanned by the winds of the OPEC oil crisis and food price explosions of the early 1970s, and soon spread like wild fire across the economy through cost-of-living indexes in labor and supplier contracts during the mid-1970s. It died down, only to be rekindled by the second OPEC oil crisis at the end of the decade.

The doubling and tripling of oil prices by a newly powerful OPEC could not have come at a less serviceable time. In an economy dependent upon oil as input for energy, plastics, and chemical fertilizer, and to propel its thirsty autos, crude and refined oil are necessities in production and consumption. The payments for the higher-priced by-products of oil were as unavoidable as seasonal hurricanes in Florida. Then, as now, the causes of the inflation were clear enough for everyone to see. Well, perhaps not everyone.

Milton Friedman, then a professor of economics at the University of Chicago, had an entirely different explanation for inflation. At the time, he was America's leading indicator of inflation. During the early 1960s, a time of tranquil goods prices, Friedman—in congressional testimony—predicted dire inflationary disaster from the "runaway spending" of the Democrats. Even then, wealthy bondholders were grumbling about the "devastating inflation rate." Fortuitously, Friedman published an important summary of his doctrine in 1970, just in time to "explain" all the inflation since and to contribute to the Wall Street ideology adopted by the bondholders. According to Friedman's doctrine, only one cause of inflation exists—the rate of growth in the nation's money supply. In line with Ricardo's doctrine, money was a veil. Had the good times of the sixties continued to roll, Friedman's doctrines themselves would have rolled over and died. Instead, the inflation made him a prophet in his own land. He won the Nobel Prize for economics during the inflationary year of 1976.

Friedman Defines a Speed Limit for Economic Growth

Friedman, following J.B. Say, considers the savings–investment nexus to be a guarantee of full employment—at least, as full as employment can get without ravaging inflation. The triumph of Friedman's ideas led eventually to placing a speed limit on the rate of economic growth. A specific level of employment, Friedman was to conclude, sets the upper limit to stable prices. This "natural rate of unemployment" was greatly to be respected. If, perchance, at the natural rate of unemployment, the government and the Federal Reserve collude to accelerate the rate of growth in the money supply, the outcome would be devastating inflation—perhaps the end of the world as we know it. Though Friedman did not consider unemployment to be a force of Nature, eventually "natural" began to imply that it was somehow determined by Nature and was thus inexorable.

As economic science continued to advance along Friedmaniacal lines, economists eventually called the natural rate of unemployment, less eloquently, the "non-accelerating-inflation rate of unemployment," or, with a brevity for which we should all be thankful, NAIRU, pronounced "Nehru." The NAIRU is an idealized unemployment rate for inflation. Any unemployment rate below the presently-decreed NAIRU causes an acceleration in inflation. If any persons are unemployed at rates of unemployment at or below NAIRU, they are voluntarily unemploying themselves; that is, they prefer idleness to working. *They*, not the wealthy, comprise the leisure class. Since the monetarists see all behavior as self-interested, they do not expect people to withdraw from their jobs to fight the otherwise inevitable great national inflation. However, brute force monetarism can be used to push people from their jobs.

Stuart E. Weiner, an Assistant Vice President and economist at the Federal Reserve Bank of Kansas City assures us that the natural rate continues to be a reliable guide to Federal Reserve actions. "Historically," he writes, "the gap between the actual unemployment rate and the natural unemployment rate has been a reliable indicator of future increases in inflation." He goes on to explain the Federal Reserve's pre-emptive strike against inflation in the absence of any signs of inflation:

> The actual unemployment rate went below the natural rate in
> advance of the increase in inflation.... That is why relying on
> current inflation as an indicator of future inflation is dangerous,
> and why the Federal Reserve has taken timely policy action.[9]

In short, Weiner is saying, Alan Greenspan and other Fed heads
have to stay ahead of the curve if a rise in inflation is to be avoided
because of the "inertia" in the inflation process and the lags in
the effect of the Reserve's policy action. Otherwise, according to
the fully-employed economists, the economy would be heading for
a great train wreck. This natural rate of unemployment went higher
and higher during the 1970s and 1980s, only to taper off a little
during the late 1990s. Remember, however, the Reserve's
admonition: price stability is a poor predictor of inflation, and the
absence of current inflation can be dangerous!

Not surprisingly, a common weave runs throughout classical
economics—Friedman's monetarism, and the thoughts of central
bankers like Paul Volcker and Alan Greenspan. Adam Smith, the
first classical economist, often used the term *natural* when writing
of wages, prices and employment. Moreover, the classical economists
had already formulated what became the basic principle of modern
monetarism—unfettered markets as the only way to manage the
real economy. Then, slowing the growth rate of money would halt
inflation without adding to unemployment above its natural rate,
or so all faithful monetarists believed. Friedman, who had once
wandered alone in the wilderness, ignored, if not demeaned, by
the reigning Keynesians, now had the ears of presidents and central
bankers. To Milton Friedman and his most devout monetarists,
money not only mattered, it was the *only* thing that mattered.

How the *Wall Street Journal* Promoted the Supply of Money as an Indicator of Well-being

Parallels between things important to Wall Street, bondholders, and
the monetarists are too obvious to miss. Wall Street began to

believe that money matters in more ways than one. The devout practitioners on Wall Street, once loving money only as an asset unto itself, began to appreciate its instrumental virtue in the glorious war against inflation. Since inflation was a natural concern of bondholders, monetarism was promoted as Wall Street's favorite idea. Moreover, Wall Street's favorite newspaper led the monetarists' crusade against the evils of inflation.

The *Wall Street Journal* is not only Wall Street's most influential information source, it has the greatest circulation of any newspaper worldwide with a daily circulation of about two million and many secondhand readers. It not only reaches the highest corporate offices but the political power centers of Washington and other world capitals as well. Moreover, the last time the *Journal* checked (in 1982), its subscribers mirrored Wall Street's clients. Nearly 90 percent owned securities with an average value of $371,900 or $603,222 in 1998 dollars.[10]

At a pivotal historical moment, the *Journal* began to cultivate the most virulent strain of monetarism, its single-cell species. Alfred L. Malabre, Jr., a graduate of the *WSJ,* has traced its natural biological trail. An economics reporter at *WSJ* at the beginning, thereafter he was economics editor for twenty-five years.[11] Following a long visit with the monetarist high priest at his vacation retreat, Malabre wrote an early story on Milton Friedman's ideas to later lament, "I mistakenly presented monetarism to *Journal* readers through rose-colored lenses and as virtually dictated to me by Milton Friedman."[12] As Malabre relates, the visit ended with his "never once hearing mention, for example, of velocity—the rate at which money turns over or, more simply, changes hands."[13]

Friedman and his loyal disciples began to tell an amazingly simple parable. As monetarism was later expressed, the linkages between money, income, and prices within *"a monetary black box"* were strong and dependable. Alan Greenspan, then merely a presidential adviser, used to tell President Richard Nixon, "You see, I have this little black box," and Nixon's eyes would glaze over.

Were it not for the money supply and its growth rate, Greenspan said, governmental institutions would have absolutely no influence on the economy. Repeatedly, we would hear that "only the money supply matters!"

Still, Malabre had let the genie out of the black box. Monetarism got still another major boost from Sam L. Nakagama, one of Friedman's former students who was then at an investment advisory firm on Wall Street. Nakagama arranged an economic conference to shine the spotlight on monetarism (beginning November 21, 1969) at Phoenix's opulent Arizona Biltmore—with a decor and cuisine sufficiently sumptuous at high season to charm even central bankers. He invited some 200 influential individuals from government, academia, private business, and the press. Among those attending was Darryl R. Francis, then President of the St. Louis Federal Reserve Bank and a rotating member of the powerful Federal Open Market Committee, the Sacred College. Prominent academics included most of the leading monetarists, Friedman being the featured speaker of the conference, flown to Phoenix on the last day by luxurious private jet.

Ordinary people were not well represented at this gathering. Many members of the dominant leisure class believe that proximity to money guarantees an understanding of it. This notion is reinforced by a second belief: those having little income not only do not understand money, but the active cultivation of their ignorance of it is good for society. Unsurprisingly, then, the gathering at the Biltmore included, among many others like them, the Senior Vice President of Chase Manhattan Bank, a partner of Lehman Brothers, and Beryl Sprinkel, Senior Vice President of Harris Trust & Savings Bank. Sprinkel later would serve as a chair of President Reagan's Council of Economic Advisers (1985–89). Nakagama invited no labor union leaders, much less idle blue-collar workers.

The speakers, including Sprinkel and Leonall Andersen, a Vice President of the St. Louis Federal Reserve Bank, extolled the undeniable virtues of monetarism. The duly-invited press—the economics editors of *Time, Business Week, Chicago Tribune, and Wall Street Journal,* and also the Editor-in-Chief of *Barron's,* the Assistant Managing Editor of *Fortune,* and senior economic correspondents from the *New York Times* and the *Los Angeles Times*—are impressed. Malabre rushed into print "an unskeptical account of monetarism's virtues" on the *Wall Street Journal's* front page.[14] *Time* graced its cover with the elfin visage of Milton.

Malabre, much to his later torment, continued to promote monetarism on the *Journal's* news pages. Lindley H. Clark, Jr., then a *WSJ* associate editor and a former student of Friedman, sang his praises on the *Journal's* famous editorial page. Clark went on to become the leading supporter of monetarism at the paper. The synergism among the *Wall Street Journal's* praise, the elegant Biltmore conference, and the special interests of Wall Street levitated monetarism from the economics underworld. Soon, its effects would help to create the bondholding class.

The Federal Reserve Contributes to the *Ideology of the Bondholding Class*

Two other forces would ensure the final ascent of monetarism and the rise of the bondholding class. The first was the increased availability of money supply data, various series of which would be carefully followed by bond traders. Before the mid-sixties, the Fed released only semi-monthly money supply figures; before 1955, only monthly data. By the late 1960s, the Federal Reserve began to report money supply figures *weekly.* The rise of monetarism and the availability of timely money supply figures were not coincidental. The Federal Reserve Bank of St. Louis was a monetarist stronghold even during the early 1960s. It had lobbied long and hard to persuade the Fed's Board of Governors to provide up-to-date figures.

The St. Louis Fed itself was the second force. While Darryl Francis, then the Reserve Bank's president, was a rotating member of the FOMC, the whirling dervish of monetarism was the tenacious and irascible Homer Jones, head of economic research, with a PhD from Friedman's home, the University of Chicago. Darryl Francis depended on Homer and his staff of economists, who were refining money supply figures and publishing monetarist articles in the St. Louis Fed's *Review*, using a substantial budget.[15] The articles always sounded the same note: the economy is naturally stable if the government stays out of the way and "the Federal Reserve properly manages the money supply."

Despite economists' belief that there is no such thing as a free magazine, the bank's *Review*, like all the Reserve Banks' Reviews, *is* free. At that price, it reached a large audience on Wall Street, in the news media, and in Washington, D.C. This information was being cast to the winds at a time when the Board of Governors judged, perhaps presciently, monetarism to be bunko economics.

The motto of the St. Louis Federal Reserve Bank, uniquely among the twelve regional banks, had a monetarist intonation. Over the entrance was written *In Hoc Signo Vinces*, or, "Under This Sign You Shall Conquer." The Latin was followed by the classical monetarist equation $MV = PT$. In that equation M represents the money supply level, V is its turnover rate or velocity, P is the average price level or price index, and T is the number of economic transactions. The "equation" is a truism because the money supply when multiplied by the rate each dollar turns over, equals the value of total transactions in the economy. During the early part of the twentieth century, Irving Fisher, a Yale economist, first wrote the monetarist equation in this form.

The St. Louis Bank's faith should not be taken lightly. The Latin is from "Constantine's Dream": the "sign" is the cross of Jesus Christ.

Money Carries the Day, Only to be Superceded by Bonds

Eventually, all these forces sustaining monetarism coalesced; the power flowed from the St. Louis Fed to the private bankers and then into the Fed's Board of Governors. As Malabre writes, "The corporate counterpart to the St. Louis Federal Reserve Bank was First National City Bank in New York."[16] First National began to court monetarism during the 1960s and continued its love affair during the 1970s under the chair of Walter Wriston. Wriston became an influential member of the Federal Advisory Council (FAC), a committee of a dozen bankers chosen by the Reserve Banks within each Federal Reserve district. The FAC, long a part of the Fed meets quarterly with the Federal Reserve Board. At one such meeting, on September 7, 1979, the committee urged the Fed governors to change the Federal Open Market Committee's operating procedure so that "monetary aggregates [would] take priority over concerns about further upward moves in domestic interest rates."[17] We may surmise that Homer Jones and the St. Louis economists wrote much of the statement.[18]

By this time, monetarism had a lot of money—abstract and otherwise—behind it. The next major appointment to the Federal Reserve Board would not only alter the economic growth path of the American economy, but greatly transform the fortunes of bondholders and ordinary people at home and abroad. Surprisingly, this pivotal appointment was officially made, not by a right-winger wearing an Adam Smith necktie, but by the first "New Democrat." As to the truth, it was Wall Street and the bondholders who selected the appointee.

NOTES

1. George Gilder, *Wealth and Poverty* (New York: Basic Books, 1981), p. 259.
2. *Ibid.*, p. 68.

3. *Ibid.*, p. 118.

4. Editorial, "Born Again Budget Balancers," *Wall Street Journal* (July 25, 1979).

5. Adam Smith, *An Inquiry into the Nature and Causes of the Wealth of Nations*, edited by Edwin Cannan, with an introduction by Max Lerner (New York: Modern library, 1937) [1776], p. 321.

6. Economists have generally missed this concordance: that both Smith and Keynes attribute savings and real investment to separate groups of people

7. The reader can find much more about Adam Smith, John Maynard Keynes, Milton Friedman, and many other famous economists in E. Ray Canterbery, *The Literate Economist* (New York: HarperCollins, 1995). For Smith's grand vision, see Chapter 4. For Keynes and all garden varieties of Keynesianism, see Chapters 11–14.

8. Extreme Smithian believers want no part of government. Smith would not agree with them. Overall, he favored government provision of military security, the administration of justice, and privately unprofitable public works and instructions. When we turn to specifics, the list runs to fifteen items, among which are the government's right to impose tariffs to counter tariffs, to punish business fraud, to regulate banking, to provide post offices, highways, harbors, bridges and canals, and so on. Even so, only if private domestic markets were unfettered would the consumer continue to reign as king. For the same reason, Smith also opposed monopolization of the production of a commodity. The radical free-marketeers, however, who came long after Adam Smith, would not have opposed the merger movement of the past twenty years.

   A welcome corrective of what Adam Smith really wrote and meant is in Jerry Z. Muller, *Adam Smith in his Time and Ours* (New York: The Free Press, 1993). Muller's treatment is much more extensive than the brief account I present here.

9. Stuart E. Weiner, "The Natural Rate and Inflationary Pressures," *Economic Review, Federal Reserve Bank of Kansas City*, Third Quarter 1994, pp. 7–8.

10. See "Basis for Strategy: A New Census of the Corporate Finance Universe," Dow Jones & Company, 1982.

11. The reader seeking more detail on the other personalities behind the ascent of monetarism can do no better than read Alfred L. Malabre, Jr., *Lost Prophets* (Boston, MA: Harvard Business School Press, 1995), Chapter 5. The book is sprightly styled.

12. *Ibid.*, p. 141.

13. *Ibid.*

14. Malabre, *op. cit.*, p. 152. I gleaned the names or titles of the participants at the conference from Malabre's Chapter 5.

15. At the end of 1995 the Bank president's salary was $209,500 while 49 "other officers" received a total of $4,436,500 or an average salary of $90,540.82. The 1,068 other full-time employees plus 75 part-time employees received a total of $34,509,764 or an average wage of $30,192.27. See Board of Governors of the Federal Reserve System, *82nd Annual Report* (Washington D.C.: Board of Governors of the Federal Reserve System, 1995), p. 293.

16. Malabre, *op. cit.*, p. 160.

17. Quoted by Malabre, *op. cit.*, p. 167.

18. Economists at the St. Louis Fed wrote most of the speeches and statements for the St. Louis District's FAC member.

———❖———

FIVE

A Wall Street—Federal Reserve Experiment Creates a Monster

The inflation beginning in the late 1960s, made worse by the OPEC cartel during the 1970s, and "explained" by Milton Friedman and the monetarists during the late 1950s led to a great and ghastly experiment by one of Wall Street's own. The experiment gone wrong created a financial Frankenstein, the consecrated bondholder. Generally, we social scientists have good reason to be humble: replicating our "experiments" is virtually impossible because the subjects are not only human, but almost never the same ones at the same times. Besides, persons usually do not like to be experimental subjects. Even so, a ghastly experiment was about to be performed on humans—powered by monetarism.

Not only was monetarism promoted on Wall Street, it depended, for its activation, on Wall Street's bond dealers and investment banking houses. Moreover, Wall Street was to name the authoritative figure who would set monetarism into motion. Though no one knew it at the time, monetarism was to be the electricity energizing an otherwise lifeless bondholding monster. In the end, as with *Frankenstein* the story, the true villains were the creators, aptly inspired by an almost religious faith in the source of the power. The victims were not only absent from the electrifying conference in the Arizona Biltmore, but from the creation itself.

Wall Street and Still More Bonding

In one sense Wall Street is just a place. It is a street with a river at one end and a chilling colonial graveyard in the dark shadows of Trinity Church's Gothic spires at the other. In between is a narrow, deep abyss filled with investment banking and brokerage firms. The permanence in their location is assured by frequent threats from the New York Stock Exchange to move to New Jersey; the mayor of New York City is willing to do almost anything to keep this abundant source of tax revenue. These Wall Street firms, protected by lax regulation, begot the mad scientist who created the maniacal forces that made a few *very* rich.

Being also a state of mind, any Wall Street madness can spread far and wide. Some of the players are at a great geographical distance from Manhattan. A key player in California, Michael Milken, the inventor of junk bonds, is not only a household name, but to many, a Faustian evil-doer. Wall Street's investment bankers provided the discarded body parts while Milken created the initial excitement attracting the bond buyers, though he had lots of help from people in Washington, D.C.

Again, Wall Street's clients were like reflections in the Street on a rainy night. Just as the new bondholding class was gathering in 1981, the *average* income of the Street's hardcore customers was $84,000 a year or $136,920 in 1998 dollars, then placing them among the top 1 percent of U.S. household incomes. On *average*, these few households owned portfolios of stocks, bonds and other financial assets valued at $331,000, or $539,530 in 1998 dollars. At the top, 5 percent of these households held portfolios greater than $1 million, or about $1.6 million in 1998 dollars.[1] Wall Street, like its *Journal's* editorial page, has *always* considered the richness of the few to be the best indicator of the robustness of the American economy. By this measure, conditions were to improve dramatically during the next two decades, multiplying those client dollar figures many-fold.

Money, in its myriad forms, has always been the lifeblood of the Street: we cannot say the same for bonds, and certainly not for junk bonds. Still, bonds have long had some standing on Wall Street because those few specializing in underwriting, arbitraging, and speculating can make much money. Moreover, as we said, these elite bond dealers and investment bankers have always been important to the Reserve and to the U.S. Treasury. If the bond-buying public is the circulation conduit for money and bonds, the dealers and investment bankers comprise the artificial pumps for bonds. The Fed and the U.S. Treasury provide transfusions, whether necessary or not.

We seldom get a glimpse of the underwriters and dealers, except those serving prison terms. However, few organizations have the time, the know-how, or the means—much less the courage—to undertake a public bond issue alone. If Ford is busy manufacturing automobiles, Exxon exploring for oil, and the U.S. Treasury intervening in foreign exchange markets, they do not have the experts nor the sales staff to sell a large new bond issue. These sales, in hundreds of millions or even several billions of dollars, demand the help of a firm that understands the capital markets and that has ready access to many individuals and institutions as lenders. Thus, for those who rely on long-term debt, the Wall street underwriters and dealers are very important.

As noted, the Federal Reserve and the U.S. Treasury have always had close friendships with these bond dealers and brokers. Then, as the Street slithered toward the 1980s, it was to name one of its own to head the Fed, a tradition that has since not been broken. Though harmony among Wall Street, the Federal Reserve, and the U.S. Treasury is hardly new, concordance ascended to a lofty level. From this new climate emerged not just the creator of a monster but of bonds.

Wall Street Selects One of Its Own to Head the Federal Reserve

On August 6, 1979, a day that should live in economic infamy, Paul Volcker was sworn in as chair of the Federal Reserve Board. President Jimmy Carter, a supremely ethical soul whose ignorance in economics and monetary policy was legendary, had made the appointment. The new chair, unknown to most people, was a familiar figure not only on Wall Street but in Washington policy circles. Most importantly for our story, Stuart Eizenstat, President Carter's domestic policy adviser, confirms that "Volcker was selected because he was the candidate of Wall Street."[2]

The tall and gangly Volcker had the kind of resumé adored on the Street. He had served for four years as President of the New York Federal Reserve Bank, the district bank directly ministering to Wall Street. Already, Volcker had served as Nixon's Treasury Under Secretary for Monetary Affairs, and had worked closely with the Reserve. Before that, he had done two turns in private banking at Chase Manhattan. At the appointment time, President Carter did not realize that Volcker would not only govern national economic policy but preside arrogantly over a transmutation in which millions of Americans would lose jobs, homes, small businesses, farms and their savings while a few would gain fortunes.

Strangely, being skeptical of monetarism at that time, Volcker was, by St. Louis's catechismal standards, a scientific heretic. Nevertheless, by the time of his appointment, the spiraling economic pressures greatly favored the ascension of monetarism as we came to know it. First, though hardly decisive, was the orchestrated instruction of the bankers on the Federal Advisory Council. Second, this was no ordinary inflation: the inflation rate had risen as high as 20 percent during 1979, following that second OPEC spike.

True to the Street's expectations, the day after the announcement of Volcker's appointment the bond market rallied and the Dow

Industrials leaped. Despite months of decline, the dollar, too, suddenly rose on international markets. With their newly-acquired understanding of the science of monetarism, the bondholders already had begun a tradition of applauding those they respected by bidding bond prices upward. The bondholders were feeling good.

Since the chair of the Federal Reserve Board needs only to please Wall Street and the bondholders, power comes easy. The power of an eminent chair such as Volcker and, following him, Alan Greenspan, is limited only by the abilities, the preferences, and the prestige of the other Fed governors on Wall Street. Volcker's stooped, rumpled features were disarming, and a cheap cigar, his constant companion, added character to his seeming bemusement toward those who could not appreciate his scientific monetary policy and who blundered off to engage in fiscal folly.

The Federal Open Market Committee, the Sacred College, is powerful not only because the Board's chair heads it but also because it buys and sells the securities that make the wheels of monetary policy turn. The FOMC includes the seven governors plus four rotating regional bank presidents, each serving every third year. Like Jesus Christ, however, monetary policy has twelve apostles. The twelfth—once Paul, as the president of the New York Reserve—is the permanent vice-chairman of the FOMC, giving him a pivotal role among the district Fed banks' presidents. Besides, not only is the New York Fed strategically located in the Wall Street financial district, the Fed's bond trading desk is on the ninth floor of the Bank building. Volcker knew from experience how he could manage the meetings of the Sacred College; he, too, had always had close contacts with the Wall Street laity.

The Embrace of the *Bond Market Strategy*

Under the Street's influence and Paul Volcker's supremacy, the Sacred College chose to change its operating procedure from a

Keynesian to a purely monetarist tack. On October 6, 1979, a historic day, the Reserve's regional bank presidents who were on the FOMC were called to Washington. The secrecy was so acute that the Fed carefully spread the presidents around the city in different hotels to avoid the ever-vigilant press. At that convivial meeting, all embraced money supply targeting, the *bond market strategy* for ending inflation; that is, the Sacred College of Bonds and Money would set a "proper" growth rate target for the money supply and then try to hit it. Afterward, Paul held a press conference for the Revelation.

Volcker and the Sacred College would now conduct monetary policy by restraining the growth in the various money supply measures—M1, M2, and M3—within various ranges. A greater emphasis in day-to-day operations would be on the supply of private commercial bank reserves (that directly influence money supply growth), with much less emphasis on confining short-term fluctuations in the federal funds rate (the rate private banks charge each other for overnight lending of their reserves which are on deposit at the Fed). With fewer bank reserves, for example, private banks have less in excess funds to lend to potential borrowers. Diminished lending, in turn, would reduce checking accounts or demand deposits since loans are deposited in various private banks. At that time, the favorite measure of the money supply, M1, comprised mostly cash and demand deposits owned by the public.

This was a sharp break from past practices. Previously, it had been the FOMC who decided the appropriate interest rate for federal funds, the private bank reserves held at the Fed. The federal funds rate had been governed through purchases and sales of government securities by the Sacred College. Since changes in this key interest rate are passed on to borrowers, the American Keynesians believed that monetary policy influenced the course of the economy through the fluctuations in the federal funds rate. If the economy is soft, according to the Keynesians, the twelve apostles might favor a lower "fed funds rate," as the federal funds rate is affectionately called; if the economy is booming, the FOMC would surely opt for a higher fed funds rate. A directive would tell the Fed's trading desk at the New York Reserve Bank to buy or sell government bills and bonds in a way designed to hit the interest rate target. If the FOMC considered interest rates too low in an overheating economy, the directive to the desk would be to "sell securities." As private banks or others wrote checks to a Reserve Bank for those securities, they would be drawing down their cash reserves at the Fed.

As private bank cash reserves decline, the banks would reduce outstanding credit. A rise in the fed funds rate would ration the smaller volume of funds lent and, ultimately, the Keynesian economists believed, all interest rates throughout the long spectrum of maturities would rise. Not only would private banks be paying higher interest rates on overnight loans, but General Motors would be paying higher interest rates for its borrowing, and so too would be the buyer of a new car or house. Less credit means less in the checking accounts composing the bulk of the M1 money supply. That the money supply slows with the reduction in bank credit is *a result, not a cause* of anything.

Monetarism was a transmutation. Volcker had adopted the Friedman–Jones principles, and the monetarist Kingdom on earth had come. Under the new procedures, an undesired fall in the fed funds rate would not prompt a fire sale of securities by the Reserve. The fed funds rate would simply be ignored, as all eyes would be on the money supply prize. Suppose the money supply is growing at a pace exceeding the range of growth targeted by the Sacred College. Then, and *only then*, would the New York trading desk sell securities, reducing bank reserves, and reining in the money supply. The targeted growth rate in M1, for example, might be in the range of 1 to 4 percent. If the actual growth rate is 5 percent, that would call for a securities sell-off. That the fed funds rate went up or down now was *a result* (of presumably many forces), *not a cause* of anything. Though, again, only money mattered, reality is not as simple as monetarism. After all, if bank reserves available for lending are reduced in the pursuit of slower growth in the money supply, we might expect the fed funds rate to rise.

As noted, the pressures favoring monetarism from the *Wall Street Journal,* Milton Friedman, Homer Jones, and the private bankers of the FAC were extraordinary. If those pressures were insufficient, international concern among foreign bankers might have tipped the balance. The international value of the dollar had been declining for a couple years. At cheaper dollars, Japanese yen and German marks buy more American goods and can exert upward pressures on that great demon, U.S. inflation. Moreover, foreign central banks—the counterparts to the Fed—hold U.S. dollars as international reserves. A decline in the dollar has two unpleasant results for these central banks; it reduces the value of their international reserves, and, also, the central bankers' power to influence their countries' exchange rates by buying and selling various currencies. Above all, central bankers do not like their powers diminished.

In September, Volcker had attended a meeting of the International Monetary Fund and the World Bank in (then lovely and peaceful) Belgrade. Verily, the club composed of the world's central bankers is a tight one, more exclusive even than the Chevy Chase membership. Each takes the concerns of his fellow travelers seriously. After all, they know what a tough daily grind it is to decide money supplies and interest rates. Though these monetary officials devote considerable thought to site selection, they often go for weeks without a trip to Paris, the Riviera, the Grand Tetons, or a favorite golf resort. Central bankers also hold contempt for anyone insinuating they know as much about money as they do. At the Belgrade meeting, foreign monetary officials urged Volcker to engage a tighter monetary policy to brace the dollar and increase foreign exports to the U.S.

Volcker, faced with a bold scientific experiment in the making that only a Dr. Frankenstein could love, might have thought that the world's bankers would go easy on him if monetarism went awry. He gambled that strict tightening of the money supply would silence these critics abroad. If interest rates edged up a bit, they would forgive him since the movement would be in the correct (Keynesian) direction, slowing the American economy and bracing the dollar. Volcker, however, had decided what he was going to do *before* the Belgrade meeting. The final decision was political: he *knew* that a slower money supply growth rate would elevate interest rates and cause a recession. With all eyes on the money supply, however, Volcker would not be blamed for soaring interest rates.[3] Besides, and we had the monetarists' word on this: the control of inflation by slowing money growth would only *temporarily* and *modestly* reduce factory output and employment. *No cost* to the U.S. domestic economy would be incurred.

The Bond Holders Get Traumatized and Become Part of the Problem

The lie was cast. The growth rate in the money supply roughly halved during the first six months of this "scientific" experiment based on misguided faith. Wall Street, bankers, monetarists, and, initially, bondholders everywhere rejoiced. The U.S. dollar did reverse its direction. However, if any glass ceilings were in their path, interest rates shattered them all as rates headed skyward. Not that interest rates had previously been modest: the fed funds rate, close to 10 percent in midsummer 1979, by early 1980 had nearly doubled, soaring to 18 percent. Even the highest rated corporations began to pay 14 percent for loans. An offering of long-term bonds by IBM sank along with the entire bond market: the early public buyers lost around $50 million as the issue went unsold. Bond prices were mired as if in a steamy peat bog in the Scottish moors.

What happened in IBM's "bond fire" sale and to Merrill Lynch and Salomon Brothers, the underwriting syndicate, became a cautionary, even chilling tale for bondholders. As noted, when interest rates go through the ceiling, bond prices go through the floor. From time to time the few syndicates who underwrite corporate or government bonds may refuse to take the bonds to market. When this happens, *the bond market collapses*. Without its precious bodily fluids or liquidity, the bond market dies. Unlike Frankenstein's creature, the market cannot be re-animated.

Such a cataclysmic event is no more welcome for the U.S. Treasury than it is for IBM and the bondholders. As government tax revenues fall short of federal expenditures, the Treasury cannot sell new issues of securities to finance its new debt. The U.S. Treasury then has no money to pay its bills. Whereas bondholders suffer capital losses when the bond market is weak, they could lose all their capital if the bond market closes and never reopens. Only those who sold in time and put their funds in the stock market or elsewhere would avoid the catastrophe. As it turned out, the Treasury's average short-term borrowing cost leaped from 9 percent to about 16 percent during early 1980.

Neither the monetarists nor the bondholders had expected the horror of a bond market collapse and soaring interest rates. Nor did they expect what happened next. Face to face with a financial Frankenstein, the Carter Administration panicked. It pressured a reluctant Volcker to invoke a little-used counter-monster, the Credit Control Act of 1969, to regulate the credit of financial institutions. The immediate reduction in borrowing had an equally quick and sickening effect on the economy. In the second quarter of 1980 the real GNP plunged at an annual rate of nearly 10 percent. Volcker's monetarism and the Carter Administration's regulatory error had caused a very sharp business recession.

Alarms went off along the aisles of the Federal Reserve. Volcker began to remove the new controls only two months after he had imposed them. The Sacred College began pumping money into the economy through Open Market Desk purchases of securities. The V-shaped recession of 1980 rode on the back of the lengthy, painful recession of 1973–75. Even so, the deep but short recession ended before the Great Monetarist Experiment.

After the genesis of monetarism by Volcker in 1979, the bondholders became part of the problem. Traumatized by Volcker's experiment, their more watchful eye on what the Reserve might do next would make bond prices increasingly volatile. Hypersensitive to Volcker's slightest move, the bondholders tried to predict the long-run future with each minute wobble in the weekly money supply data. If, contrary to the predictions of the growing industry of Fed watchers, M1 rose or fell moderately, bond prices and interest rates would spasm. If M1 grew "too quickly," bond prices would slump in anticipation of future tightening, causing interest rates to soar. By emphasizing the money supply above all else, the Reserve had contributed to the money supply fetish and jitters of the bondholders. M1 became the leading indicator for the financial market. Moreover, the anxiously awaited prognostications of the Fed watchers led, as noted, to even more volatility.

Animating a Greater Monster

By now, Carter was out, due in great part to what monetarism had wrought despite warnings from White House advisers of the consequences of Dr. Volcker. It was an economy in which only the infectious optimism of Ronald Reagan and supply-side economics, the economics of joy, could turn back the darkness, or so it was thought.

Reagan not only rode into the White House on a White Horse, but on the back of Volcker's economic recession that helped to defeat Jimmy Carter. As Reagan came to power, the recovery from the Carter Administration's 1980 recession was incomplete: the unemployment rate still hovered near 8 percent. Volcker and Reagan faced the continuation of the stagflation malaise, a condition of simultaneous inflation and unemployment afflicting Great Britain and Western Europe as well. Of the twin abominations, both Paul Volcker and Ronald Reagan—by then both scientific monetarists under the influence of Friedman—considered inflation by far the greater evil.

Like Malabre at the *Wall Street Journal*, Reagan had mastered monetarism at the feet of Milton Friedman. Reagan fervently believed that the sole cause of inflation was a rapidly growing money supply. Moreover, he believed, as did Friedman, that monetarism could defeat inflation without a noticeable decline in production or increase in unemployment. Worse, Reagan believed that Volcker had failed because he had not persevered in his first duel with the inflation demon. In an influential meeting with Volcker, Reagan urged him not only to return to tight monetary policy but to an *even tighter* monetary policy. A more formidable monetary monster had to be animated.

Having failed to slay the inflation monster with one of his own making, Volcker once again cranked up monetarism. Though it had been tested in a failed experiment, perhaps its voltage had simply been too low. The Reserve again slowed money supply growth after mid-1980 even as it turned up the voltage of monetarism. Keeping its hands off the monetary switch, the Reserve continued to decelerate the growth in the money supply in 1981, hoping perhaps to create a better monster. Still a recent convert and thus a singularly devout monetarist, Volcker might have blamed the credit controls for the 1979–80 recession.

The cooperation between the self-proclaimed "politically independent" monetary authorities and the Reagan Administration was inspirational, what with the White House and the Fed in unaccustomed agreement: the money supply would grow by no more than a meager 2.5 percent per year. A few blocks from the Fed's marbled Sacred Palace, White House staff were singing hosannas about how nominal gross national product (GNP) would be growing at an annual rate of *12 percent* between 1980 and

1984. Any economist failing to believe in the religion of the money supply was turned into salt by the *Wall Street Journal*.

What happened next had not been anticipated by the monetarists nor by Reagan's supply-siders. Even Ronald Reagan's optimistic glow could not prevent the calamity. By 1979 and 1980 the line of "voluntarily" unemployed workers was rapidly growing but apparently not fast enough to keep inflation under control. Still, following the monetarists' prescription to the decimal point, Paul Volcker managed to increase the unemployment rate to a level unseen since the Great Depression, even while greatly increasing the employment of staff economists at the Fed. Real GNP plummeted. Only the unemployment rate was Heaven-bound as it steadily climbed to 8.4, 8.8, 9.5, and, by the end of 1982, to 10.8 percent. For the monetarists, this should have been Heaven on earth. What had gone so horribly wrong?

Inflicting the "Necessary Pain" on the Working Class

Even if we accept the monetarist's arithmetic, Volcker's monetary policy does not add up. We need look no further than *In Hoc Signo Vinces* followed by $MV = PT$, the classical equality for monetarism and the motto of the Federal Reserve Bank of St. Louis. In the modern monetarist equation of Milton Friedman, real output or real GNP replaces the T. If we express all values in the equation in percentage changes or growth rates, the growth rate in the money supply plus the growth rate in its velocity equals inflation plus the growth rate in real GNP. That is, the modern monetarist equation becomes *Percent Change, M + Percent Change, V = Percent Change, P + Percent Change, Real GNP*. The sum on the right of the equal sign is the growth rate in *nominal* GNP.

In this way, the great promise of monetarism reduces to simple, and wholly embarrassing, arithmetic. Reagan–Volcker's planned pace for the money supply was a meager 2.5 percent, while promising to generate an amazingly rapid 12.0 percent nominal

GNP growth rate for 1980–84.[4] Suppose President Reagan's advisers had asked the obvious question: "How great would the percentage change in the income velocity or turnover rate of money have to be to give their targeted money GNP growth rate (on the right hand side of the equal sign) of 12.0 percent?" The answer, of course, is 12.0 percent minus 2.5 percent, or 9.5 percent. The growth rate in the *velocity of money*, the variable Friedman failed to mention to Malabre, would have to be an astounding 9.5 percent! Yet, the *historical average growth rate* in velocity was *only 3 percent* for the entire postwar era, 1946–1980. Only a *cockeyed* optimist would expect a future rate of 9.5 percent! More importantly, this historical 3 percent growth rate of velocity added to a 2.5 percent growth rate for money (again, summing the two rates) would allow nominal GNP to grow *only* 5.5 percent a year. At a White House inflation wish rate of 6 percent, the real growth in GNP would be –0.5 percent annually (5.5 – 6.0). *Real GNP declines!* In fact, that's what happened.

Again, in 1981–82, as during the Great Depression, job prospects were appalling, and expected returns from investment dismal and increasingly uncertain—seemingly a Keynesian situation. Households and corporations, however, not only held onto money but placed it in highly liquid financial assets, reducing the income velocity of money. Contrary to the ideas of either Adam Smith *or* Keynes, personal and corporate savings were going into financial assets instead of into real business investment. Without rising spending by consumers and business, output falls. Thus, Volcker's tight monetary policy only diminished inflation at the steep cost of a deep recession, just as it had before.

Administrations as remote as Eisenhower's (1953–61) and as recent as Carter's (1977–81) had shown what a sufficiently stringent monetary policy could do. If we look only at the full business cycle, a period including recession and recovery, the cycle of 1979–84 looks much like the Nixon–Ford–Carter years of 1973–79. Each era got off to a fast start with hyperinflation inspired mostly by OPEC's crude-oil price increases (and worrisome food–price inflation in the first period); in each era Volcker created a severe economic downturn to slow inflation, though the second time around the Reaganauts claimed that ending inflation would be painless. Dr. Volcker was the "scientist" doing the monstrous arithmetic not only in the denouement of the Carter administration but also in the early Reagan years.

Richard Nixon was to express regret that he never understood "what those people over at the Fed were doing." Jimmy Carter fails even to mention Paul Volcker in his memoirs. President Ronald Reagan, too, understood monetarism only through the imaginary, essential black box. He believed what they told him. However, Volcker knew better; he *knew* pain would come, *necessary pain*, he thought, but his cautions were overwhelmed by Reagan's upbeat economics of joy. Though celebrated on Wall Street as its science-based savior, Volcker was the arch-enemy of America's factory workers and the middle class.

Volcker knew that the pain would visit the hinterlands, not Wall Street. Moreover, in his words, "the administration generally supported our efforts to restrain money growth in 1981, even at the expense of ferociously high interest rates." He barely conceals his enthusiasm for the afflictions, as he adds, "the fact is, from my own admittedly partial and prejudiced perspective, there was substantial support in the country for a tough stand against inflation, for all the real pain and personal dislocation that seemed to imply." We can only imagine home buyers and unemployed construction and auto workers demonstrating at the Reserve Board in Washington, D.C., clamoring for more "transitional agony" in the interests of price stability.[5] We can only imagine, like a Mary Wollstonecraft visualizing life made better from the corpses of jobs. In fact, home builders, Realtors, and auto dealers mailed hundreds of keys to the Fed's Sacred Palace, symbolizing unbuilt houses and unsold cars. Despite the pain inflicted on ordinary people, the power of Wall Street and the bondholders over public policy in Washington had been established.

In the end, only Wall Street saw goodness emanating from the monstrous Monetarist Experiment. Thereafter, not only would the bondholding class gain dominance, its members would become very rich. Joyfully, we remained, as Reagan put it, "a country where someone can always get rich," or even a few.

NOTES

1. See "Basis for Strategy: A New Census of the Corporate Finance Universe," Dow Jones & Company, 1982.
2. As quoted by William Greider, *Secrets of the Temple* (New York: Simon & Shuster, 1987), p. 47.
3. A complete, detailed account of the Volcker era at the Federal Reserve Board is provided in Grieder, *Ibid.*, Chapters 11–17.
4. An alternative measure of the money supply, M2, was relatively stable during this time. The Federal Reserve, however, was using only M1 as its guide. Later, the Fed would look at a variety of measures of the money supply. M2 includes not only currency, checkable accounts and traveler's checks (M1) but also small-denomination time deposits, savings deposits and money market deposit accounts, money market mutual funds shares (non-institutional), overnight repurchase agreements, overnight Eurodollars, and a consolidation adjustment. Obviously, as Wall Street invents more instruments in which liquid assets can be held, whatever comprises the money supply changes. A third measure, M3, includes larger denomination deposits plus financial instruments of long maturities. The search for the "correct" measure of the money supply goes on.
5. Paul Volcker and Toyoo Gyohten, *Changing Fortunes: The World's Money and the Threat to American Leadership* (New York: Times Books, 1992), p. 176. Volcker's Phrase "transitional agony" appears on the following page.

SIX

The Rise of the Bondholding Class

Ronald Reagan "is the man to whom we Americans owe a debt that we will never be able to repay."

Rush Limbaugh, *The Way Things Ought to Be*
(New York: Pocket Books, 1992)

Only in retrospect are the conditions that fostered a new, powerful bondholding class plainly discernable. First, as already established, a self-regarding ideology is required. Second, as elementary as it sounds (because it is), to have a bondholding class, bonds are needed—lots of bonds. Third, for what had been a financial instrument duller than a Cubs' baseball game before Sammy Sosa, bonds must become exciting. Fourth, odd as it may seem, even for the rich, extra funds must be generated to sponge up historically massive amounts of bonds.

As it turned out, the federal bonds were unexpected windfalls from Dr. Volcker's monstrous Monetary Experiment combined with Reagan's wild budgets. Michael Milken, the king of junk bonds, not only supplied the excitement but *still more bonds*. The sorely needed mad money to buy the bonds was supplied by Reagan's lopsided tax cuts. Meanwhile, having crafted and promoted the ideology, and having taken the Federal Reserve, Wall Street had only to penetrate the nation's capital to fulfill these minimal conditions.

Once upon a time, the fable goes, Wall Street considered the free market to be the litmus test for what was spiritually correct, whereas it believed the White House and the Congress to be hell-bent on redistributing income and wealth from the rich to the poor. Not only was Wall Street's penetration of Washington, D.C. successful, the frequent complaint emanating from New York and the capital that they have different agendas has been silenced. We next consider how it all happened.

Wall Street and the *Bond Market Ideology* Penetrates Washington, D.C.

It is one thing to influence national economic policy through ideas, but it is quite another feat to govern that policy. The Street could not control the American itinerary at great cultural distance; it had to go to Washington. Taking the Sacred Palace of the Fed was easy. However, setting up a beachhead in the White House and Congress required going beyond the control of money to domination of the nation's political agenda. For that, Wall Street had to sell "trickle-down" economics. In recent times, the idea itself had Wall Street origins.

Unmitigated monetarism inadequately served the Street. Though monetarism would end inflation, it provided no basis in itself for tax cuts for the Street's clients, the bondholders. The *bond market strategy* lacked "scientific" support for cutting capital gains and other taxes. Luckily, a new school of economists, the "supply-siders," provided a lifeline from capital gains to a reason to have more of them. Whatever supply-side economics lacked in academic substance, its embrace by Milton Friedman, leading to resounding endorsements from the editorial pages of the *Wall Street Journal*, indemnified it.

Wall Street, still giddy from its infatuation with monetarism, fell hard for supply-side economics. Without the *Journal* as Wall Street's organ, the relationship with "supply-side" economics would not have been consummated.[1] Worse, the conservative media orchestrated the full monty of the *bond market ideology* or naked Wall Street capitalism. While most of the monetarist prescriptions for inflation came from authentic PhDs or economist-doctors, most supply-siders, by contrast, were not economists at all but journalists. Still, their soft-core ideas were persuasive on the Street.

This media event began with the appointment of Robert Bartley—a shy but sprightly writer still in his thirties—to the *Journal's* editorial page, the most influential business editorial page in the United States, perhaps in the world. In turn, Bartley hired Jude Wanniski, a self-confident refugee from Las Vegas, who went on to be an economic adviser to the 1996 GOP presidential candidate and year-2000 GOP presidential aspirant Malcolm (Steve) Forbes, Jr., the publisher of *Forbes* magazine. Neither Bartley nor Wanniski was trained in economics but they shared an interest in Washington politics and its effects on the national economy. Wanniski quickly became the supply-side leader.

Earlier, while working for another Dow Jones newspaper, the *National Observer*, Wanniski had met a young economics professor from the University of Chicago, Arthur B. Laffer. Wanniski and the fast-talking Laffer, much alike, became firm Washington friends. Laffer convinced Wanniski and Bartley that tax cuts and a tight monetary policy would ignite inflationless economic growth. In the fullness of media time, Laffer's twin ideas became Reaganomics. The tax cuts, bent to favor the rich, would lead to such an explosion in savings, production, and employment that any initial loss in revenue at the Treasury would be more than offset by revenue gains. Laffer could capture all of this wondrous stuff— or so he said—in one simple curve, the Laffer curve.

Though no hard evidence could sustain Reagan's faith in the Laffer curve, incantations wafted from the supply-sider faith that a reduction in tax rates would flood the Treasury with tax revenues. With exploding tax revenues paying for a shrinking government, federal budget deficits would end. Most economists, to their own credit, believed otherwise; tax rates were well below this range of perversity.[2]

Still, the game was underway on Wall Street. Once Wanniski deployed the *Wall Street Journal's* op-ed page to pitch Art's curve, Reaganomics was ready to play ball. Notably, Wanniski also wrote a longer article featuring the Laffer curve in *Public Interest*, a magazine edited by conservative Irving Kristol, a frequent *Journal* contributor and guru of the New Right. Someone showed Wanniski's article to Ronald Reagan, who was challenging President Ford (unsuccessfully) for the 1976 presidential nomination. Intrigued, Reagan met with Laffer. Later, Wanniski's modestly titled book, *The Way the World Works*, gave the Laffer curve celebrity status. Meanwhile, these conservatives had brought other Republicans into the fold.

It is dangerous to underestimate the power of the *WSJs* editorial page, perhaps the most elite medium of all. Without the *Journal's* huge circulation and prestige, the Laffer curve probably could not have been lobbed across home plate. As Bruce Bartlett, a Washington-based political consultant and supply-side architect put it, "the *Journal*, particularly its editorial page, under the leadership of Robert Bartley, is one of the most intellectually stimulating publications in America. Moreover, it has been the vanguard of neoconservatism [the New Right] and supply-side economics." He goes on to say that his book *"Reaganomics": Supply Side Economics in Action* "probably could not have been written without the *Journal*, a fact amply demonstrated in the footnotes."[3] With Bartley in control of the editorial page, the supply-side players had unlimited access to the business and political world.

In this critical turning point in history, ideology and dogma in the guise of good science served the *bond market ideology*. Luckily for the rich, as Ronald Reagan's political star was ascending, so coincidentally was the New Right. Its ideology blended stunningly not only with Reagan's, but Milton Friedman's as well. While the

Federal Reserve was building up the money supply at just the right rate, Reagan, adopting their approach, would balance the federal budget by ending social welfare programs, and the rich would be freed by tax cuts to increase their savings, assuring a rapid growth in real business investment. It is central to our story that the magic of "trickle-down" economics and aggressive deregulation liberating financial institutions not only created the bondholding class but continue to nurture it.

The Initial Deployment of the *Bond Market Strategy*

So, it came to pass, the *bond market strategy*, later to be deployed by Alan Greenspan, was first embodied politically in Reaganomics. The centerpiece of supply-side economics, the wildly misnamed Economic Recovery Act of 1981, cut personal tax rates for the rich and gave handsome but ineffective tax credits for business investment. Additionally, Reagan raised defense spending, cut non-defense spending, deregulated various industries, and, finally, would *balance the federal budget by 1984*, the year that George Orwell had "the clocks striking thirteen." The federal government's social welfare role, expanded by the New Deal programs of the 1930s, was reduced; its military presence was greatly enlarged along with the penal system. Reaganomics went as far as destroying labor unions, beginning with the air traffic controllers, whom non-union workers replaced.

As Bartlett correctly wrote, "in many respects, supply-side economics is nothing more than ... Say's law of markets rediscovered."[4] The savings-to-investment connection revealed to George Gilder, the author most frequently quoted in Reagan's speeches, the truth: "to help the poor and middle classes, one must cut the tax rates of the rich."[5] According to the *bond market ideology*, enlarged personal savings would automatically become new factories and equipment and the benefits would trickle down to lazy, undeserving workers. This notion provided the "moral grounds" for lowering marginal tax rates for the rich. Moreover, entrepreneurs would play their historically heroic role once they were freed from the shackles of taxation. David Stockman, then Reagan's director of the Office of Management and Budget (OMB) and once an unabashed supply-sider, confessed in a Christmastime 1981 interview, "Kemp-Roth (the name of the original supply-side tax bill) was always a Trojan horse to bring down the top rate." The supply-side theory, in Stockman's view, was really new clothing for the (*yes*) naked, once-discredited doctrine—the old "trickle-down theory."[6] Dogma not only overcame reason then, the bondholders' ideology is still with us.

Let there be no mistake about the intent behind the *Ideology* and the *Strategy*. The Street wants to make the rich richer. That goal not only fits Wall Street's ideology but suits its own moneymaking desires. In this, though actions never came close to fitting the script, Wall Street and the bondholders not only succeeded wildly during the final quarter of the twentieth century, the Clinton Administration built them a bridge to the twenty-first.

In the course of the initial success, bonds, lots of bonds, were created. They were created both in Washington and on the Street. Moreover, many huge tax cuts for the rich were to follow the avalanche of bonds. Those tax cuts continue to be made in Washington. Behind the mask of economic science, the dangerous duo of monetarism and "trickle-down" economics finally created the richest class of people on earth, ever.

Where the Government Bonds Came From

Had the government revenue targets been military ones, the supply-siders would have missed them by roughly a continent. The nominal GNP growth rate during Reagan's first presidential term was not, of course, at the scripted, but wildly improbable, yearly rate of 12 percent. In midsummer 1981 it was the *unemployment rate* that was approaching 12 percent. *Budget deficits* began to shatter historical records. A slumping national income meant sluggish tax revenues, especially at the lower tax rates.[7] Reagan's tax cuts combined with the explosion in military spending and the deep recession took the national debt from $908 billion to $3.2 trillion, or *more than treble the amount accumulated by all of his thirty-nine predecessors, beginning with George Washington.* Soaring federal budget deficits and debt accumulation did not end with Reagan's second term. President George Bush comforted those habituated to continuity as the federal deficits continued their rise, nearly reaching $400 billion by fiscal year 1992. The national debt, at last a heavyweight, weighed in at around $4.0 trillion in 1992.

Bonds, not money, were being created in historic amounts. The money would, nevertheless, soon follow through interest payments and capital gains. Reagan, a great fan of John "Duke" Wayne, doubtless could imagine Squadron Leader Duke loading those bonds aboard one of those new, expensive bombers. Then, in one last heroic mission, Duke commands, "Daarop those bonds on the heathens. We'aall shaw those bastards!" "Yes, sir," barks a pilot, "Bonds away!" In the noir Hollywood ending, ordinary people were routed.

Michael Milken Adds to the Bonds and to the Excitement

With the path to liberated markets being smoothed by Milton Friedman, the freeing of markets for moneymaking became a moral imperative for Reagan. Friedman had expressed his mantra of freedom in 1970: those businessmen who speak of the "social responsibilities of business" are "unwitting puppets of the intellectual forces that have been undermining the basis of a free society these past decades."[8] The sole responsibility of business, said Friedman, was to increase its profits, a faith echoed in Reagan's speeches. Word about the "magic of the market" spread quickly from the Reagan White House to the countryside. The key phrases on Wall Street were: (1) The Reagan Administration is against all government regulations affecting *any* market, including bond markets; (2) If money can be made by doing something—anything—it is an immoral act not to "just do it" (with needless apologies to Nike). Michael Milken was a natural by-product of the *bond market ideology*.

Attitudes, for sure, had to have changed. Not only had the rarified pleasure of taking great risks with money vaporized after the Crash of 1929, the idea of risk aversion had become popular among professors of finance by the 1960s. The most brilliant of these professors rediscovered an idea, once proprietary knowledge only to chicken farmers: "You should not put all your eggs in one basket." Since the eggs-in-a-basket parable did sound a bit simplistic, and since professors of finance detest barnyard metaphor, William Sharpe, the late John Litner, and Jack Treynor instead deployed the more elegant name, the capital asset pricing model. Since Sharpe went on to share a 1990 Nobel Prize in Economic Science for this seminal idea, we perhaps should take it seriously. Not holding all your eggs in one basket became known as *diversification*.

Mostly we are risk-averters, say these professors; therefore, we should select a portfolio of securities with risk-aversion in our hearts, investing in public utilities and avoiding casinos. The value and riskiness of this entire portfolio are what concern its holder, not the value of any particular security in it. After all, if the value of half the assets in our portfolio declines by 15 percent and the other half rises by 15 percent, we are no worse off. The pricing model provides a measure for the amount of an asset's *risk premium* or the difference between the asset's expected return and the risk-free interest rate (the interest rate on a security that has no chance of default such as a U.S. Treasury bill). Doubtless, diversification sounds as American as scrambled eggs.

Having made their case, or basket, as it were, the professors quickly qualified it. We cannot eliminate entirely some risks from holding different securities in a portfolio. In fact, the only risk that diversification can eliminate is risk unique to the asset and is *diversifiable risk*. Diversification cannot erase the other risk; it is awkwardly but accurately called *undiversifiable risk*. The measure of undiversifiable risk is Greek to most people; in fact, it is Greek even to finance professors. They call it *beta* (β). Though the calibration of beta is dazzlingly simple, we need only understand how it was deployed by Michael Milken.[9]

Beta is the bête noire of finance. The greater a security's beta, the greater its undiversifiable risk and, the beast being what it is, the less likely that the risk can be diversified away. The risk-averter, they advise, should avoid such securities. If the security with the high beta, however, also has a high expected return, the purchase may seem worth the extra risk. For instance, if Netscape bonds have a beta of 10, the expected rate of return on Netscape bonds should be ten times that of a "safe" portfolio.[10] The value of beta is an estimate of the amount of an asset's *risk premium* or the *extra return* required to compensate the buyer for the extra risk of holding the asset. Even the risk-taking buyer, perhaps a player like Donald Trump, being otherwise "rational," wouldn't buy securities with extra risk unless he expects an extra reward for it. Even the risk premium of an entire market compared with safe, 90-day T-bills can be calculated.[11]

Not every professor of finance agrees with orthodox opinion. One of those offbeat professors, W. Braddock Hickman, in an analysis of corporate bond performance for 1900–43, had shown how a *diversified* long-term portfolio of low-grade bonds yielded a higher rate of return, *at the same risk* as an otherwise comparable portfolio of blue-chip bonds. Another study of bond returns for 1945–65 reached the same conclusion.

Michael Milken, an intense business student at the University of California at Berkeley during the mid-1960s, was reading Hickman's landmark study of low-grade and unrated bonds while other students were mellowing out on marijuana. Later, as a securities salesman at Drexel, Milken preached the gospel of

Hickman. At first, most of Drexel's customers were unwilling to buy higher yield securities. To Milken, however, the higher yield on low-grade bonds simply reflected a risk well worth taking at such high expected returns. Milken was convinced that the *only* problem with low-grade debt was its lack of liquidity or quick convertibility into money.

Milken's view bears repeating: the *only problem* with low-grade debt was its *lack of liquidity*. Eventually, Milken's own intensive research dispelled customers' initial aversion to high-risk bonds. Such bonds included "fallen angels"—bonds issued by well-known companies, such as Penn Central Corporation, that had fallen in price as these companies got into financial trouble. In Milken's view, buyers underestimated those "risky" companies' abilities to pay interest on their bonds. Put differently, Milken told customers that the bond players were *irrationally* "risk-averse": the bond market had been sullied by those golfing widows at Chevy Chase. Realistically, he suggested, a well-diversified portfolio of high-return low-grade bonds would provide a higher rate of return than ordinary bonds *and* no more risk.

Eventually, Milken's sales ability solved the "lack of liquidity" problem. He attracted a group of financiers who saw no stigma attached to low-grade securities. As their returns met or exceeded their expectations, the early buyers became enthusiastic backers of Milken and clients of Drexel.

By early 1977, when Wall Street's plan to take Washington by land, sea and air was in its infancy, Milken already controlled a quarter of the national market in high-yield securities. He had become a *market-maker*. Using a technique mastered by the Great Houdini, Milken's own key unlocked the door to liquidity (of a different kind, of course). Milken could assure the holder of bonds that he would buy their bonds whenever the holder wanted to cash out or go liquid. In turn, Milken could resell the securities, keeping any difference between the "buy" and "sell" price he accrued. In practice, just as Houdini had once monopolized magic, Michael Milken *became* the junk bond market.

Since they did not publish the "buy" and "sell" prices, only Milken and a few colleagues knew of the widening spreads between these prices, an increasing source of riches for Milken. Milken controlled *both* the *new issues market* and the *secondary or resale market* for junk bonds. The Securities and Exchange Commission, the main regulatory agency for the securities markets, did not register the offerings and the Milken Market went unregulated, just as Milton Friedman, Ronald Reagan, and the supply-siders fancied. Milken always operated with more knowledge than any buyer or seller because he *was* the low-grade bond market.[12] If such a thing as "a market" could ever be personified, *he* was it. Those buyers and sellers on the other side of the market might as well have been smoking something; they were no match for Milken's secret information. Thus, much of the "magic" of this market came from Milken's concealment of the key to it. Houdini, too, would have been impressed.

By the 1990s, as the market in low-grade bonds made a comeback (only to falter by 1998), colleagues in finance and economics winced when someone referred to them as "junk bonds." They would retort, "these are high-yielding bonds with large betas!" In fact, Michael Milken, in an uncharacteristically candid moment, did call high-yielding bonds, "junk." According to Meshulam Riklis, who controlled the Rapid-American conglomerate, and who was one of Milken's first clients, "he [Milken] looked at my bonds and he said, 'Rik, these are junk!' "[13] Since the term stuck, Milkin doubtless regretted this brief flash of honesty. More to the point, junk bonds epitomized the revolutionary shift toward risk-taking in the bond market: brokers began to use betas as the basis for "*good* expected returns" on securities. A half-century trend favoring risk aversion and opposing excessive debt ended during the 1980s.

Back when the bond market and Ozzie and Harriet defined stability, there was little reason to use betas. Truth in labeling abided. Some corporate and municipal bonds were classified as "low-grade bonds," a warning label sufficient then to keep most buyers away. Whatever else he might have done, therefore, Michael Milken and those who made his system work should be given credit for making these low-grade bonds alluring. His system nonetheless depended upon the players on Wall Street doing what they always do, moving wherever money is to be made. Despite an understandable earlier reluctance to sense excitement in the world of bonds, the Street came to embrace bonds with a passion rivaling its new lust for slow economic growth.

Milken's initial creation of junk bonds could never alone have created the *degree* of excitement about to invade the bond market. As important as junk was, several other forces were to radiate not only out of Wall Street but also out of Washington, D.C., giving bonds a glitz and making a few people extremely rich. The spreading harmony between Wall Street and Washington was new and, therefore, all the more welcome on the Street. We next consider those final forces.

Junk Bonds Lead to LBO Mania and to Still More Bonds

Despite the slippery slope on which the junk bond market was built, it led to a new era of leveraged buyouts (LBOs) during the 1980s, more feed for the bondholders' trough, and, ultimately, to the downsizing of the working class. Though *being* the junk bond market was highly lucrative, Michael Milken saw still bigger money in mergers and acquisitions. A corporation, a public company, would be bought out by a group of financiers with money generated by selling junk bonds to insurance companies, banks, brokers, and savings and loan associations (S&Ls). In this wonderful arrangement the financiers did not have to use any of their *own* money. Moreover, all those handling the transactions, including the

CEOs selling their own companies, and Milken with his widening spreads between buy-sell prices, made tens of millions of dollars. Milken's salary plus bonus by 1982 was already $45 million, or $72 million in 1998 dollars.

Kohlberg Kravis Roberts & Co. (KKR) became the dominant takeover artist.[14] In turn, insurance companies, banks, and S&Ls virtually stopped financing the buying of capital goods, drilling for oil, or building houses; instead they lent billions to KKR in their purchases of junk bonds from Milken. KKR completed nearly $60 billion in acquisitions during the 1980s, culminating in the purchase of RJR Nabisco for $26.4 billion in late 1988, then the largest takeover in history and sufficiently notorious to become not only a book but a TV movie.

Since Milken and KKR were entrepreneurs in the eyes of the Reaganauts, ample government assistance was forthcoming. A conglomerate rush—the merger of unrelated enterprises—was encouraged by both tax policy and by an antitrust policy most notable for its aggressive laxity. On the heels of a historical record of mergers of companies in 1981 and 1982, the arrangement of mergers had by 1983 become a growth industry led by a legendary Texas tycoon by the misnomer of Slim Pickens.

Fortuitously, by 1985 Michael Milken and his Drexel colleagues had more client money than they could place. To increase the supply of junk bonds, they began to finance corporate raiders such as Pickens, Carl Icahn, Ronald Perelman, and KKR. The KKR executives borrowed more money through Drexel between 1984 and 1989 than any other client of the junk bond firm, one of the most symbiotic relationships ever. These takeovers of large corporations generated billions of dollars' worth of junk bonds, for even the use of leverage diminishes the value of outstanding bonds of former blue-chip corporations to junk. Milken's salary and bonus continued to climb—exceeding $440 million in 1986 alone.

Conglomeration and its consequences are symbolized by the bidding war for Marathon Oil Company. Mobil tried to buy

Marathon. Contrary to the claims for the effects of the supply-side tax incentive program, Mobil expressed an interest in buying *existing* oil reserves rather than going to the time and trouble of actually looking for new reserves. In its boldest gamble since the company was put together by Andrew Carnegie and J.P. Morgan in 1901, U.S. Steel bid against Mobil for Marathon.

Even though Mobil raised its ante and took its case to the Supreme Court, the Court ruled in favor of U.S. Steel because it was not then and had never been in the oil business. As a result of the acquisition, U.S. Steel (now USX Corporation) became the nation's twelfth largest industrial company. As I later relate, the merger mania set off by junk bonds not only had effects on the bondholders, it was to alter the prospects of wage earners at USX and most other corporations.

What happened to RJR Nabisco should have raised a yellow flag against the coming financial turbulence in the 1990s. By the spring of 1990 it nearly sank into bankruptcy because of financial problems resulting from its efforts to keep its junk bond debt afloat. KKR, too, was close to sinking. These savings, including those from seniors' social security checks, went not into new software development or factories but into securities with values eroding in the high tide of debt. However, unlike many senior citizens and the S&L's, not only did KKR survive the storms, but by the mid-1990s it was again listing shares of companies it owns on the New York Stock Exchange and expanding its operations.

Provisioning Funds to the Rich to Buy the Profusion of Bonds

Everything required for the creation of a new, but nonproductive leisure class was in place by the early 1980s. As we go beyond the depth charge of federal deficits, the explosive force of junk bonds, and consider the final force, we, at last, can fully explain the rise of the bondholding class. Though bonds are necessary for the existence of a bondholding class, they alone are insufficient. The working class cannot be expected to snap up $3 or $4 trillion in new federal bonds, especially when this volume is printed and distributed over such a brief historical period. Only the very rich, super-rich, and supra-rich could cope with such massive issues. A new concern comes to the fore: could even wealthy persons afford these new bonds? The question was a frightening one on Wall Street where the bonds were being underwritten by the investment bankers and where most of the values in portfolios were being held.

As to the truth, the great concentration of ownership of bonds among the wealthy is no secret. Though the Federal Reserve has never officially drawn a connection between debt finance and the rich, its own data confirms what most people have always suspected and Wall Street has always known. When the bondholding class was beginning to take flight, the Federal Reserve Board's survey of consumer finances showed that families in the top 2 percent—nearly or actually the super-rich—owned some 39 percent of corporate and government bonds and 71 percent of tax-exempt municipals. The wealthiest 10 percent, the simply rich, then owned 70 percent of the bonds and 86 percent of tax-exempts.

In accordance with the *bond market strategy*, however, to unleash economic growth, America's wealthiest citizens needed even more income and wealth. The final initiative creating the new bondholding class was, fittingly, Reagan's massive program of tax cuts for the rich. Consider the reductions in the *effective* income tax rate, the true rate paid rather than simply the tax rate from the IRS schedules. The effective income tax rate on the super-rich, the top 1 percent, had been reduced by 7.8 percentage *points* by 1984. The effective tax rate for the very rich, the top 5 percent, dropped by 4.2 percentage points and, for the simply rich, the top 10 percent, 3.1 percentage points. Moreover, the top tax rate on unearned income from interest payments fell steadily from

70 percent in 1980, to 50 percent in 1982, to 38.5 percent in 1987, and to 28 percent in 1988. Thus, not only did the rich enjoy much higher incomes—be it from salary, stock options, interest payments, or capital gains—each family could keep a much larger share of its gains.

Tax cuts for the rich paid for the bonds! The amount of income freed by tax cuts for the rich would seem unbelievable if they did not happen to be known. Tax breaks for the very wealthy enabled them to buy something like $700 billion of Reagan's new bond debt. Even the distribution of these holdings was tilted toward the upper 1 percent or super-rich, and still more to the upper ½ percent or supra-rich. The *average* tax break for the super-rich, the top 1 percent, was $52,621 by 1989. The total value of these tax cuts for 1982 through 1990 was nearly *$2 trillion* (in 1985 dollars). By 1992, under President Bush, the average tax break for the super-rich had risen to about $78,090 on incomes averaging $676,000. In this instance Big Government made a difference for a select group of slightly more than a million families. Most, if not all, of these extra dollars went into securities portfolios. Not only were the bonds—in massive quantities—initially created during the Reagan years, but so were the means to buy them. What's more, the tax breaks continue to this day.

Incredibly, over two full terms, the Reagan Administration *came perilously close to not creating enough new bonds for the rich.* Milken's junk bonds were sufficient to diminish the gap between amounts supplied and demanded. That rich people existed—even before Reagan and Milken—became part of the problem: excluding financial institutions and the federal government, the rich *already* owned most of the remaining existing bonds, well before their unneeded tax cuts. While Volcker's recession combined with Reagan's budgets were taking the national debt or the value of bonds outstanding to $3.2 *trillion,* Reagan's tax cuts had given the rich only a $2 trillion windfall for their purchase, leaving precious few newly-engraved bonds for private banks, insurance companies, the Federal Reserve, and foreigners to buy!

Interest payments by the Treasury were greatly accelerated early on by Volcker's tight money policies, abetting the debt-to-wealth shift. The Treasury had to rapidly expand its debt to make these payments: in this way, it capitalized interest by converting it into new bonds. Bonds continued to fall from the sky. As a result, federal expenditures on interest soared from $96 billion in 1981 to $216 billion in 1988, only to go still higher to $241 billion in 1996. By the early 1990s interest payments would become the third largest category of federal spending, threatening to knock national defense spending off its number-two perch.

Among households, the interest payments blessed the few holding the bonds, while crowding out federal expenditures. Since only 3 percent of all families then directly held any bonds, the top 1 percent of wealth holders, the super rich, got half of all interest payments going to households, while the top 10 percent got virtually all of it. Compound interest alone was creating new millionaires and billionaires. While the payment of interest continues to be good news for the bondholding class, it is crowding out federal expenditures that could benefit other citizens. Today, the payment of interest on the national debt to the very rich, not the debt itself, is the major problem.

Let there be no mistake regarding who benefitted from the deficits. The yearly tax benefits for the *very rich* combined with exploding twice-yearly debt *interest* payments *exceed the full increase in the yearly pace of federal deficits beginning with Reagan's first year*! In 1998 Americans paid as much in taxes as interest payments to the bondholders as they paid to run the navy, air force, army, marine corps, intelligence agencies, and the defense administrators and staff. That's about 14 cents of every federal government dollar spent! Largely because of the growth of the government bond market, 13 cents of each dollar of personal disposable income (personal income after income taxes and social security deductions) was coming from interest payments by 1996. In bold contrast, only four cents of each dollar of income came from stock dividends.

For Wall Street, those interest payments and tax breaks alone were not good enough. As it turns out, capital gains in the secondary or resale markets would become an even more important wealth source than the spiraling interest.

Anticipations

At a casual glance, seeing where all those federal funds and tax breaks went is difficult. To the ordinary citizen the funds had disappeared with barely a trace, as if the checks had been written in invisible ink. Yet, it was the visible hand of the U.S. Treasury that provided enormous amounts of mad money to bondholders during these years. As an article of "trickle-down" faith, the rich can be given more money out of gratitude, presumably for hiring workers—though not so many that the unemployment rate falls below its natural rate. Seldom, in the annals of history, however, has a government come so swiftly and magnanimously to provide such massive financial resources to the wealthy.

Coming to the aid of the rich was good for Wall Street. Not only had the bond issuers and bond buyers given investment bankers more business, but ideology had given the new bondholding class reason to blame any future capital losses on unemployment rates falling below Friedman's natural rate, breaking the speed limit for economic growth. To Wall Street, "trickle-down" economics confirmed the *ideology of the bondholding class*; it was scientific capitalism.

Wall Street capitalism, prematurely portrayed in the editorial pages of the *Wall Street Journal*, began, not with Reagan or even Milken, but with Paul Volcker. "Trickle-down" economics coupled with Volcker's industrial-strength monetarism not only complemented the *ideology of the bondholding class,* it defined the Street. Good luck continued to reign for Wall Street and the new bondholding class. Unable or unwilling to reduce deficits, Bush left it to Democrat Bill Clinton to cut the deficits by some 60 percent during his first term, move to a balanced budget sometime in 1998, and build his proverbial bridge to the twenty-first century with budget surpluses. Now that the bondholding class holds the bonds, it has reason to make bonds scarce, and, all the better, to raise their prices.

Those who say that the age of "trickle-down" economics, as old as Adam Smith's seminal ideas, ended with the Volcker-Reagan experiments either have not been paying attention or have been beguiled by the *ideology of the bondholding class*. Next, we see how Alan Greenspan embraced—with a fervor that would have embarrassed even Ronald Reagan—the *bond market strategy*. If the Washington media had kept as close an eye on Alan Greenspan as it did on Monica Lewinsky this final assault on traditional American capitalism might not have happened.

NOTES

1. For still more details on this *Wall Street Journal* connection and influence, see again, Alfred L. Malabre, Jr., *Lost Prophets* (Cambridge: Harvard Business School Press, 1994), Chapter 6. Malabre's account is consistent with that of Bruce Bartlett, *"Reaganomics": Supply Side Economics in Action* (Westport, Connecticut: Arlington House, 1981), Chapter 11.
2. For a more detailed history of Reaganomics and its consequences, see E. Ray Canterbery, *The Literate Economist: A Brief History of Economics*, 2nd edition (Singapore/River Edge, NJ/London: World Scientific, 1999) and, by the same author, *The Making of Economics*, 4th Edition (Singapore/River Edge, NJ/London: World Scientific, 2000).
3. Bruce Bartlett, *"Reaganomics": Supply Side Economics in Action* (Westport, Connecticut: Arlington House, 1981), p. viii.
4. Bartlett, *op. cit.*, p. 1.
5. Gilder, *op. cit.*, p. 188.

6. Quoted by William Greider, "The Education of David Stockman," *Atlantic Monthly*, December 1981, pp. 46–47. Stockman's confessions had been made to journalist-friend Greider.

7. In reaction to the massive tax revenue losses, in 1982 Congress repealed a scheduled further increase in accelerated depreciation allowances and eliminated safe-harbor leasing, a 1981 provision that allowed unprofitable companies to sell their tax credits and depreciation write-offs to profitable companies. These 1982 tax changes left an improvement in the expected return from plant and equipment investment of about 17 percentage points (rather than 28 percentage points) above the pre-Reagan tax treatment return. In such a deep economic slump, however, sales were not sufficient to warrant investment in new capacity and the tax cuts could provide no stimulus.

8. Milton Friedman, "The Social Responsibility of Business is the Increase in its Profits," *New York Times Magazine*, September 13, 1970. Reprinted in Thomas R. Swartz, and Frank J. Bonello, Editors, *Taking Sides: Clashing Views on Controversial Economic Issues*, 3rd Edition (Guilford, Connecticut: Dushkin, 1986), p. 22. A rebuttal is offered by Robert Almeder in a companion piece, pp. 28–36.

9. Suppose on historical average a 1 percent rise in the NASDAQ composite index leads to a 10 percent rise in Netscape. The beta for Netscape would be 10 ($^{10}/_1$). Suppose on historical average a 1 percent rise in the S&P 500 produces a 0.5 percent increase in the price of GM stock. The beta for GM would be a meager 0.5 ($^{0.5}/_1$). Thus when NASDAQ fluctuates (down and up), the price of Netscape fluctuates ten times as much, whereas on the S&P 500, GM fluctuates less than the overall market. The higher risk of Netscape is based on its greater volatility.

10. If Netscape's beta is 10, its expected return in excess of the 90-day T-bill rate should be ten times the difference between the return on the entire stock market and the T-bill rate. Thus if the overall market return is 8 percent and the T-bill rate is 4 percent, the risk premium on Netscape would be a mind-numbing 40 percent [$10 \times (8 - 4)$]! In turn, the expected rate of return on Netscape should be 40 percent to chance the risk of holding it. As it turns out, the price of Netscape during the Great Bull Market of the 1990s exceeded 40 percent several-fold.

11. The risk premium of the whole market is the expected return for the completely diversified market portfolio minus a "risk-free" interest rate such as the annualized 90-day T-bill rate.

12. Many more details about Michael Milken can be gleaned from a book by Pulitzer Prize-winning reporter James B. Stewart's *Den of Thieves* (Simon & Schuster: New York, 1991). The reader will find here, besides Milken, many other Wall Street criminals from the "anything goes" era of the 1980s that has been revived during the 1990s.

13. Quoted by Connie Bruck, *The Predators' Ball* (New York/London: Penguin Books, 1989), p. 39.

14. The complete story of KKR is told in George Anders, *Merchants of Debt: KKR and the Mortgaging of American Business* (New York: Basic Books, 1992).

———◆———

SEVEN

The Final Assault on the Clinton White House

Greenspan haunts every budget meeting, though his name never comes
up directly. Instead, it's always our "credibility" with Wall Street. It is
repeatedly said that we must reduce the deficit because Wall Street needs
to be reassured, calmed, convinced of our wise intentions.

> Robert B. Reich, *Locked in the Cabinet*
> (New York: Alfred A. Knopf, 1997)

Historically, a frequent complaint has emanated from New York
and Washington: "Those politicians inside the beltway do not
understand Wall Street's needs." Unlike so many disputes, the
quarrels between the Street and Washington have ended. The head
of the Federal Reserve System, two successive Treasury secretaries,
and the bondholding class, itself a joint product of Washington
and New York, have moved Wall Street's agenda into the White
House. As President-elect, Bill Clinton virtually turned over White
House economic policy to Alan Greenspan and to the Treasury
heads, all choices of Wall Street. By mid-April 1993, the
administration had embraced the preferences of the financial market
players for budget deficit reduction and free trade, a dream
program for Eisenhower Republicans. Meanwhile, Clinton
maneuvered to dilute Greenspan's power. In that endeavor, as I
relate, Clinton failed.

Greenspan and Clinton: An Unholy Alliance

The initial alignment of Clinton and Greenspan seemed as unlikely as that of Venus and Mars. In the 1950s, Alan Greenspan was well to the political right of the Eisenhower Republicans. Greenspan was drawn into the tight little New York circle led by Ayn Rand. As for Dwight D. Eisenhower, Rand considered him a closet communist. Greenspan had been one of the first students at the Nathaniel Branden Institute, the "think tank" founded to further the ideas of Ayn Rand. Rand's other followers called Greenspan "the undertaker" because he always dressed in a black suit, much like the one he wore to her funeral. Greenspan later took to wearing only blue, perhaps so he would seem less the villain to blue-collar workers.

Greenspan was a member of a radical right group known to themselves as The Collective and, to Rand, as the Class of '43, named for the year of her novel, *The Fountainhead*. Summing theologically her philosophy, Rand evokes radical individualism as the theme of *The Fountainhead*, which she called "individualism versus collectivism, not in politics, but in man's soul."[1] Its hero, architect Howard Roark, embodies a philosophy of pure self-interest. He designs a gigantic government housing project for the poor only under the condition that he designs it *his way*. In the end Roark cannot save the project from the many evil characters opposing him in the name of some greater good, such as taking from the rich and giving to the poor. Thus, Roark is justified in destroying his butchered creation with a charge of dynamite! The poorly housed are left with rubble, but Roark has saved Rand's philosophical theme: the "do-gooders" put the heroic entrepreneur in the position of having to blow up the project.

The Collective converted Greenspan into a lover of free markets, a man not only suspicious of do-gooders but having a righteous hatred of government. Greenspan told the *New York Times* in 1974, "What she [Rand] did—through long discussions and lots of arguments into the night—was to make me think why capitalism is not only efficient and practical, but also moral."[2] Whatever irony attends a free-marketeer becoming the world's most powerful bureaucrat is exculpated by the revelation that Greenspan, the Howard Roark of central banking, has been the lonely hero freeing Wall Street from the chains of government.

Greenspan never wandered far from his Randian roots, nor from Wall Street. In 1954, he and an older bond trader, William Townsend, established the New York-based consulting firm Townsend–Greenspan & Company. The company not only made Greenspan a millionaire, but introduced him to the biggest banks in New York. At Rand's prodding, Greenspan entered the political arena as the director of domestic policy research for Richard Nixon's presidential campaign. Staying on as an informal Nixon adviser, the future central banker easily bridged the ideological gap between Wall Street and Washington. From Townsend, Greenspan learned how inflationary expectations could depress bond prices and increase long-term interest rates, something he never forgot.

The volatile mixture of Randian philosophy, Wall Street values, and Washington reality, nonetheless, sometimes exploded. In 1968, for instance, Greenspan created a problem for Nixon by setting in motion a proposal to free Wall Street from regulations. Since many on Main Street did not trust Wall Street, the idea of *regulating* Wall Street was very popular. Nixon had to reverse Greenspan. Later, as President Ford's chief economic adviser, Greenspan proposed a sharp reduction in government spending during the presidential election year of 1976, presumably to douse the flames of inflationary expectations which were feeding rises in long-term interest rates.[3] As the country entered its deepest recession in fourteen years, Greenspan somehow persuaded Ford to ignore the recession and attack the inflationary menace at a time when unemployment already stood at 8 percent! Voters, unsympathetic, defeated Ford and elected Jimmy Carter president. Greenspan himself was involuntarily unemployed from government for a time, returning nonetheless to his high-priced consulting work; he never became a digit in the natural rate of unemployment.

Greenspan never strayed from his radical ideology, though at the Fed he stated it with less clarity. In a 1966 essay for Ayn Rand's newsletter, Greenspan declared gold the ultimate weapon of the haves against inflation, a way for the "owners of wealth" to "protect" themselves against government schemes to "confiscate the wealth of the productive members of society to support a wide variety of welfare schemes."[4] In other essays he attacked antitrust and consumer protections laws. Later, in a thinly veiled attack on the government's case against Microsoft, Greenspan displayed a deep philosophical doubt about antitrust enforcement. He said, "I would like to see far more firm roots to our judgments as to whether particular market positions do, in fact, undercut competition or are only presumed on the basis of some generalized judgment of how economic forces are going to evolve." But, he added, there "ought to be a higher degree of humility" when enforcers make such projections.[5] When Greenspan raised the fed funds rate, he nevertheless lacked, if anything, humility.

In sharp, dramatic contrast to Greenspan's pedigree, Clinton was a Southern populist who had governed the poor, backward state of Arkansas. He was one of the New Democrats; they were more centrist than the old Democrats, but they nonetheless wished to retain the social programs from Franklin Roosevelt's New Deal. They still believed that the federal government had an important role in maintaining full employment. It was, they believed, the responsibility of the federal government to increase opportunities for the poor, because the rich had the resources to care for themselves. Moreover, Clinton had run for president on a platform of public investment in the infrastructure such as roads, airports, bridges, and schools. By the time of his run for a second term, however, these issues had long since been abandoned unless "building a bridge to the twenty-first century" is considered a new infrastructure.

Why would the Clinton White House agree instead to an alliance with Greenspan? No doubt deep concerns among those being appointed to positions in the U.S. Treasury contributed to this end. The U.S. Treasury's dependence on the bondholding class to purchase its securities (including the foreign bondholders, especially in Japan and the United Kingdom) had greatly increased when the Reagan–Bush governments turned their backs on the truly conservative method of financing government from tax revenue.

Besides, Clinton was hardly the first Democrat president to be undone by Wall Street. After all, Alan Greenspan's ineptitude helped defeat Ford and, ironically, elect the *first* New Democrat. Later, however, the Reserve got even. Paul Volcker's first recession had inspired the electorate, at last, to answer Jimmy Carter's plea for self-denial by sacrificing Carter's presidency. We turn now to the travail of the second New Democrat president in his battle of wits with Volcker's successor.

Greenspan's Bond Market Strategy

What was once merely an anti-inflationary neurosis at the Federal Reserve crossed an invisible psychological border into a psychosis, culminating in the zero-inflation policy championed by Greenspan. A new way of thinking emerged: slow economic growth was *good* because it led to higher bond prices and hence a bullish stock market. Interest rates were to be kept low not by an easy money policy but by managing to keep the economy soft. Even the hint of a speed-up in economic growth created a chill in the pristine air of the Sacred Palace. If necessary, the Reserve would raise short-term interest rates so that longer-term or bond interest rates might fall. This commanding view is manifestly an extension of Wall Street's *bond market strategy*.

Greenspan outlined his new philosophy to Clinton alone in the Governor's Mansion in Little Rock shortly after Clinton's election to his first term. No single economic policy could do more good for society than a drop in *long-term* interest rates. These rates

128 *Wall Street Capitalism*

matter most to businesses with large debts and to people paying mortgages. The Fed could control short-term interest rates but long-term rates would not drop unless the "the bond market" was convinced that the White House was going to reduce the federal deficit.

Greenspan imagined bondholders and traders to be "highly sophisticated," by which he meant that they expected the federal budget deficit to continue "to explode."[6] With such vast federal expenditures, inflation would inevitably soar. In Greenspan's single-minded view, the budget deficits from government spending, not soaring oil prices, had induced the double-digit inflation of the late 1970s. Wary investors then demanded higher long-term returns because of the expectations on deficits. This unfavorable spin on federal deficits was the new twist in the post-Reagan *bond market strategy*.

With deficits under control, Greenspan said, market expectations would change. Bond traders would have more faith in their mantra, price stability, and long-term rates would drop. Since homeowners had increasingly used refinancing as a source of consumer credit, they would buy more automobiles, appliances, home furnishings, and other consumer goods. This borrowing and spending would wonderfully expand the economy. Moreover, as the bondholders realized lower yields on bonds, they would shift money into the stock market and stock prices would take off like a flock of geese. Finally, in this congenial environment, economic growth from deficit reduction would increase employment. By the end of more than two hours of "bonding," the new president-elect had signed on to Greenspan's version of the *bond market strategy*.

Deficit Hawks at the Treasury Come to the Aid of the Bond Market

Greenspanspeak might not have carried the day except for the deficit hawks circling Clinton's original agenda. The lead hawk and surely the one with the greatest wingspan was Lloyd Bentsen, the Treasury Secretary designate. Leon E. Panetta, then the new budget director, also sounded the alarm that the budget deficit was shooting out of control. By the turn of the century, it would be $500 billion, "a truly unmanageable level."[7] Alice Rivlin was selected deputy to Panetta precisely because she was of the same species. Though distrusted by the consultants who had brought Bill to Washington, and despite compulsive foot-in-beak media relations, Rivlin's deficit demeanor ultimately put her on the top perch at Budget when the President reassigned Panetta to the White House staff aviary.

The success of this *bond market strategy* would depend on the stimulus the economy would get from the promised fall in long-term interest rates. Alan Blinder, then a designated deputy director of the Council of Economic Advisers (CEA) and by 1995 Vice Chairman of the Fed, was among those at a critical agenda-setting meeting just 123 days before the inauguration. Blinder concluded that falling long-term interest rates could offset the adverse effect of a 1.5 percent lower economic growth rate arising from a reduction in government spending (and in the deficit) of $60 billion if the bond traders' inflation premium (based on expectations) evaporated. "But after ten years of fiscal shenanigans," warned Blinder, "the bond market will not likely respond."[8]

At Blinder's revelation, Clinton's face turned red with anger and disbelief. "You mean to tell me that the success of the program and my reelection hinges on the Federal Reserve and a bunch of fucking bond traders?"[9] The others at the meeting now agreed that that indeed was the case (with expletives deleted)! At that defining moment Clinton perceived just how much of his fate was passing into the hands of the unelected Alan Greenspan and "the bond market."

Vice President-elect Albert Gore said that such "boldness" was the essence of Franklin D. Roosevelt's program. "Look at the 1930s," he reminded everyone. "Roosevelt was trying to help people," Clinton shot back. "Here we help the bond market, and we hurt the people who voted us in."[10] Panetta told Clinton he had no choice. If he did not act, a balanced-budget amendment might pass Congress, forcing Clinton to surrender his presidency to a few members of Congress. Apparently, if the White House were to raise a white flag, hoisting it over the Sacred Palace of the Reserve was far better than over the dome of Congress. Besides, Panetta warned, the Reserve would probably raise short-term interest rates if the deficit kept going up.

Public Infrastructure Is Sacrificed to Reduce the Federal Budget Deficit

Clinton's economic team came to conclude that without Greenspan's cooperation they were doomed. Bentsen went to Greenspan to assure him that the team had moved toward deficit reduction. "The Fed chairman, first among deficit hawks, smiled at the news."[11] Bentsen concluded that Greenspan would be supportive within broad limits. Even the amount of the deficit reduction was set (at $140 billion) by Greenspan and passed along to Bentsen who passed it along to Clinton without attribution.

In the second week of Clinton's presidency, Greenspan dropped his final bomb: after 1996, the interest on the debt would explode, and "a financial catastrophe" would follow. Bentsen was there along with Robert Rubin, then head of the National Economic Council and subsequently replacement to Bentsen as Secretary of the Treasury. They agreed. With visions of stock market crashes, depression, and collapsing banks dancing in his head, Clinton assured the three that a major deficit reduction plan was already in the works. Clinton, the extraordinary mix of true Democrat, populist, Southern pulse-taker, man-of-the-people, and brainy policy student was out: deficit hawks and the Washington–Wall Street establishment had swooped down and stolen Clinton's presidency.

The outcome for Clinton's own agenda was worse than he had thought at the time. Without Clinton's knowledge, Congress had decimated his investments because of the caps placed on spending for the years 1994 and 1995 as part of a 1990 budget deal. Panetta had always downplayed the importance of the caps; therefore, their devastating effects went unanticipated by the rest of the economic team. Once told, Clinton's temper erupts a second time. "I don't have a goddamn Democratic budget until 1996. None of the investment, none of the things I campaigned on."[12] That, of course, was the case. In a separate account by former Secretary of Labor Robert Reich, Clinton stalks the room, fuming: "We're doing everything Wall Street wants!"[13] That, too, was the case.

What were the immediate consequences of the *bond market strategy?* Gradually the 30-year bond rate did come down, from 6.8 percent to below 6.0 percent, and the capital gains of bondholders went up. There followed an undramatic but steady expansion of GDP. Interest-sensitive spending on residential construction, plant and equipment investment, and consumer durables accounted for all of the growth that occurred in 1993. In those interest-rate sensitive sectors, real GDP rose by 11 percent while the non-interest-sensitive sectors showed virtually *no growth*. Greenspan and Bentsen credited the growth to "the financial markets strategy." Greenspan had claimed that each percentage point decline in the long-term rate would boost GDP by $50 to $75 billion: Bentsen rounded this up to $100 billion.

Greenspan Breaks His Promise

The Greenspan–Clinton alliance nonetheless had the life span of a butterfly. In January 1994 Greenspan told Clinton and his economic advisers that inflation expectations were mounting, driving long-term rates to 6.3 percent. Two weeks later the Fed raised short-term rates, with the Fed raising rates a third time on

April 18, 1994. The long-term benchmark rate moved to 7.4 percent, higher than at any time in Clinton's first term. Again, the Fed was raising short-term interest rates in the hope of slowing the economy and *thereby* lowering the long-term rate. Greenspan had broken his promise to the President to bring interest rates down if Clinton narrowed the deficit.

The Federal Reserve Board's official account, transmitted to Congress on February 21, 1995 is: "The Federal Reserve continued to tighten policy over the year and into 1995, as economic growth remained unexpectedly strong.... Developments in financial markets—for example, easier credit availability through banks and a decline in the foreign-exchange value of the dollar—may have muted the effects of the tightening of monetary policy." Firms and households were going deeper into debt (as Greenspan *had* promised) and the dollar was falling; however, these were now "reasons" for turning the monetary screws even tighter.

By early 1995, signs of an economic slowdown appeared. As we know, the same parts of the economy that are very sensitive to interest rate reductions are equally or even more sensitive to interest rate increases. Moreover, a Republican-dominated Congress was pushing for deficit reduction though spending cuts and greatly reduced tax rates for the rich, using Reaganautic rhetoric. Meanwhile, President Clinton was taking a beating in the polls, despite having achieved the only significant deficit reductions since the Nixon Administration.

The President's angry outbursts revealed his undeniable frustration. After all, his advisers told him that a small and rich minority of the population in the bond market (again, the top 10 percent hold 86 percent of net financial assets and the top 1 percent, nearly half) would dictate the President's own agenda. The millionaires and billionaires—those *most active* in market speculation—have only 400,000 to 500,000 votes among themselves (not counting "dollar votes" of the investment bankers and other professionals on Wall Street). Despite this, most of Clinton's economic advisers embraced The Bond Market as a new American icon.

The embrace seems complete as we read the 1995 *Economic Report of the President*, written by Clinton's Council of Economic Advisers (CEA). The CEA expresses a renewed emphasis on deficit reduction, as if the President has not done enough for Alan Greenspan and The Bond Market: "A primary economic reason for reducing the federal deficit is to increase national saving, in the expectation that increased saving will, in turn, increase national investment in physical capital.... The implication is that increased national saving should be associated with increased productivity." In this way, the *Report* also embraces Say's Law in which saving is not only a social virtue but the direct and reliable route to greater real capital accumulation: the *Wall Street Journal* editorial writers could have written this message.

Worse, the 1997 *Economic Report of the President* claims that interest rates would have been higher had deficit reductions not taken place, ignoring the unmistakable fact that Greenspan had raised the fed funds rate nearly 50 percent against inflation's ghost in 1994—*after* the deficit reduction legislation had been enacted. Is it any wonder that historical evidence suggests no close, positive relationship between federal deficits and interest rates? Though Clinton had *reduced* the deficit steadily, interest rates *went up*, not only in 1994, but in 1995 and 1997. *Greenspan* had raised interest rates in the face of declining federal deficits. Moreover, despite three years of compelling evidence—every estimate of the NAIRU had predicted a rising inflation rate, but it did not rise—the council speculates that lower unemployment itself may reduce the natural rate of unemployment.[14] If this is so, fighting inflation by *raising* unemployment, since that only raises the threshold natural rate of unemployment at which inflation takes off, is disingenuous!

Even the 1998 *Economic Report* fails to dismiss NAIRU. The council's estimate of a 5.5 percent NAIRU for 1997 should have led to a 0.3 percent increase in inflation instead of an actual

0.4 percent *decline*. This result, writes the council, "would appear to pose a challenge to models of price inflation based on the concept of a NAIRU." The council nonetheless lays the blame of NAIRU's temporary failure to a decline in computer prices, a judgment that happens to be wrong. Moreover, this report, like all Clinton-era reports, carefully avoids a serious discussion of monetary policy, much less any criticism of Alan Greenspan's policies.[15]

When all is said, using traditional Democrat Party rhetoric to rationalize the *Bond Market Strategy* is devilishly difficult.

The Consequences of Alan Greenspan's "Independence"

How did the Democrats come to this sorry state of economic affairs? The Fed's "independence" is based as much on convenience as necessity, ceded as it was during World War II and reclaimed during those Eisenhower years. Yet, renowned journalist Bob Woodward has Greenspan, sensitive to presenting an image contrary to his assumed "independence," agonizing over the propriety of his sitting next to First Lady Hillary Clinton at the President's first State of the Union address. Nevertheless, Greenspan was there and looking more the peacock than the hawk.

Unlike the Independence Avenue that runs from the Congress and parallel to the South Portico of the White House, however, the "independence" of the Fed is a one-way street. In Woodward *and* Reich's reporting, Greenspan manipulates Clinton and Bentsen, and Bentsen manipulates everyone else. Greenspan's Fed, demanding that the White House and Congress never meddle in monetary policy, held the White House economic agenda in bondage.

As noted, the historical power of the Fed has always derived from its unmatched ability to create an aura of mystery about the regulation of money and bonds. These matters are said to be way beyond the grasp of novices. But, if the Fed were so smart, why did it allow its own entrapment by the bondholder class? The short answer: Greenspan, once simply a member of the Collective, was a charter member of the bondholder class. Until April 1997 and his marriage to NBC-TV correspondent Andreas Mitchell, Greenspan had most of his personal assets in a blind trust. He then liquidated that trust so the couple could make joint financial plans. At the end of 1997, his own $3.5 million in financial assets were mostly in short-term Treasury bills ($2.4 million) and in bonds ($600,000). He held mostly T-bills, he said, "to avoid any conflict of interest." Since the Fed conducts monetary policy by buying and selling T-bills, this is like the head of the Securities and Exchange Commission saying that he holds only stocks "to avoid any conflict of interest."[16]

The Federal Reserve by now had created a new set of expectations against which it was powerless to avoid sloth and recessions. Stock markets go into mini-crashes with each upward wiggle in short-term interest rates, not because the speculators expect inflation but because they expect recession down the road from the higher prime and long-term rates that are guaranteed whether inflation takes form or not! The traders expect recession because the Reserve has had a phenomenal postwar record in its creation. The stock traders sold if they expected that Greenspan expected that the bond traders would expect inflation followed by the recession created by the Greenspan's expectations about their expectations. These expectations' impulses are completely out of control! As it handles these new impulses, the Federal Reserve's grasp now extends beyond the reach of the Constitution.

Clinton's Quandary With Greenspanmail

The lower interest rates at the beginning of the Clinton years did at least for a while help with jobs and the economy. Meanwhile, the President, at Greenspan's and the Treasury's bidding, had more than halved the federal deficit by 1996. Despite being held hostage by the bond market, Clinton achieved a major increase in the earned income tax credit (a negative income tax). This credit goes to those workers whose earnings fall short of $27,000. He also temporarily increased income tax rates at the very top of the income distribution, the source of financial market speculation. Both actions went under the Grand Old Party knife in the Gingrich-led Congress in 1995. Worse, incumbent Clinton chose to deploy notorious political consultant Dick Morris during the 1996 reelection campaign, probably because the economic well-being of the typical American family—long in the doldrums—was slipping perceptably. Morris, however, decided that to be re-elected, Clinton needed to do still more of the same by campaigning on the GOP agenda.

Clinton, an intellectual and pragmatist, probably considered all the options short of the *bond market strategy*. Still, his choices were limited. The White House could have avoided being Greenspanmailed only by going directly to the people: if Clinton had not gotten the deficits down, Greenspan would have raised short-term rates *immediately*, rather than waiting until later. The impeachment or replacement of Greenspan during Clinton's first days in office were the only other, improbable, options. Clinton did not have the votes in a GOP-controlled Congress that was in Wall Street's pocket. The problem rested with the tremendous and unchallenged power of Wall Street and the Federal Reserve against a President reluctant to use his political capital.

Despite the *bond market strategy* being in disarray, job improvements during the campaign, Clinton's adoption of the Republican agenda, and a lackluster campaign from Bob Dole, who had yet to endorse Viagra, was sufficient to reelect Clinton in 1996. The bond market still fears strong economic growth; the stock market still fears higher interest rates despite its speculative highs in 1996–99. In early September 1998, when Greenspan merely hinted that he was as likely to *lower* as to raise interest rates, the Dow made its then-largest point rise ever, a 380-point leap in one day.[17] If anything, the activities of the Good News Bears had heightened during these years as the Dow swung wildly—hundreds of points from week to week, sometimes from day to day, sometimes *within* the day.

Clinton's Aborted Efforts to Change the Agenda at the Reserve

Clinton's shift of Alan Blinder from the Council of Economic Advisers to the vice chairmanship of the Fed was not only an attempt to moderate Greenspan's policies, but to provide an heir apparent. However, the Republican congressional victory in 1994 ended White House hopes that Blinder could gain Senate approval and replace Greenspan. A carefully orchestrated effort by Greenspan and others to discredit Blinder on Wall Street as one too willing to tolerate "some inflation" to keep the economy growing now had the support of Congress. As to Wall Street, "the constituency for easy money—low rates—at the Fed has just lost one of its most outspoken champions," sniffed Fed watcher Stephen S. Roach, chief economist at Morgan Stanley & Co., upon Blinder's departure from the Fed.[18]

Though Blinder's resignation left two unfilled seats among the seven Fed governors, the GOP's capture of Congress guaranteed that President Clinton would nominate Greenspan for a rare third term beginning March 1996. Moreover, Greenspan probably helped select Clinton's other two Fed nominees—the Office of Management and Budget (OMB) director Alice Rivlin, her hawkish wingtips now touching those of Greenspan himself, tapped for vice-chair, and St. Louis economic consultant Laurence H. Meyer, as a governor. Both agree that the economy can't grow much beyond 2.2 percent a year without rekindling the fires of inflation.

Clinton's first choice to replace Blinder as vice chair was Felix Rohatyn; he too could not win Senate confirmation. Rohatyn not only has written extensively about his concern for the financial fragility of the economy but had called for the Fed to worry less about goods inflation. Though managing director of the Lazard Frères investment house and a high mandarin of capitalism, Rohatyn, not only a maverick on Wall Street, but a liberal Democrat, is distrusted there as much as Greenspan is revered.

Robert Rubin and the Investment Bankers Move into the White House

The bond market continued to inhabit Bill Clinton's thoughts as he agonized over balanced budget agreements with Congress during early 1997. Not only Robert Rubin, but each of the other men responsible for getting the President's budget through Congress, had left a successful career in investment banking. Erskine Bowles, a political moderate and venture capitalist from North Carolina, became chief of the White House staff. The new head of the OMB, Franklin Raines, helped run mortgage giant Fannie Mae. All three bankers could slip unnoticed into a moderate Republican administration. Some Democrats were wishing that they had; these party members were beginning to worry that Clinton's channels to the progressive community were closing. In any case, they signed on to the 1997 Budget Reconciliation Act and capital gains tax reductions that greatly benefited wealthy families, and forecast federal surpluses as far into the future as the eye could see.

Rubin, who moved up to replace Bentsen as Secretary of Treasury on January 10, 1995, had spent most of his working life at Goldman, Sachs Co. in New York, one of the world's most profitable investment banks. An upper one-percenter in the income and wealth distributions, Rubin commuted by private jet between the tony Jefferson Hotel in Washington and his Park Avenue home in New York. Boyish-looking for his 1938 birth year, Rubin had long been not only a New Democrat but a centimillionaire exuding the calm, deliberate airs of the polished investment banker he once was. Beginning as an option trader in 1970, Rubin was, by the decade's end, one of a quartet of elite arbitrageurs known as the "four horsemen," one of whom was Ivan Boesky. Rubin went on to revive Goldman Sachs' bond department and become co-chairmen of the firm in 1990. Having come up through the ranks of bond and stock traders, Rubin was to fret greatly over what the financial markets might "think."

During negotiations over Clinton's 1994 budget, Rubin had advised the President to ease up on his "tax the rich" rhetoric, which Rubin warned would increase class divisiveness. His apparent fear that the rich will rise up and revolt against the poor appears excessive. Then, when Secretary of Labor Reich suggested, on November 21, 1994, an attack on Republicans for seeking a capital-gains tax cut and corporate tax cuts, and the use of the presidential bully pulpit to let people know about the great increase in income and wealth concentration, Rubin blanches.

"Mr. President," Rubin interrupts, "you've got to be *aw-ful-ly* careful to maintain the confidence of the financial markets. You don't want to sound as if you're blaming corporations."[19] Later, on December 7, when Reich suggests eliminating some of the tax loopholes of large corporations, Rubin responds, "The financial markets would take it badly." Then, when Reich suggests that corporations should be required to count advertising outlays as an investment for tax purposes, saving the Treasury billions, Rubin responds, "the financial markets would take it very badly." When on Wall Street, Rubin bought and sold for the bondholding class; now, he had become one of its most influential spokesmen.

The Bondholders Legacy: Ending the Progressive Agenda

In his second term, President Clinton abandoned domestic economic policy concerns and was looking to foreign policy achievements as a way to elevate his historical place among American presidents. He had fought Greenspan and Wall Street and had lost, first, as President-elect, turning domestic economic policy over to Greenspan, then, turning the White House over to a corporate investment banking strategy. Progressives were deeply disappointed. (Besides, by late 1998, while Greenspan's words still were moving financial markets, the House of Representatives was impeaching the President.)

Despite an introverted personality and a solicitous treatment of his colleagues, Chairman Greenspan emerged historically as the most powerful leader of the nation's central bank and an acknowledged spokesman for deregulation and privatization. Within the Reserve, he minimized challenges to his decisions by deft maneuvering. His anti-inflation phobia won raves from the bondholding class and from Wall Street generally. In his third term Greenspan answered to no one. He had more power over the American economy and much of the global economy than any other person.

Robert Rubin had always been on Greenspan's team. Working quietly behind the scenes, Rubin not only helped to persuade Clinton that federal deficit reduction was his top priority, but put a subtle pro-business stamp on the presidency. In December 1996, as Clinton made his cabinet appointments for his second term, he not only named Rubin as secretary of the treasury, but as "captain of the team." Then, he sent Rubin and Greenspan to San Francisco in early September 1998 to negotiate with Japan's finance minister, ironically, attempting to push Japan toward an expansionary fiscal policy.

Meanwhile, Greenspan and Rubin had a lot of help from the GOP. A revitalized Republican Party, dominating Congress in 1994 (for the first time in forty years), became a cheerleader for the bondholding class. During 1995, several GOP candidates for the presidency, the least of whom, former economics professor Phil Gramm, were recycling the Reagan–Kemp supply-side tax ideas. These ideas enjoyed greater respectability in the proposed supply-side tax cuts of Republican nominees' Bob Dole and Jack Kemp of Kemp–Roth. The superficially mainstream resurrection of financial capital gains and inheritance tax-cut proposals, not only from the

Gingrich–Gramm and Dole–Kemp Republicans but from the White House, enjoyed sufficient respectability to make bi-partisanship seem an oxymoron.

In the end, the centerpiece of the 1997 tax bill signed by Clinton was a cut in capital gains taxes and other tax benefits for the rich. The richest 1 percent of households once again benefitted by far the most, with each paying $16,000 less in taxes. The bottom 20 percent of U.S. households saw their taxes *rise* by an average of $40 a year. The second 20 percent saw no change, and the middle 20 percent gained only $150 a year. Finally, the GOP legislation that passed the House in 1998 to eliminate the U.S. tax system by the year 2003 was a thinly veiled effort to replace it with a tax system still more favorable to the rich. A tie vote in the Senate tabled the bill. New Democrats, it has been said, are the pragmatists who are able to compromise with the GOP. By that standard, if by no other, Bill Clinton is the most compromised Democrat president in history.

These forces have sustained a class rich beyond common imagination during the twentieth century. Soon, euphoria combined with price volatility would engulf the sale of bonds, public and private, providing new profit opportunities for daily traders. After huge capital gains had given the bond market long-denied respectability, playing the bond market—joined at the hip by a gyrating but bullish stock market—required the agility of a racquetball champion. The bondholding class, carved out of soaring inequality and now operating in a newly deregulated financial environment, would contribute mightily not only to the reversal of fortunes of the lower 95 percent of families, but to the creation of a financial casino.

The completion of the "Reagan Revolution" continued to be promoted by then Speaker of the House Newt Gingrich and his GOP majority, as well as by *Forbes*, the magazine, Steve Forbes, the presidential candidate, and by *Barron's,* a publication devoted to bonds—not to mention the editorial page of the *Wall Street*

Journal, a page still devoted to those of sufficient wit to hold great wealth. It continues, too, to be supported by the Milkin Institute, a nonprofit organization funded by Milkin's junk bond fortune. President Clinton, while ending his first term, signed a welfare bill that he said he disliked, ran a 1996 presidential campaign mostly from the GOP platform, and was reelected. In 1997 Clinton signed onto a "trickle-down" package of capital gains and inheritance tax cuts. In winter 1998 the President was impeached by the GOP he had emulated. *That* is the way the world *really* works.

We next consider the ramifications of the *bond market strategy* and the bondholder's legacy for the huddled masses.

NOTES

1. Quoted by Ayn Rand's biographer, Barbara Branden, *The Passion of Ayn Rand* (Garden City: Doubleday & Company, 1986), p. 132.
2. Quoted by Steven K. Beckner, *Back From the Brink: The Greenspan Years* (New York: John Wiley and Sons, 1996), p. 12. Beckner first became acquainted with Greenspan through his writings on the virtues of laissez-faire economics and the gold standard in Ayn Rand's journal. Later, Beckner covered Greenspan as a financial journalist in Washington. For the most part, Beckner's book is laudatory, though what Beckner praises Greenspan for, others might condemn him.
3. See Beckner, *op. cit.*, p. 15.
4. Alan Greenspan, "Gold and Economic Freedom," *The Objectivist*, July 1966, reprinted in Ayn Rand, *Capitalism: The Unknown Ideal* (New York: Signet Books).
5. Alan Greenspan, Testimony Before the Senate Judiciary Committee, U.S. Congress, June 16, 1998.
6. Bob Woodward, *The Agenda: Inside the Clinton White House* (New York: Simon & Schuster, 1994), p. 69.
7. *Ibid.*, p. 82.
8. *Ibid.*, p. 84.
9. *Ibid.*
10. *Ibid.*, p. 91.
11. *Ibid.*, p. 98.

12. *Ibid.*, p. 165.

13. Robert Reich, *Locked in the Cabinet* (New York: Alfred A. Knopf, 1997), p. 105.

14. For a detailed critique of the 1997 *Economic Report of the President*, see James K. Galbraith, "The Clinton Administration's Vision," *Challenge*, July–August 1997, pp. 45–57.

15. Once again, for details on the contents of the 1998 *Economic Report of the President*, as well as an explanation why falling computer prices did not alter the inflationary environment, see James K. Galbraith, "The Economic Report of the President for 1998: A Review," *Challenge*, September–October 1998, pp. 87–98.

16. For the complete story regarding the Greenspan portfolio, see the Washington AP Release by Dave Skidmore, "So, Where Does Greenspan Put His Money? Not in the Stock Market," August 19, 1998.

17. The day was Tuesday, September 8, 1998. The percentage gain of 4.98 percent, however, was only the 58th largest ever in percentage terms.

18. Quoted by Louis Uchitelle, "No. 2 at Fed Tells Clinton He Is Leaving," *The New York Times*, January 17, 1996, pp. C1, C3.

19. As quoted by Reich, *op. cit.*, p. 207.

III.

THE BAD NEWS FOR ORDINARY PEOPLE

EIGHT

Surfing Today's Volatile Bond Market

Repercussions of the *bond market strategy* extend well beyond the bondholding class itself. Its expanding resources are increasingly devoted to speculation, giving bondholders the power to move not only the bond market but—directly and indirectly—stock markets. The great divide came from new wealth sufficient to make speculation in bonds appealing. Even when this class confines its activities to the bond market, it still has dramatic effects on other markets. Worse, this ability gives the bondholders fearful power over public policy, especially the policies of the Federal Reserve and the White House. Moreover, the bondholders define their own best interests as universal; they can only be, at best, 5 percent correct.

The way bondholders became a financial weathervane for all markets came about innocently enough. The rough rule of thumb used by the widows of Chevy Chase was not contrary to workers' well-being: the widows favored the rapid economic growth then benefitting not only bondholders, but workers. Moreover, the widows did not trade at the sharp gilded edge, hoping to tease still greater returns out of capital gains. Now, not only would the new bondholding class fear inflation, but any speed-up in economic growth, employment and wages that might tempt the Federal Reserve to raise interest rates in a preemptive strike against *expected* inflation. Perhaps it is poetic justice, but Alan Greenspan made the life of bondholders more complex.

Looking for new ways of judging how the American economy is performing, the bondholders began to use clues found in future bond price changes, not only as a guide to the bond and stock markets, but to judge public policy. Not only do the holders and dealers now watch every move in bonds, their *reactions* to movements in bond prices have important consequences. In particular, the bondholding class has become very judgmental regarding the Fed's actions. No longer favoring rapid economic growth and strong employment conditions because these conditions no longer favor bond prices, the bondholder's view of what is good about the economy conforms better with what is best for Wall Street. From these developments came a still greater division between those who hold financial assets and those who work for a living.

The Bondholders Seek New Ways of Measuring Economic Performance

In the search for new clues, there are a few important things to remember about bonds. As noted, when the interest rates on coupon bonds move, the prices of bonds (even those about to be issued) move *in the opposite direction*. (A reminder: the bonds continue to pay the same *amounts* of annual interest or fixed income.) Imagine a teeter-totter with the price of a bond sitting at one end and its interest rate at the other; when the price end teeters toward the ground, the interest rate end totters upward. Moreover, a price change in a bond from a movement in its interest rate will be greater, the longer the maturity of the bond. Though there is very little difference between the interest return at purchase time and the yield to maturity of Treasury bills (because they mature in one or a few months or, at most, 52 weeks), the bondholders nonetheless watch yields on bonds maturing in five years or more with the intensity of a teenager in front of *Baywatch*. A 30-year bond is considered especially risky.

Finally, while the face value of a bond, even of a Czarist Russian bond, never changes, the prices of all bonds change continually in the closely watched *secondary* or resale bond market.

Beginning in the late 1970s, escalating in the 1980s, and continuing through the 1990s, bond prices have become highly volatile and merit closer watching. As the swelling amounts of money going in and out of the market make bond prices increasingly volatile, bonds become more like stocks, and require those new clues. Still, the vast majority of Americans do not have a clue; they pay little heed to daily movements in bond prices, not out of ignorance, for intelligence is no guarantee of wealth, but from lack of anxiety, for their stake is so small. They still watch most closely whether they will have a job tomorrow.

The Bond Surf Is Up

The bondholder, once navigating waters as still as those of Minihaha, is now navigating something more akin to the Pipeline at Oahu's North Shore. Increased wealth held in narrow channels has shaped market waves into hollow cylinders into which an unwary surfer can disappear and, only with considerable luck, reemerge before the wave swallows him. The bond market, once for timid widows, is now host to surfers who would not be intimidated by waves at Waimea Bay in March. Like the Jekyll and Hyde nature of Hawaii's beaches, the bond market can change character from one day to the next, or even within five minutes after the release of a favorite clue or indicator.

For example, one week before a major new issue of Treasury bonds in early August 1996, bond yields plunged as much as half a percentage point, boding well for the prices of any new bond issues. On Tuesday, August 6, the market showed remarkable strength despite the prospect of $10 billion each of new 10-year notes and 30-year bonds. Buyers greeted the first leg of this major Treasury refunding and exploding supply of bonds with a yawn.

Never mind Jekyll and Hyde, what could account for this wonderful reception for such a large new offering?

In the Goldilocks Economy, we recall, *bullishness* comes out of *lackluster* economic news. Through much of July the financial players had feared possible reports of improved employment numbers and higher inflation prospects that might lead Fed chair Greenspan to raise interest rates at his August meeting with the Sacred College. Early in July, bonds (and stocks) had rallied on "favorable" news on the inflation and employment front; prices for raw materials and factory employment had fallen off a cliff in July. Then, a report revealed weaker-*than-expected* growth in the manufacturing sector in July. News seldom gets better than that for the Good News Bears!

Anxious bondholders nonetheless remained concerned; perhaps the unemployment rate would drop before the bond auction. Luckily, the unemployment rate went up! John "Rocket" Spinello—chief strategist at Merrill Lynch, chief bond cheerleader, and Fed Watcher—put it best: "The anxiety balloon was punctured with respect to the likely action [by the Federal Reserve] following last week's data," he exclaimed ebulliently as the new bond issues were launched. The data, he added, suggests *less likelihood* that the Fed will raise rates, meaning there is "more willingness to buy, even though we're at lofty levels." However, he was more cautious about the bellwether 30-year bonds because of their notorious volatility. "Buying those bonds is a career decision, where most of the money in the bond market can be made or lost," he cautioned.[1]

One way to gauge risk is to rely on a statistical measure called, oddly enough, the standard deviation.[2] First, the expected return of an investment over a selected period is averaged. Second, we measure how much returns have deviated from that average during the same period. The waves at Waimea have a low standard deviation between May and September, as fishing boats bob lazily at anchor in Waimea Bay. Then, suddenly, during winter, weather transforms Waimea into a fearsome spectacle of ocean power, with waves sometimes reaching twenty or thirty feet high. Sometimes, a wave on a "big day," a day with "deviations" much greater than average, can swallow a surfer on the "inside" and, sadly, bury them under tons of water. In recent times those individuals and institutions which have ventured into the bond surf have sometimes disappeared under tons of bonds and reemerged less than whole.

A picture of monthly long-term Treasury bond yields (interest rates) between January 1977 and January 1998 confirms the shift from serene waters to turbulent surf. The yields—reflecting opposite movements in prices—are plotted in Figure 8.1. For Treasuries, as for corporate bonds, the mid-sixties was like Waimea in summertime. The standard deviation was only 2.5 percent; that is, long-term bond prices varied from their average values by only an estimated

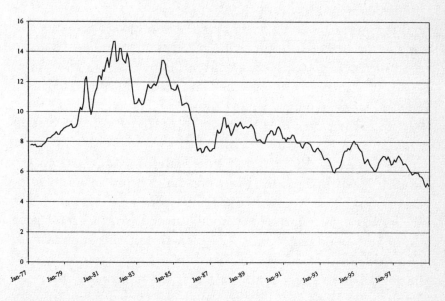

Figure 8.1 Thirty-year Treasury Bond Yields, February 1977 to December 1998

Source: Board of Governors of the Federal Reserve System
NOTE: The data are for the first day of each month.

plus or minus 2.5 percent. At the time, in the 1970s, the surf seemed to froth with the two energy crises, but, in retrospect, that decade exhibited month-to-month calm.

For long-term bonds the 1980s was like winter in Waimea. During the Reagan–Bush years of 1986–90 bond prices deviated 12.6 percent from their average. (This variation or volatility, of course, is also an "average," hiding the still greater monthly volatility.) Generally, bond prices looked like foaming surf, as did their corresponding yields. Volatility of long-term Treasuries decreased to 8.9 percent between 1991 and 1995; apparently bipartisan waves because they were shared about equally by Republican Bush and Democrat Clinton. However, these movements still look like winter in Waimea compared with historical experience. In the fourteen five-year periods from 1926 to 1995, *only four* periods experienced higher volatility than the 1991–95 period.

Volatility during the early 1990s, too, was even greater than our multi-year measure would suggest. The bond market had its worst year *ever* in 1994; then, in 1995, it had one of its *best* years. In truth, prices and yields of long-term bonds have made waves during the nineties that only the most daring surfer would ride. The yield soared from a 22-month low of 5.77 percent in October 1993, to 8.16 percent only a year later; it then fell below 6 percent in December 1995. By mid-1996, it had risen to around 7 percent. On the second Friday in March 1996, interest rates exploded and Treasury bonds suffered the worst one-day collapse in fifteen years, driving *their* yields skyward. Again, the rises in yields reflect the fall in the capital value of the bond; anyone who had purchased the 30-year bond in January had already lost the equivalent of more *than one and a half years' worth of interest payments* by mid-March. On the second Friday of June, within minutes, the price of a $10,000 face-value Treasury bond plummeted $250, as many public bondholders joined brokers as daily traders, or what the stock brokers call "day traders."

Explaining Bond Price Volatility

Many explanations, of varying reliability, have been offered for the swell in volatility. According to the folklore of the bondholding class, of course, inflation is its great enemy. In a financier's classic, Princeton professor Burton G. Malkiel flatly states that by the 1970s and 1980s "inflation accelerated and bond prices became more volatile."[3] Little wonder why, then, the bondholders say, "If inflation were vanquished, the giant waves would recede and still waters would prevail."

At the risk of mixing a metaphor, this wisdom now seems to hold little water. Though considerable inflation in goods and services prices *sometimes* accompanied the other four volatile eras going back to 1926, the inflation rate during the nineties was lower than during the mid-1960s. Inflation, demonized by bondholders, was steady; swaying like the mildest of trade winds, it languished in a narrow band of 2.5 percent to 3.5 percent during the early nineties. By 1998, U.S. goods inflation was approaching zero.

Something had changed dramatically. Not only were bondholders no longer content to buy and hold, their sensitivity to even mild inflation or their expectation that the Federal Reserve would react to distantly-perceived mild inflation had increased. Their own preference for low inflation had been achieved, but apparently low was not good enough for the Sacred College, or so bondholders believed.

When funds move out of the bond market, they go somewhere. The Federal Reserve's *Flow of Funds Accounts* shows outflows of $43.4 billion away from bonds after 1994, when 30-year Treasuries lost about a tenth of their value. As a result, some unlucky bond funds holding such Treasuries lost nearly a fifth of their value.[4] Despite all the claimed advantages from diversification, this painful experience kept many American players out of the market in 1995. The now high yields (and low prices) nonetheless proved irresistible to foreigners. The inflow of money from the foreign contingent of the bondholding class is what made 1995 the third-best year ever for bonds. The 30-year Treasuries were up about a third as Greenspan finally eased interest rates.

Some of the funds of the American bondholding class quickly flowed into stocks as substitute assets. Already in the midst of a long bull market, the American stock market began to perform even better. In the first half of 1996, while $121 billion was cascading into the stock market, bonds enjoyed only a $9 billion trickle. Though $121 billion may sound like a lot of money, it isn't to some: of 1995's Forbes Four Hundred—the four hundred richest Americans—the *top sixteen alone* had a total net worth *greater than $121 billion.* All that money flowing into the stock market during those six months might have come from only sixteen families! Money flowing in and out of bonds *did* cause their prices to change. As a matter of fact, bonds and stocks have become very much alike.

The historical role of bonds has been reversed. Contrary to the preferences for interest income for widows in an earlier era, capital gains on bonds now dominate the total return, much as with stocks having near-zero dividends. And, again, as with stocks, increased bond market price volatility guarantees total returns on long-term bonds greatly different from their interest rates. For instance, the price of a 10-year bond per $100 of face value rises from $84.70 to $100 when its yield falls only from 12.75 percent to 10 percent. The quick 18 percent capital gain overshadows the 2.75 percent annual loss in yield. In the other direction even modest declines in interest rates cause capital values of long-term bonds to swing downward wildly and the risk to capital becomes a major concern not only to wealthy individuals and brokers but to managers of financial institutions such as commercial banks.

When capital gains rule, not only do the resale markets become far more important, but their volatility leads to greater sensitivity to even remote hints of inflation. It is no longer enough to know what is presently happening, the asset holders must have a guide to the future even if the future is unknowable. Thus, we cannot easily dismiss the bondholder's fixation on inflation without considering the connections between employment, inflation, interest rates, and the heads of the Federal Reserve—even when the connections are imaginary.

Why *Expected* Inflation in Commodities is the Bondholder's Worst Nightmare

As ever, a self-serving mythology beclouds the bondholders' view of inflation. In the Wall Street parable, just as prices of goods can be expressed in real prices or money prices adjusted for inflation, so too can bond yields be put in inflation-regarding values. Commodity inflation deflates the money or nominal interest rate into the *real rate of interest*, seemingly important to the bond market players.[5] Suppose, the parable goes, that William Wrigley makes a loan to the U.S. Treasury for one year by buying a 5-year T-note. If the nominal or stated annual interest rate is 8 percent, Wrigley will have 8 percent more dollars at the end of the year. But, if he *expects* the Consumer Price Index (CPI) to rise 10 percent during the same year, despite his having 8 percent more dollars at the end of the year, Wrigley expects to be paying 10 percent more, collectively, for his airplane fuel, Cabernet Sauvignon, dinner at the club, and the latest computer software. He can buy only 2 percent less in goods value at the end of the year and, tragically, be 2 percent worse off in real terms.

The inflation of concern is always an *expected inflation* because a bond trader buying a 5-year note at a stipulated yield does not have figures on the *future* inflation rate. The bond trader can only have *expectations* about what the inflation rate might be during the next five years. Wall Street might believe that Alan Greenspan knew precisely what inflation would be in the future, but he, too, had only *expectations* about it. Worse, his own actions could *alter* others' expectations. Even if inflation expectations are ill-informed, wildly off track, or derived from illusions of grandeur or deep-seated paranoia, they nonetheless are critical to the bondholders. The lenders, be they William Wrigley or anyone else, are less willing to make a loan to the U.S. Treasury, or so the parable goes, if they expect to pay more for their goods and services five years from today.

As with all parables, this one contains some fantasy. First, it is not the real interest rate that concerns bondholders, but the *negative effect* of a rising nominal interest rate on *bond prices*. Second, it *is* the interest rate, not the bond prices, that concerns *stockholders* because a rising interest rate signals higher costs for businesses and consumers (though the falling bond prices will eventually make them attractive again). Figure 8.2 confirms how, during the Great Bull Market in stocks of the 1980–90s, their prices have generally moved in the opposite direction to the yields on long-term Treasuries. Moreover, the falling bond yields meant soaring bond prices. Third, the financial asset holders are not truly worried about the higher cost of necessities. Since Mr. Wrigley is rich, he feels no pinch from the inflated prices of food, clothing and basic shelter. The bondholder worries, not about inflation, but about its depressing effect on bond prices and the depressing effect of rising interest rates on stocks as bond substitutes. All of which brings us to the specific auguries of inflation monitored today.

The Closely Watched Harbingers of Inflation

Bondholders, increasingly sophisticated, try to anticipate inflation or anticipate the Federal Reserve's anticipation of inflation. Taking their cue first from the monetarists, a rapidly expanding money supply was believed to indicate that inflation would accelerate and capital losses in bonds would be just around the corner. Since reducing inflation through a tighter money policy takes a great amount of time, the Reserve has to make preemptive strikes. The

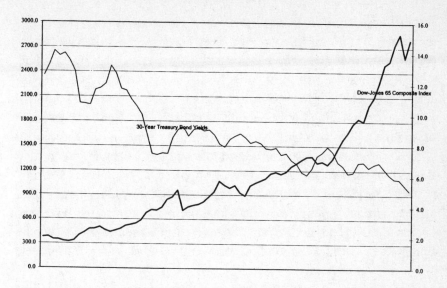

Figure 8.2 Stock Prices and Yields on long-term Treasuries, 1980–99
Source: Board of Governors of the Federal Reserve System

Reserve, like the military, has to be the first to see the enemy, in order to defeat it. As Alan Greenspan said in early 1998, "History teaches us that monetary policy has been most effective when it has been preemptive."[6] Then, the Reserve's own actual or expected behavior becomes a leading indicator of inflation among the bondholders.[7] If the Reserve begins to slow the money supply or to raise the fed funds rate, or, as in this instance, Greenspan *hints* that he might, inflation must be just around the corner. Sometimes the bondholders acted on what the Fed watchers said *they* thought Greenspan meant or was thinking. These expectations regarding the expectations of Alan Greenspan became the leading indicator of inflation.

Though the money supply was closely watched from the late 1970s to the mid-1980s, thereafter the effect on bond prices from anticipated money supply movements began to diminish.[8] After all, by the mid-1980s even Paul Volcker had abandoned monetarism and was targeting the fed funds rate. The bondholders began to respond to announcements regarding consumer prices, producers' prices, and the unemployment rate.[9] They knew that these clues were the ones watched closely by Volcker and, later, by Greenspan, and therefore by the Fed watchers.

Though a falling employment rate has long been a harbinger of inflation, by the early 1990s unemployment figures took on special significance as the Good News Bears began to prowl. Regardless of the indicator, the bond players react more strongly to "surprises"—any *unexpected* movement or movement larger than *expected* in an unemployment figure. Finally, not only have the favorite clues changed from time to time, their effects can be stronger or weaker depending on what else is going on in the economy or abroad.

Though the universe of indicators today is not simple, it is not hopelessly complex. To help sort things out, the primary dealers and interdealer brokers in bonds set up GovPX, Inc. in 1991 to improve the public's access to U.S. Treasury security prices. Since GovPX data covers five of the six major interdealer brokers, it accounts for two-thirds of the interdealer broker market. The most actively traded security among the brokers is the 5-year Treasury note.

In the most detailed study to date, Fleming and Remolona use GovPX data from August 1993 to August 1994 to identify the largest bond price movements and the most active trading episodes from every five-minute interval across the global trading day.[10] The largest price movements came within about fifteen minutes of the announced values of selected indicators, most of which have fixed dates and times for release. Of the top 25 price movements, the largest bond price decline (of 0.59 percent) came immediately after the release of the August 5, 1994 employment report. The employment figure exceeded what was expected by only about 54,000 jobs. However, it was a time of great uncertainty regarding whether Greenspan was about to raise the Fed funds rate for the fifth time in six months. (Recall that 1994 was a bear market year in bonds.)

Improvement in the employment picture has become the leading cause of bond price declines, confirming the presence of the Good News Bears. The next most important influence on bond price deterioration is an increase in the producers' price. Increases in consumer prices and the fed funds rate targeted by the Fed also result in significant bond price slippage (the Reserve began to announce its target for the fed funds rate at its February 1994 meeting). Movements in the same indicators—in about the same order of importance—lead to heightened bond price volatility. Moreover, movements in these indicators compared with what the bond traders expect—the "surprise" component—not only alter bond prices in a significant way, but have tremendous effects on price volatility.

If *employment* is better than *expected*, bond prices plunge. If the producers' prices rise by more than *expected*, bond prices plunge. If the fed funds target rate is higher than *expected*, bond prices plunge. Beyond these obviously important indicators, Fleming and Remolona found that other good news for workers such as improvements in industrial production, consumer confidence, new home sales, durable goods orders, construction spending, or housing starts also mean lower bond prices. Contrary to what Wall Street, Alan Greenspan, Robert Rubin, and even Bill Clinton has told us, however, changes in the *federal budget deficit* has *no* measurable effect on bond prices.

The 25 greatest *surges* in trading activity in the Fleming–Remolona study all came within 70 minutes after a release of the value of an indicator, 19 of them within half an hour. The greatest surge, consisting of 33 bond transactions worth a total of $240 million (in face values), came in a five-minute interval 20 minutes after the July 29, 1994 report of a *slowing GDP*. Employment, producers' prices, and retail sales releases appear to be important for both price movements and trading surges; the fed funds target rate actions are influential to bond price movements, as are housing starts for trading surges. While bond price movements occur rapidly, high trading activity persists for an extended period of time after the indicator is released.

Does the great importance of employment on bond prices and trading volatility mean that inflation is, well, an inflated foreteller of bond price softness? Not at all: favorable employment conditions weaken the bond market because the bondholders know that Alan Greenspan or whoever heads the Fed believes that a tighter labor market will lead to wage acceleration and that those escalating production costs will be passed along as inflation. The same can be said for most of the secondary indicators—swelling consumer confidence, new home sales or improved construction activity. These clues are not themselves adverse; it is the *fear* that any sign of economic improvement will lead the Federal Reserve to *expect* inflation. In turn, in the minds of the bondholders, hikes in the fed funds rate lead to billowing nominal interest rates, slumping bond prices, and those dreaded capital losses.

Bond Yields as Clues to Stockholders

The fed funds rate is under the *direct control* of the Sacred College of Bonds and Money. The Sacred College can alter the reserves of the private banking system (out of which the federal funds are lent overnight by the banks) by buying and selling government securities. An expected fed funds rate hike (as the College sells securities) signals that the Reserve is getting really serious about fighting inflation. Not only does an expected higher fed funds rate signal an urgent need to get out of bonds maturing in more than two years, the prospect for both higher bond yields and a recession is usually scary to stockholders. Stocks are dumped, not out of fear of immediate losses, but from *expected* higher bond yields plus the *expected* recession from the *expected* further hikes in the fed funds rate. The stock market goes into a swoon—much like the lady of the plantation during the Civil War: the market takes a dive because people sell their stocks, not because of any bad news for the ordinary working American. From this we can trace a *direct connection* between the actions of the Reserve, bondholders, *and* stockholders.

Luckily for the financial market players, there were no further fed funds rate increases between mid-1995 and 1999. By then, Greenspan's *bond market strategy* had created the greatest financial bull market in American history. Since, as it turned out, he overdid it, it is difficult to miss the irony. By December 1996, when Greenspan famously talked about the "irrational exuberance" of the stock market players, he believed that stock prices were overvalued by about 20 percent. Rather than raising the fed funds rate to tame the markets, however, Greenspan tried to talk them down. Since the fed funds rate is even more powerful when the financial markets are speculative and uncertain, he knew that an abrupt, surprising fed funds rate increase could cause panic and the greatest stock market crash in American history. Still, the stock market made one of its historically great one-day plunges in reaction to Greenspan's admonition, only to recover quickly during the following days.

Greenspan was in a quandary. He sensed inflation was again just around some corner, but he did not want to alarm his constituency on Wall Street, despite his being comfortable in his role as the scourge of working Americans. Greenspan could not breathe a sigh of relief until the Asian crisis set in by summer 1997. With the collapse of several Asian currencies, Greenspan expected a slowdown in U.S. exports to that part of the world. In turn, a worsening trade balance would slow the economy. By then, not coincidentally, the Dow had risen several thousand more points.

Thus, we have not lost sight of those few in whom America's financial holdings are so wonderfully concentrated, the bondholding class served so well by Greenspan's bond market strategy. With such great financial asset inflation, the rich were getting richer every which way. As noted, most bondholders put their money in securities simply because they have more money than they can possibly spend on goods and services (I do not mean to imply that they have limited imaginations regarding purchases), all of which brings us full circle to the prices that matter most.

The Uncontested Inflation in Pecuniary Decency

Since inflation dominated public policy concerns during the final quarter of the twentieth century, it is important to be doubly clear about which inflation the bondholders deplore. Notably, the bond market first captured the imagination of the Republic during an era when "conspicuous consumption," as the irrepressible Thorstein Veblen called it, regained respectability.[11] President Reagan set the tone with his lavish inauguration in 1981, lasting four days and including nine formal balls, with performances by Frank Sinatra and Charlton Heston. Soon, the supra-rich were using three jet aircrafts for a family-values spring trip to Florida or to the Caribbean—one plane for the adults, one for the children, and one for the servants and other baggage.

Still, the cost of being in the bondholding class seems to go up yearly. By 1997 *Condè Nast* came up with a vacation package costing more than $170,000, the going price (per person) for a 103-day world cruise on the *Crystal Symphony* in a penthouse with a veranda—alas, not including wine.[12] Bond and stock salespeople now were spending as much as $25,000 a week on limousine services, flowers, and other perishables. A duplex on fashionable Fifth Avenue a few blocks north of the Plaza went for $27 million. Hatteras Yachts of New Bern, North Carolina began to build 92 feet to 130 feet custom yachts at a base price of $8 million. A decade earlier when a rising tide was raising more than a few yachts, the biggest vessel the company built was a little 70-foot cruising yacht, selling as late as 1994 for a modest $1.5 million.

None of these expenditures are essential. In an act Veblen called "pecuniary decency," what the super-rich consume is unimportant compared with what the consumption *represents*. In Los Angeles the rich can rent a stretch limousine equipped not only with a hot tub but a helicopter pad, apparently to impress airborne dates. Luxury jets, chartered for corporate executives, facilitate overnight shopping trips to one coast or the other at $25,000, serving the even higher purpose of vanity. A business executive buys Renoir's paintings, not because he admires them, but because he can brag about their prices.

The appeal of emulation stems from the startling inequality even among the super-rich bondholders. To be super-rich in 1996 (top 1 percent) the entry-level adjusted gross income was only $200,000 with net worth merely $2.5 to $3 million. A *Worth*–Roper Starch survey of these one-percenters found that 57 percent didn't consider themselves "rich" (and only a quarter thought themselves "upper class") though their *average* family income was about $675,000.[13] Those earning the entry-level income of $200,000 no doubt thought themselves to be in the middle, though the true middle (median) was only about $31,000. Still, in the prior year of 1995, some 70,000 households filed tax returns reporting incomes in excess of $1 million. They represent about one fifteenth of the super-rich. Though a great distance separates the bottom of society from the bondholding class, the distance between the bottom and the top of the super-rich is much, much greater.

If true fear of inflation exists among the bondholders, it is surely not because luxuries might become more expensive for those at the very top. High prices are often essential in distinguishing a luxury from a commonplace good. Alan Greenspan or any other Federal Reserve head has never contested inflation in pecuniary decency. Moreover, if the multimillionaire buys an adequate beach vacation home for $1.6 million, the house will appreciate with inflation, greatly overwhelming whatever losses might be expected from purchasing higher-priced foodstuffs for his chef's preparation.

Besides, by the end of the century the rich were buying 20,000-square-foot houses for demolition to make way for a more suitable 40,000-square-foot shelter.

Reagan's inaugural parties at the leading edge of the rise of the bondholding class now seem bourgeois. Near the end of the nineties, the good times were being celebrated in more lavish parties in the Hamptons at the cozy east end of Long Island. The most frequently overheard comment was "thank God for Alan Greenspan." Having achieved the sluggish economy, Greenspan had not recently raised interest rates. Still, by summer 1998 there was some sense that the dancing, networking, and shoulder-rubbing with Kim Basinger and Alec Baldwin could not go on forever. It could be like that memorable Long Island party that Scott Fitzgerald's Gatsby threw during the Jazz Age. It ended badly.

And so, we arrive at a shameful conclusion. It is never so much the inflated price of rice, beans, and potatoes at the source of the angst of the bondholding revelers; it is the rising cost of pecuniary decency and *the rise in nominal interest rates (from inflation)*, a plummeting stock market, and the prospect of having no place to put their capital gains. Even this is not the whole truth; a deeper truth, even if it is less flattering to the bondholding class, often prevails.

Beyond Rational Returns

Since they cannot see inflation until it happens, the bondholders' disquietude concerns those indicators which fuel their expectations of rising inflation, because the expectations—mythical though they often are—are the stuff of the bondholders' "reality." If, for example, enough wealthy bondholders truly *believe* that government deficits cause inflation (even if they really don't) and the deficits continue, they will *expect* inflation, sell their bonds, and drive bond prices down and interest rates up. Self-fulfilling prophecies more persistently move markets than do prophets. In this respect the great enemy of the bondholding class is the bondholder and his inflation-regarding *expectations*. So much the worse for rationality because the absence of current inflation offers no cure for the inflation neurosis.

Some of the consequences do not appear rational for American society either. Even if the professors were correct before, even if America was once a nation of risk-averters, it has become a nation of risk-takers. The debt grew, the number of financial instruments exploded, and those who failed to speculate increasingly fell behind in the race toward elusive pecuniary decency. Large betas, those elusive measures of risk, are now used to select the "best" bonds and stocks. If an expected rate of return is minimal, it means that the company must be a laggard. One certainty remains: the bondholders are getting richer, much richer, at the expense of others. Having had too much of a good thing, however, risks are rising even for the rich.

Spiraling volatility in the bond market, once common only to stocks, puts the players at greater risk. They look even more anxiously at indicators and for quick financial fixes. Volatility has led not only to a greater variety of indicators but to still more financial innovations such as derivatives, assets whose value "derives" from that of the underlying assets such as bonds. Seemingly, more "knowledge" and more derivatives have not only made speculation more profitable but have made the steadiness of the financial markets crumble. As we next relate, these risks to financial markets have not only spread to the rest of the economy, but are palpable.

NOTES

1. As quoted by Suzanne McGee and Charles Gasparino, "Bond Prices End Flat as U.S. Three-Year Sale Fails to Stir Up Much Excitement for Investors," *Wall Street Journal*, August 7, 1996, p. C19.

2. A frequently used formula for this standard deviation, σ, is the square root of $\sum \rho_i (R_i - R^e)^2$, where ρ_i is the probability of realizing R_i or the realized return, and R^e is the expected return. Before the square root is taken, the formula would give us the variance of returns.

3. Burton G. Malkiel, *A Random Walk Down Wall Street* (New York: W.W. Norton, 1991), p. 209. Whether we agree or not with Malkiel, this book is a great read.

4. The exact percentage changes, respectively, were a loss of 11 percent on 30-year Treasuries, a loss of 17 percent on some bond funds, and a gain of 34.1 percent on 30-year Treasuries in 1995.

5. Professors of economics and finance use the Fisher equation, named for Irving Fisher, a famous economist at Yale during the 1920s and an iconoclastic inventor and founder of a company that merged with Remington Rand, Inc. As stated in the text, the Fisher equation is $i_r = i - \pi^e$. Alternatively, stated as the nominal interest rate, $i = i_r + \pi^e$, where i is the nominal interest rate, i_r is the real interest rate and π^e is the expected rate of inflation during the period the security is held. A more precise calibration of the Fisher interest rate is given by $i = i_r + \pi^e + (i_r \times \pi^e)$, since $1 + i = (1 + i_r)(1 + \pi^e) = 1 + i_r + \pi^e + (i_r \times \pi^e)$ and 1 can be subtracted from both sides to give the first equation. However, for small values of the real interest rate and the expected inflation rate, the last term (a product) is very small and can be ignored, giving us the simpler equation.

6. In testimony by Alan Greenspan before the Subcommittee on Domestic and International Monetary Policy of the Committee on Banking and financial Services, U.S. House of Representatives, February 24, 1998.

7. An early study on the effects of the money supply (M1) on bond prices and yields is N.G. Berkman, "On the significance of weekly changes in M1," *New England Economic Review*, May–June, 1978, pp. 5–22.

8. This shift in focus is noted by G. Dwyer and H.W. Hafer, "Interest Rates and economic announcements," *Review*, Federal Reserve Bank of St. Louis, 1989, pp. 24–46.

9. The shift toward the CPI, PPI, and joblessness is illustrated by M. Smirlock, "Inflation Announcements and Financial Market reaction: Evidence From the Long-term Bond Market," *Review of Economics*

and Statistics, 1986, pp. 329–33 and by T. Urich and P. Wachtel, "Market Response to the Weekly Money Supply Announcements in the 1970s," *Journal of Finance*, Vol. 36, 1981, pp. 1063–72. The more recent studies such as T. Cook and S. Korn, "The Reaction of Interest Rates to the Employment Report: The Role of Policy Anticipations," *Economic Review*, Federal Reserve Bank of Richmond, 1991, pp. 3–12 and A. B. Krueger, "Do Markets Respond to More Reliable Labor Market Data? A Test of Market rationality," unpublished paper, Princeton University, 1996, point towards the moving power of employment data.

10. Michael J. Fleming and Eli M. Remolona, "What Moves the Bond Market?" Research Paper No. 9706, Federal Reserve Bank of New York, February 1997.

11. See Thorstein Veblen, *The Theory of the Leisure Class* (New York/London/Victoria: Penguin Books, 1994) [1899], a volume in Penguin's "Twentieth Century Classics." This classic is not only amusing but remains quite modern.

12. "How to Travel Like a Millionaire," *Condè Nast Traveler*, January 1997, pp. 27–33.

13. Richard Todd, "Who me, Rich?" *Worth*, September 1997, p. 73.

NINE

Risks Become Palpable as Bonds are Traded for Chips

Spiraling volatility in the bond market, once common only to stocks, put the institutional players at greater risk, leading many to look anxiously for financial instruments that might lessen that risk. Wall Street has willingly supplied more derivatives or "chips" that, it claims, will lessen risk. Derivatives are financial instruments whose values "derive" from those of the underlying assets—in the case at hand, bonds. Increasingly, not only are the speculative players playing with these chips, some began using *imaginary chips* to leverage the ordinary ones, a majestic conversion that began with bonds and interest rates. Though derivatives are as old as tulip bulb futures, the presence of notional or imaginary financial "assets" valued at a multiple of the real economy was unprecedented. Moreover, the variety of new bond derivatives increased faster than the acumen of their traders. Yet, undeniably, volatility and leveraged derivatives led to greater *potential* capital gains (and losses): speculators love volatility even as they create it. This great financial transformation led to new perils for financial markets, the gravest of which was the threat that the entire securities casino may close down.

Still, if the very wealthy are to speculate, they must not only have a goodly supply of chips but plenty of games to play. The new means of corporate acquisition, takeovers by leveraged junk bonds, provided not only red chips to go with the blue but some new games. Then, as bond speculation heightened volatility, even normally conservative commercial bankers got into the game. Wonderfully deregulated financial institutions became remarkably innovative in begetting new financial instruments in which bond proceeds and interest could be stored momentarily for quick appreciation or leveraged for still greater gains.

On Wall Street, *every* new instrument is said to meet "a need in the marketplace." Otherwise, the security wouldn't exist! Wall Street's needful language serves, as ever, a higher purpose. It conjures images of *les misérables*—crippled orphans, aging widows, and homeless children—milling about the graveyard of the Trinity Church. Their palsied hands are reaching out for the solid nourishment derivable only from another mutated bond or for the liquid nourishment derivable only from an "asset" based on a debt backed by a second debt backed by a third debt and so on, to the bottom of the universe of bonds. The Wall Street broker's failure to meet a need in the marketplace is a sin punishable by purgatory in a place like Fargo or, upon second offense, a sentence to sell Italian shoes in Chinatown.

The common denominator championing not only the bondholding class, but the full freedom to trade bond derivatives was Alan Greenspan. Not surprisingly then, Greenspan has left his mark on many financial catastrophes. Because of his distrust of every regulator except himself (playing that heroic Randian role), he is often at the scene of the accident when high-flying financial markets and institutions collide with reality.

More than anyone, Greenspan created expectations that joined the stock and bond markets at that gyrating hip. More than anyone, he engineered the Great Bull Market in securities. Greenspan went on to accelerate deregulation of banking and financial markets, leading to massive mergers and creating banks and other financial institutions "too large to fail." As we add still another chapter to his catalog of blunders, we find Greenspan arranging the bailout of a huge "hedge fund" dealing in the derivatives that he does not want regulated. Yet, financial fragility, a creature of the bondholding class, cries out for the kind of financial regulations inimical to an Ayn Rand, a Milton Friedman, or an Alan Greenspan.

In truth, neither Paul Volcker nor Alan Greenspan could control volatility once the bondholders became irrational speculators. The demons they unleashed took on lives of their own. The markets for securities or real estate—whatever the instrument of excess—eventually collapse and a credit crunch ensues. Ultimately, even Greenspan had to come to grips with the realities of financial excess and mass hysteria. Patsy Cline-like "crazy" behavior—manic, obsessed, haunted, mesmerized, and orgasmic—leads to abnormal outcomes. At such times, as Thomas W. Lamont, J.P. Morgan's partner, told the governors of the Stock Exchange on October 24, 1929 (Black Thursday) "Gentlemen, there is no man nor group of men who can buy all the stocks that the American public can sell." The same sometimes can be said for bonds. When the bondholders overdo financial opportunities, a mania follows that must somehow have an end, usually an atrabilious end. This madness of crowds or popular delusions has had a long history—including tulipmania in early seventeenth century Holland, the Mississippi–South Seas bubbles in eighteenth century France and England, the Great Crash of 1929, and the financial market panic on October 19, 1987.[1]

When Bonds Fail to Move Stocks

More often than not, as noted, bond and stock prices moved in the same direction—up—during the final two decades of the twentieth century. As we know, this symmetry was not accidental. Wall Street, the Federal Reserve, the U.S. Treasury, Congress, and even the White House have been increasingly responsive to the preferences of the bondholding class. Generally, keeping bondholders happy kept the shareholders happy. (Of course, to repeat, these are often the same people, ready to substitute equity for debt instruments and vice versa at opportune moments.) Bondholders do not want the capital losses from rising bond yields and the shareholders loathe rising interest rates. The Goldilocks economy of slow growth has been masterminded to serve *all* securities holders.

As a result, the 1980s and the 1990s were decades for paper profits, much like the 1920s. During 1982, a year of near-depression for those preferring work, long-term taxable bonds had annual total returns of about 40 percent. The once-dullness of bonds turned iridescent. Though common stocks did not do as well, during the final six months of 1982 alone, they appreciated by more than 28 percent, whether measured by the Dow or the S&P 500. Judged by total returns, 1983, too, was a very good year for paper. Bonds and stocks again took off together during the mid-1980s.

Those exceptional times when movements were not in tandem were perilous. In 1987 the prices of bonds and stocks were moving in *opposite* directions, a very bad omen. Bonds dropped sharply during the first three quarters while stocks appreciated about 30 percent. However, on October 19, 1987, the Dow Jones industrials dropped 508 points, then the largest single-day decline in history, representing a loss of about $500 billion in financial wealth. Bonds rallied as stocks fell. Within seven lean days, stock prices had dropped by nearly a third. This pattern of events is pictured in Figure 9.1 (the Moody's Aaa are the highest-rated corporates). As corporate bonds moved out of the vortex of low yields, stock prices, with a slight pause, began to drop, the Dow bottoming at 1,384 in the spider-like configuration.

Uncharacteristically, a decade later, contrary movements in bond and stock prices occurred again. As the effects of the Asian crisis began to cut into U.S. corporate profits by summer 1998, bonds began to rally. Later that year, another financial crisis developed

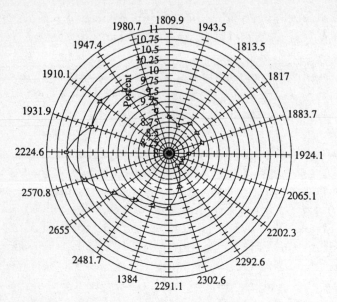

Figure 9.1 Corporate Aaa Bond Yields and the 1987 Crash
Sources: Board of Governors of the Federal Reserve and Dow Jones

in Brazil and was soon spreading throughout Latin America. When enough dark clouds hang over the economy, declining profits can turn the Goldilocks economy into recession at the expense of stock prices, as happened during the Great Crash of 1929.

What I have just said merits restatement. By dint of definition, the Goldilocks economy is delicately balanced between an economy "too hot" and an economy "too cold." It really must be *"just right."* The collapse of the Asian economies and the Latin American crisis were *good* insofar as they slowed the American economy enough to end the modest growth in workers' wages. However, if the U.S. economy languished, the Asian depression and its domino effects would provide *too much* of a good thing. The balance by early 1999 could not have been more precarious, nor more menacing, if not for the bondholding class, then for ordinary people. Once again, concerns were shifting toward the failure of entire markets.

When the Market Fails, it is Systemic

During the final quarter of the twentieth century, the securities market players reacted quickly and decisively to even modest movements in closely-watched economic and financial omens. Of course, a market player's worst terror is a crash in the market they happen to be in and the resulting inability to sell their assets (illiquidity) or, if they can sell, then only at great losses. Though rationality is much more reputable, its respectable defenders eventually have to deal—sometimes by denial—with panics, if for no other reason, because they happen.

Risk has a way of making itself obvious at once to many players. Fear is contagious and quickly infects virtually everyone until crowd psychology drives asset values away from their fundamental or true economic values, much as the history of manias suggests. Speculative bubbles, a product of crowd euphoria, move asset prices from their conventionally expected values.[2] Selecting from two brands of behavior—collective rationality or irrationality—we can plunk for those who say that crashes can't happen, or we can observe wildly gyrating securities prices, minute-by-minute, on CNN.

During tulipmania in Holland, the Mississippi-South Seas Bubble, the Crash of 1929 which ended the Jazz Age, and even the stock market crash of 1987, not only entire markets, but economies were at risk. In these manias it was not a matter of whether one tulip bulb or another was rising or falling in price, nor was it a matter of Radio rising in price and Wright Aeronautic falling. The markets for every bulb and every stock disappeared. Betas became irrelevant; entire systems failed. Though in the crash of 1987 assurances from the Federal Reserve as lender of the last resort restored liquidity, such assurance may be inadequate if the global financial system fails.

The lack of liquidity is the most severe problem with a system-wide failure. *Liquidity* is the measure of the quickness with which we can turn an asset into cash without incurring great costs. A market with many buyers and sellers exhibits liquidity, but even the bond market is not immune to a liquidity crisis. When insufficient buyers exist, the few investment bankers are not going to agree to underwrite new issues, even issues of the U.S. Treasury. An unopened bond market ends liquidity as the bondholders know it. Unlike the women who get "prettier at clos'en time" in the country song, noth'en about a clos'en bond market is pretty.

When the system fails, diversification loses whatever powers it might have had. Nor does current liquidity offer a permanent guarantee of being able to sell before incurring losses. The worst-case scenario involves a market whose liquidity depends upon the sales ability and manipulation skills of one or a few persons. Liquidity in the Milken junk bond market, as we will see, depended on one man. As we will also discover, in the 1998 collapse of Long-Term Capital Management, the high-flying hedge fund, its highly leveraged positions made liquidity fleet. These cases threatened the entire financial system and thus, the American and, now, the global economy.

The Crash of Milken's Bond Market

Consider first the story of the Milken Market. On March 29, 1989, the authorities indicted Milken on ninety-eight counts, including racketeering charges. Soon, in a sweeping consent decree, the Securities and Exchange Commission (SEC) virtually took over Drexel, which agreed to pay Milken $70 million for his equity in the firm. Without Milken's sales genius, however, Drexel could not pedal the junk bonds. Instead, the firm ended up having to buy the junk paper out of its own capital, leaving Drexel with a giant portfolio of its own junk.

Previously, when Drexel's large bond issuers had threatened default, Milken had restructured the debt, usually with even more leverage, resembling nothing so much as a pyramid scheme. Now, however, the remaining sales force at Drexel was unable to "roll over" weak debt into new junk bonds. Besides, Drexel's big clients such as Columbia Savings and Loan and Executive Life, were stacked to their ceilings in junk bonds and could not ingest more. The companies built on the piles of junk paper began to crumble. Integrated Resources and the giant retailer Campeau Corporation collapsed into bankruptcy. Columbia and Executive Life eventually joined the crowd.

The entire Milken Market pyramid collapsed with the October 1989 "minicrash" of the U.S. stock market. Takeover stocks led the 200-point market plunge on October 13, then the second-greatest points drop in its history. The whole junk bond market collapsed as issuers of those bonds began to default on their obligations. As a result, junk bonds yielded a negative 11.2 percent for 1990. Michael Milken and his brother remained the big financial winners. A member of the Forbes 400 since 1986, Michael held $700 million in net worth in 1998, his brother, $525 million.

Alan Greenspan and Junk Bonds Contribute to the Savings & Loan Debacle

Milken's junk bonds and even Alan Greenspan's consultancy played pivotal roles in the monumental collapse of the savings and loan industry. In the prototypical case, the notorious Lincoln Savings & Loan, not only outright thievery, but trading in junk bonds and foreign currencies contributed to an expensive failure. Heavily involved with Michael Milken and Drexel Burnham, Charles Keating transformed Lincoln from a home mortgage lender to an Arizona land developer, junk bond lender, and player in the takeover market. The S&L's knew this non-mortgage business of junk bonds as "direct investments."

The potential for financial disaster from speculative investments led the Federal Home Loan Bank, a regulatory agency, to impose a 10 percent limitation on such direct investments. Greenspan, a former head of President Reagan's Council of Economic Advisers, had by now returned to his lucrative position as a private consultant. He wrote a laudatory letter dated February 13, 1985 for Keating supporting his application for exemption from the 10 percent rule. In his letter to the Federal Home Loan Bank of San Francisco, Greenspan described Lincoln Savings & Loan as "an association that has, through its skill and expertise, transformed itself into a financially strong institution that presents no foreseeable risk to the Federal Savings and Loan Corporation," the depository insurance agency for the industry.[3] Greenspan, who Wall Street ultimately decided was the only one sufficiently trustworthy to head the Reserve after Paul Volcker, not only was paid $40,000 for writing the letter, but endorsed the soundness of Keating's use of insured deposits to buy junk bonds from Milken.

Unfortunately, by the end of 1987, Lincoln's interest-bearing liabilities exceeded its interest-bearing assets by more than $1 *billion*. Lincoln's *negative net worth* doubled during the next year. Keating, if not Greenspan, knew that he was working Jessie James' territory. Though Keating controlled Lincoln Savings & Loan, he refused to be an officer or director. Asked why, his reply was that he "did not want to go to jail."[4] In this way, junk bonds, though still flying high, not only led to the collapse of an entire industry, but to great losses by senior pensioners and a bailout by taxpayers. As for Alan Greenspan, his remarkable record of mistakes costly to ordinary Americans remained intact.

Junk Bonds and Other Bond Innovations Create Commercial Banks "Too Big to Fail"

Deregulation in the financial industry—begun earnestly under Jimmy Carter, a *cause célèbre* under Ronald Reagan, and heroically inspired by Alan Greenspan—stimulated takeovers. By 1998 the ten largest banks, headed by Citicorp (now Citigroup) in New York, held more than a third of all commercial bank assets. After a flurry of mergers, the trillion-dollar bank was within reach. With the trend toward faster consolidation, probably no more than ten giant banks will soon dominate the industry. Ironically, the junk bonds (abetted by Greenspan) that ravaged the S&L industry reduced the need for banks (now being deregulated by Greenspan), turning consolidation from a luxury into a necessity. Such giant financial institutions would soon prove "too large to fail."

Corporate junk bond financing was eating into the banks' loan business by the mid-1980s. Selling bonds directly to the public became easier, thereby bypassing banks. Things that, in the 1970s, only the *Fortune 500* companies were able to do, could now be emulated by lower-quality corporate borrowers by issuing junk bonds. Though this market slowed sharply after Michael Milken was indicted in 1989, it was rekindled, even to conflagration, in the 1990s. By the end of 1998 the telecommunications industry, which, given an explosive growth of the Internet and other digital services, was touted as having the "safest plays" in the junkyard. With Merrill Lynch's junk-bond index well above Treasuries, Margaret Patel, a portfolio manager, was advising us, "even if you don't see a lot of capital appreciation in high yield, and all you do is earn the coupon, you can still do as well as you'll probably do in equities." Besides, junk bonds were increasingly viewed as "less risky" than stocks.[5]

In commercial banking, however, junk bonds got a lot of help from two other forces. First, the commercial paper market, the market for short term debt issued by large banks and corporations, has been growing rapidly, expanding from $33 billion outstanding in 1970 to more than $500 billion at the end of 1993. With improvements in information technology, credit risk can be more quickly evaluated, making it easier for corporations to borrow in this money market. Second, at a time when converting everything into debt instruments was becoming routine, *securitization*, the process of transforming otherwise illiquid financial assets (such as residential mortgages and automobile loans) into marketable capital market securities, became irresistible. Roughly two-thirds of all residential mortgages, amounting to more than $1 trillion, are now securitized.

If it seems as if something has been created out of nothing, it probably has been. Let there be no mistake about it: Securitization is a means whereby the issuers of a new security entice people to *lend money on loans* as collateral or backing. And, securitization is not slowing. Rock star David Bowie, once the opening act for the Rolling Stones, sold $55 million in bonds against future royalties from past hit songs. Prudential bought the entire package, which pays a 7.9 percent yearly return over ten years. Once these bonds began to rock and roll, they became simply a piece of "the rock." Other stars such as Rod Stewart soon found Bowie's act easy to follow.

Sources of new bonds for the bondholding class appear inexhaustible. A plethora of financial innovations was moving the financial casino toward completeness, a gambler's paradise. The financial casino was even more efficient than those in Las Vegas or Atlantic City because the only chips required were mere key stroke entries in the computers used for trading and settling trades. The next step would be to invent mere numbers to be bought and sold—much like trading ether. Nobody would care what they were. This new market need was met by *derivatives* of bonds.

Financial Derivatives to Cover Rising Bond Risk Threaten the Commercial Banking System

The derivatives deeply and widely feared by students in the universities, if not secondary schools, are from the calculus. The meaning is similar since each is derived from something else or is a "higher order" and yet further removed from its base value. In financial markets, derivatives are financial contracts whose value depends on some underlying assets, real or financial, such as houses, commodities, bonds, currencies, or interest rates. We have reason to fear these derivatives even more than their mathematical species. They have invaded the banking industry, once considered conservative because it once was. In a classic Catch-22, Alan Greenspan and the banking industry embraced derivatives as devices for coping with spiraling bond market volatility.

Since banks hold and issue debt-paying interest, they are exposed to the perils of interest-rate fluctuations on both sides of their balance sheets. Of course, that has always been the case. However, astonishingly volatile bond prices and interest rates created the need to reduce rising risks. Unsurprisingly, the astounding growth in bank-related derivatives has been driven by contracts based on interest rates, the majority of which are in interest rate swaps, said by the Reserve to be a "low-cost way for banks to manage their exposure to interest rate fluctuations."[6]

An *interest rate swap* is pretty much like it sounds. An investment banker gets two bankers together—for a fee, of course—and one banker agrees to pay the interest it earns on *fixed*-rate assets to the second banker; in turn, the second banker agrees to pay the first banker the interest *he* receives on *variable*-interest assets. The swap can balance the values of assets and liabilities held by each bank in fixed interest and rate-sensitive interest instruments. However, only if the types of assets and liabilities are *perfectly matched* would a bank be completely free from interest rate risk. Banks which speculate can intentionally maintain an imbalance between the values of like assets and liabilities.

It gets worse; derivatives are not on the balance sheets of banks because, well, they are not balance sheet items. I suppose that one day during the 1980s bankers got together and said: "Look, our balance sheet assets and liabilities are highly volatile; the best way of reducing this volatility is to buy and sell contracts in imaginary financial instruments that *never appear on the balance sheets!*" It was a brilliant idea, judging from the rapid growth in derivatives. Off-balance sheet activities as a percentage of commercial banks' assets have doubled since 1979. Banks' holdings of off-balance-sheet derivatives stood at a notional, or an underlying, value of roughly $15.6 *trillion* in a more modest $6.7 trillion *real economy* at the end of 1994 and about twice the then value of the U.S. stock markets. The notional principal of outstanding exchange-traded and over-the-counter derivative contracts increased from less than $2 trillion at the end of 1986 to more than $20 *trillion* at the end of 1994, an average annual growth rate of 140 percent.[7] (The notional principal amount is the number by which the interest rates or exchange rates in a derivative contract are multiplied to calculate the settlement amount.)

The bulk of these exotic ventures is conducted by a handful of dealer banks who specialize in such contracts. Only six banking corporations, mostly in New York, control about 85 percent of the commercial banking derivatives market. The replacement value of these derivatives was about $500 billion at the end of 1994, compared with less than 40 percent of this value or $200 billion as the capital base of the twelve largest dealers. The replacement value is the unrealized capital gain or loss of the contract at current market prices. Besides interest rate swaps other derivatives of the banks include interest rate futures, forward contracts, and options (plus various foreign exchange rate contracts). Stock market index futures and options comprise much of the balance of the derivatives market.

Derivatives get complicated very fast. An entire book devoted to the subject could not hedge, as it were, all the possibilities. Since the dealers can differentiate their products by customizing derivatives, the possibilities are nearly endless. I am content to suggest two things: first, derivatives have become big business that banks and other institutions expect to continue to use and, second, we know things can go wrong with derivatives because they already have. Derivatives enable banks to leverage debt instruments and put customers' money at risk. The line between prudent hedging by a bank or other party and speculation is painfully long and thin. A central issue is whether a financial institution is entitled to issue or trade an enforceable gambling contract that would be illegal if anybody but a financial institution traded or wrote it.[8] An interest rate swap is a bet that interest rates will not go a particular direction, and is no different from a bet at a gaming table in Las Vegas.[9] We next consider just how enormously the gamblers can lose.

Bets on Bonds Go Wrong at Long-Term Capital Management: Greenspan Arranges a Bailout

What with the revival of the junk bond market by the mid-1990s and the ecumenical use of interest swaps by commercial banks, it was only a matter of time before junk bonds and derivatives would be combined in a newly unregulated financial institution. This wonderful invention, the *hedge fund*, would accept funds only from the very rich, borrow money from the banks and brokerages it did business with, leverage those funds with interest swaps, and make money out of key strokes on its computer. Though "hedge" used to denote the covering of risk, the hedge fund makes its money by speculating with derivatives. Those banks and brokers lending to the hedge fund also could put their own funds in it, which sounds like a conflict of "interest." The funds' play is not restricted to interest swaps, they can choose among about three thousand derivatives. At no time are these funds contaminated by contact with crude oil, timber, pork bellies, steel, mining, manufacturing, or anything even remotely resembling real output.

Let us be clear. Hedge funds answer to no oversight institution, either state or federal, even though the funds make speculative, multibillion-dollar bets with borrowed money in markets around the world. Among other laws, hedge funds can operate under a neat little 1996 amendment to federal securities laws that exempt from regulation the funds of fewer than 500 "sophisticated" institutions or individuals—those that invest more than $25 million or $5 million respectively. Once again, the insinuation is that only those of great wealth understand proper relations with money whereas the huddled masses need be regulated to avoid self-inflicted wounds. Ordinary people must put funds in tightly-regulated mutual funds that have high fees, commissions, and other restrictions.

Today there are perhaps 600 hedge funds in the U.S. One which has long been touted as perhaps the "best" is Long-Term Capital Management. More exclusive than most, the minimum amount that LTCM would accept from a "sophisticated" member of the bondholding class was $10 million. It boasted the rocket scientists who not only wrote the book on derivatives but shared a 1997 Nobel Prize in economics for writing it—LTCM partners Myron Scholes and Robert Merton. Its brain trust also included insider David Mullins Jr., former Vice Chairman of the Federal Reserve Board. The hedge fund was founded by a former Vice Chairman of Salomon Brothers Inc., John Meriwether. While Mullins was at the Fed, Meriwether was one of the "Masters of the Universe" dealing in bonds in the 1980s at Salomon, a career disrupted in 1991 when he resigned in the midst of a Treasury bond bid-rigging scandal. In Mullins view at the time, trying to corner the Treasury bond market was not sufficient reason to impose new regulations on bond underwriters.

Despite having doubled its money from 1994 to 1997, LTCM was essentially bankrupt by September 1, 1998. Not to worry, Alan Greenspan and other Reserve officials considered Long-Term Capital Management, if not too big to fail, too big on the balance sheets of Merrill Lynch, Goldman Sachs, J.P. Morgan, and other financial giants to be allowed to fail. On September 23, 1998, Greenspan was busily arranging the last-minute rescue of LTCM. As the company teetered on the edge of collapse, executives from Wall Street's largest brokerages, investment banks and commercial banks held round-the-clock meetings with Fed officials. Then, with Greenspan's blessing, New York Fed President William McDonough put the chieftains of Merrill Lynch, Travelers Group, Salomon

Smith Barney, Goldman Sachs, Credit Suisse First Boston, and others together on the 10th floor of the bank, twisted a few arms, and brokered the bailout of what was, essentially, a partnership of high-tech gamblers. Not since J.P. Morgan had huddled with the bulky bankers of his day during the Great Crash of 1929, had so many financiers come to such quick agreement.

No one giant could afford to resist McDonough's arm-twisting. As to LTCM, it had received a faxed offer earlier in the day from a group consisting of Warren Buffett, Goldman Sachs and American International Group—Buffet et al. offering to buy out the fund's contributors for $250 million, and to put another $3.75 billion into the fund's capital. The managers would be fired. The Federal Reserve came through with a better offer for the contributors and the managers who were not only retained but paid a fee by the contributors to the bailout.

In early 1995, Alan Greenspan told Congress that "although ... derivative instruments ... may have facilitated ... possible riskier strategies, it would be a serious mistake to respond ... by singling out derivative instruments for special regulatory treatment."[10] Worse, just *ten days* before the bailout, Greenspan had told a congressional hearing why regulation of hedge funds is unnecessary: "Hedge funds are strongly regulated by those who lend the money," he explained, "they are not technically regulated in the sense that banks are, but they are under a fairly significant degree of surveillance."[11] Despite the "technically *un*regulated" nature of such hedge funds, Greenspan and the New York Fed convened the heavyweights of Wall Street to raise $3.65 billion within 24 hours. Without a sale to Buffet or a bailout by the Fed, Long-Term would have been Long Gone. Ironically, on the *same day* of the bailout, the Federal Reserve Board was approving the merger of Citicorp and Travelers Group Inc. (one of Long-Term's creditors), creating the world's largest financial services company—at $750 billion, definitely "too big to fail."

As it turns out then, commercial banks need not be holding derivatives to incur losses associated with them. If the banks are lending to financial institutions that are buying derivatives on credit, the banks share the risks of the derivatives' holders. The reverberations are illustrated by the deferred collapse of LTCM. Since almost every major Wall Street securities firm and commercial bank had lent enormous sums to LTCM, its collapse could have forced a fire sale of securities and shaken confidence in an already fragile global financial system, bringing down some Wall Street giants with it.

As Peter Bakstansky, spokesman for the New York Fed said, "You had a very large entity that was hemorrhaging, with very large exposures at stake." Furthermore, the risk was systemwide: "We are always interested in the potential for systemic upset and contagion, particularly when large amounts are involved," Bakstansky added.[12] That is, LTCM and the giant financial institutions tied to its fate were "too large to fail." After all, it controlled high risk, global financial holdings "worth" about $125 billion— enough to buy AT&T. At about $80 billion in debt, not only does LTCM owe more money than most nations, it has more than a *trillion* dollars of complex derivative contracts with banks, brokerage houses, and others. Rather than LTCM itself, these giant Wall Street banks and brokerage houses themselves were the ones bailed out.

Though the precise operations of hedge funds are as secret as the meetings of the Sacred College, we do know generally what they do. LTCM specializes in bond arbitrage, whereby it places complex and highly leveraged bets on the differences between interest rates on various kinds of bonds. Its core placements, based on complex computer models, were in the U.S., Japanese and the larger European markets. It was betting that the high interest rates on junk bonds would move toward, or converge on fault-free U.S. Treasuries. With the Asian turmoil beginning in mid-1997 and culminating in the Russian political collapse and consequent financial problems in Latin America by autumn 1998, those holding riskier bonds dumped them and bought U.S. Treasuries. Thus, interest rates, rather than converging, widened even more. LTCM had made its bets in the wrong direction.

The game with bonds and chips was played this way. Suppose that 5-year junk bonds historically have a yield four percentage points above 5-year Treasuries because of their higher risk (higher betas). The Scholes–Merton computer model might predict that when the yield differences widen to, say, six percentage points, the yields will converge back to only four percentage points. At a six percentage-point yield gap, Long-Term Capital Management places a bet on the gap narrowing, agreeing to exchange the expected lower yield on $5 billion of junk bonds in exchange for the expected higher yield on $5 billion of Treasuries. This "interest rate swap" involves only a "notional" amount, the $5 billion, and, wonder of all wonders, neither party owns the underlying securities, nor anything else, only the *obligation to pay the differences* in yields. From this bet grow the gambler's profits—unless, of course, as it happened, the bet is in the wrong direction. Though its contributors were not told about it, LTCM played the same game with stock price differences between merging companies.

Actually, LTCM's actions were more reckless than simply gambling. It was highly leveraged, having borrowed from Wall Street most of the funds it was putting on the table. On the day its true condition was revealed, LTCM held $100 billion in speculative positions on its balance sheet and was down to only $2.3 billion of capital. At its peak, the company reportedly had a debt load *100 times* as great as its net assets, or ownership capital. This would be like putting down only $10,000 of your own money on a $1,000,000 house on a south Florida barrier island known to be in the direct path of a category-5 hurricane. Moreover, the fund had off-balance-sheet derivative contracts valued "notionally" at $1.25 *trillion*. Alan Greenspan feared, rightly, that further liquidation of LTCM's positions would weaken not only the bond markets of the troubled Asian, Russian, and Latin American economies, but the U.S. financial markets as well, creating a panic.

As it turns out, Greenspan and Rubin had been protecting hedge funds and the derivatives markets from regulation for a long time. They, along with Securities and Exchange Chairman Arthur Levitt and Commodity Futures Trading Commission chairwoman Brooksley Born, comprised the President's Working Group on Financial Markets. Ms. Born, alone among them, had been warning about the risk of unregulated over-the-counter derivatives by now having a notional value of nearly $30 trillion. Greenspan, Rubin and Levitt had tried to muzzle her because Wall Street had complained to the Reserve, the Treasury, and the SEC that Ms. Born's statements were already disrupting markets and creating fears that some investors would sue to get out of money-losing transactions, arguing that derivatives *should* have been regulated. Mr. Greenspan argued that hedge funds' sophisticated players already provide plenty of oversight and regulation would be counterproductive.[13]

When asked about the "bailout," Treasury Secretary Rubin and former head of Goldman Sachs testily replied, "That wasn't a bailout.... What the Federal Reserve Bank of New York did was to convene [a meeting]. These creditors made their own private-sector decisions."[14] Still, the twisting of arms by McDonough could be heard as far away as the Trinity Church graveyard. Moreover, the financial giants knew that if they did not agree to the bailout, the Federal Reserve would not come to their rescue when they are in trouble, which may be soon. Since the global financial system was hanging in the balance, the Federal Reserve had to use either the private creditors' funds or its own in the rescue. If the private creditors would have voluntarily bailed out Long-Term Capital Management, why would the Federal Reserve believe a meeting was necessary?

Generally, the bondholding class welcomed the news of the bailout. It eased fears of a wholesale liquidation of the fund's bond portfolio. For a while at least, the bailout, together with Greenspan's interest rate reductions improved the tone of the overall bond market. The bailout also raised the possibility that the Fed would have to be that much more accommodative on interest rates; Greenspan was promising as much in congressional testimony the day of the bailout. The bondholders, at least, could sleep a little better at night.

Since LTCM is one of the "smaller" and "better" of the hedge funds, other minefields are out there. After all, none will reveal what is on their balance sheets and the Federal Reserve doesn't want to know. In fact, early in October 1998 the U.S. dollar endured its biggest two-day drop in a quarter century as panic selling swept the world's $1.5 trillion-a-day foreign-currency markets. This free fall was blamed in large part on hedge funds that had been betting on the dollar.

Can the Federal Reserve Be Trusted to Do the Wrong Thing Again?

Some persons learn from their mistakes. However, Alan Greenspan had taken an uncharacteristically clear position when he talked about financial derivatives. In a speech in lovely Coral Gables, Florida on February 21, 1997, he urged a less cumbersome approach to regulating securities trading, especially derivatives and financial futures. "The less you interfere in the markets, the better," Greenspan said. "I've always believed that." Greenspan said he saw no need for regulating off-exchange derivative transactions, adding that the Commodity Exchange Act was an "inappropriate framework" for oversight of such trades. Financial innovations are to be encouraged because they increase the "efficiency" of financial markets. After all, what could be more reassuring than billions of complex wagers that are not even on the balance sheets?

Wall Street Capitalism

Following Alan Greenspan as he danced through the financial markets was like watching someone delicately walking through a minefield but stepping on every mine. When the financial markets explode next time, can the Federal Reserve be trusted to do the right thing? Will it do the right thing if (or when) a trillion-dollar bank collapses under the weight of margin calls? With the Reserve approving not only massive bank mergers but the underwriting and dealing of securities, the new banks may be too large and too compromised to save.

Just as Greenspan (and others) told the S&L's that they could do anything they wanted, he sent the same message to commercial banks and hedge funds. Besides, in international markets where the New York banks deal, there is *no* lender of last resort. As people discovered in Indonesia, the International Monetary Fund is an unreliable ally. As with the S&L bailout, taxpayers could end up picking up another very large tab at a time when the United States needs more than ever a strong and reliable banking system.

The Great Speculative Bond Casino

Not only has the bondholding class changed the rules for economic success, it has transformed the bond market into a casino. Small depositors were not the only major losers in the junk bond fiasco, so too were taxpayers and the economy as a whole. Yet, the buyout experts are back, doing a brisk business, and Wall Street is supplying still more financial innovations, instruments placing the bond market at risk to the manipulations of a single trader.

The winner-take-no-prisoners attitude has spread even to the commercial banking community. If the Reserve has its way, however, commercial banks will continue to be part of the problem rather than a way out. Greenspan's aggressively lax regulation and his bailout of LTCM spotlights the cozy relations between the Federal Reserve and Wall Street bankers and dealers. Greenspan has endorsed a sweeping Republican plan to roll back the depression-era walls erected between banking, securities and insurance firms. The proposed bank holding company structure would encourage further mergers among financial firms like the giant Citicorp and Travelers Group insurance-brokerage company and give the Federal Reserve more power to deregulate. In his typical Catch-22 style, Greenspan views the Bank Holding Company Act as essential because "the proliferation...of new financial products that enable risk unbundling have been increasingly combining the characteristics of banking, insurance, and securities products into single financial instruments."[15] One begins to wonder whether Wall Street capitalism is unlike crony capitalism.

Since ordinary people are in the direct path of cyclonic financial markets, we next consider the consequences for them. Not only permanent employment but wages were taken out by financial storms. One storm in particular—that developing over Asia and engulfing much of the global economy—would create still more difficulties for mainstream America. Worse, the bondholders would contribute mightily to the historic shift toward greater income and wealth inequalities. For ordinary people, the worst may be yet to come.

NOTES

1. For an example of how some economists have rationalized irrationality, see Yangru Wu, "Rational Bubbles in the Stock Market: Accounting for the U.S. Stock-Price Volatility," *Economic Enquiry*, April 1994, 309–319.

2. For a critique of "rational bubbles," see E. Ray Canterbery, "Irrational Exuberance and Rational Speculative Bubbles," Presidential Address to the International Trade and Finance Association, *The International Trade Journal*, Spring 1999, 1–22.

3. The full content of Greenspan's letter can be found as Appendix C of Martin Mayer's, *The Greatest-Ever Bank Robbery: The Collapse of the Savings and Loan Industry* (New York: Macmillan Publishing

Company, 1990). A full reading of the letter will inspire little trust in Greenspan's leadership of the Federal Reserve System. A dedicated reader of Mayer's book will come away with a complete understanding of what happened to the savings and loan industry, and why. See, too, Martin Mayer, *The Bankers: The Next Generation* (New York: Truman Talley Books/Dutton, 1997), Chapter 12.

4. From testimony of Patricia S. McJoynt, Senior Vice-President of the Federal Home Loan Bank of Seattle, October 31, 1989, before the House Banking Committee, in *Investigation of Lincoln Savings & Loan Association* (Washington, D.C.: U.S. Government Printing Office, 1989), Part 3, p. 160.

5. "Bonds: So Long, Easy Plays," *Business Week*, December 28, 1998, pp. 158–61.

6. Federal Reserve Bank of Cleveland, *Economic Trends*, June 1995, p. 15.

7. See David Folkerts-Landau and Takatoshi Ito, *et al.*, *International Capital Markets: Developments, Prospects, and Policy Issues* (Washington, D.C.: International Monetary Fund, August 1995), p. 18.

8. As Martin Mayer has suggested, the most important common law precedent goes against the banks. When interest rate swaps between an English borough council and some London banks went the wrong direction, the borough refused to pay off, "arguing that playing in derivatives was something they had no legal authority to do, and the banks should have known it." See Martin Mayer, *The Bankers: The Next Generation op. cit.*, p. 330. The case won by the borough cost the British and American banks about $600 million.

9. Interest rates moving in the wrong direction is what undid the Orange County (CA) pension funds. Robert Citron, the Orange County treasurer, had used reverse repurchase agreements (repos) to borrow against security holdings so that still more securities could be bought with the loan proceeds. (A repo is a contract between a seller and a buyer that stipulates the sale, and later repurchase—say, in a month—of bills, notes, and bonds at a stated date and price.) This process was then repeated until, on paper, the pension fund had assets of $20 billion instead of only $7.5 billion. Alan Greenspan is again implicated in the outcome. Citron was betting that interest rates would stay constant or fall in the new non-inflationary environment.

This was during the same year (1994) when Greenspan raised interest rates six times to slay the imaginary inflation monster. When interest rates soared instead of falling, the value of Citron's repos based on the underlying but falling bond prices, also declined significantly, for a loss of $1.5 billion. In defense of Citron's speculation, Greenspan was among the few persons on the planet expecting inflation during 1994 or since. For the details on Orange County, see the wonderful little book by Philippe Jorion, with the assistance of Robert Roper, *Big Bets Gone Bad: Derivatives and Bankruptcy in Orange County* (San Diego: Academic Press, 1995).

10. From remarks by Alan Greenspan, Chairman, Board of Governors of the Federal Reserve System, Congressional Testimony on January 5, 1995.
11. Quoted by Anita Raghavan and Mitchell Pacell, "A Hedge Fund Falters, So the Fed Beseeches Big Banks to Ante Up," *Wall Street Journal,* September 24, 1998, p. 1.
12. Quoted by Raghavan and Pacell, *Ibid.*
13. For the entire story regarding this conflict within the President's Working Group on the Financial Markets, see Michael Schroeder, "CFTC Chief Refuses to Take Back Seat in Derivatives Debate," *Wall Street Journal,* November 3, 1998, p. 1, 8.
14. "A Talk with Treasury Chief Rubin," *Business Week,* October 12, 1998, p. 126.
15. Alan Greenspan, Chairman, Federal Reserve System, testimony before the House Banking Committee, February 11, 1999, concerning financial services "reform."

TEN

❧◆❧

The Bondholding Class and Alan Greenspan Downsize America

While recent decades have been excellent for the new bondholding class, their effect has been pernicious for most people. Moreover, the bondholding class values leisure and lassitude—not for others, since for the middle class, these are afflictions, but for themselves. After all, richness gained from financial markets does not come directly from exertion. Still, bondholders would be benign if their gains meant no losses for others. For the bondholders, financial success has not depended upon good things happening to the *real* economy in which production takes place. Those working for a living are left to ponder, not the prospect for profits sharing and golden parachutes, but the fate of manufactured products, especially those made for exports in a romanticized global economy. As the American economy headed into the 1990s, the unemployment casualties continued to mount; white-collar employees were also affected because the working-class earnings stagnation could not be contained. We now expand our concerns beyond the rich.

Chairman Greenspan Uses the Unemployment Rate to Enforce the Speed Limit on Economic Growth

Since the bondholding class has a special interest in avoiding inflation, the *bond market strategy* adopted by Alan Greenspan was especially appealing because of its natural bias against inflation and full employment. The Sacred College of Bonds and Money has been willing to give the bondholders what they want. Successive White Houses and Congressional majorities have gone along with this either because they came to believe that great inequalities are good, or else because they were powerless to do anything about them. Monetary policy which targets phantom inflation at the expense of real economic growth and sustained full employment *is* the bondholders' legacy.

A couple of inconvenient outcomes from this strategy, however, require justification by the bondholding class. First is that great anomaly whereby financial asset hyperinflation is considered *good* whereas even modest goods inflation is considered *bad*. Though no true distinction can be drawn between the acceleration in goods prices and the acceleration in financial asset prices, Alan Greenspan—or Paul Volcker for that matter—has not argued for a zero inflation rate for securities. The restoration of some self-serving tenets of classical economics makes the anomaly go away, or so the legatees think. Since only the rich have the resources to save great amounts and these savings are held *increasingly* as financial wealth (so the parable goes) financial asset hyperinflation is not only a natural result of the wealthy doing well while doing good, but bullish securities markets make every American richer. We will return later to evaluate the reliability of this self-serving parable.

A second inconvenient outcome is a slower growth in employment than workers desire. The Federal Reserve tells us that its hands are tied. If the unemployment rate drops below its natural rate (recall the Non-accelerating-Inflation Rate of Unemployment or NAIRU), inflation will soar. Thus, the Reserve has no choice: it must not allow the unemployment rate to rise above its natural rate. Yet, no such natural rate of unemployment exists for those peddling securities on Wall Street. Why not? For the answer, see inconvenient outcome number one, above.

Perhaps it is only a minor embarrassment, but the natural rate of unemployment is sufficiently ill-behaved to give natural law a bad reputation. The true inconvenience has been to the working class. The unemployment rate at which inflation accelerated kept rising during the 1970s as oil and food prices soared. Figure 10.1 shows how the natural rate (estimated by one of the Fed's banks—hardly a source biased against its stability) has bounced around, eventually reaching 7.3 percent in 1978–79, only to fall back to 6.3 percent by 1994.[1] This was no problem on Wall Street where employment in the securities industry was booming during most of the 1990s.

Since the natural rate is considered a reliable guide to Federal Reserve actions, Alan Greenspan found it necessary to fight inflation before the natural rate flashes the accelerating signal. Thus, like a driver stopping his SUV a half block from a red light, Greenspan had to slow down money growth and raise interest rates *before* the unemployment rate fell to its natural rate! Unfortunately, no one unemployment rate has been *the* natural rate. Again, it mattered not what the unemployment rate was—be it the 5.1 percent of the early 1960s or the 6.7 percent of 1981—it was the going natural rate. Moreover, though the estimated natural rate was 6.3 percent for 1994–2000, the *actual* unemployment rate, at 4.3 percent in May 1998, had reached a 28-year low. Inflation exhibited near price stability—up at just a 0.9 percent annual rate. Though no acceleration in inflation was in sight, the unemployment rate rose to 4.5 percent during the next month on the way to 4.7 percent.

Remember, however, the admonition from the Pope of Wall Street: price stability is a poor predictor of inflation. The Reserve fretted about impending inflation throughout 1996–97. In early summer 1998, though the Asian crisis had begun to slow the American economy, Greenspan told Congress's Joint Economic Committee that evidence of a slowdown "still is sparse." "Tighter economic policy," a euphemism for higher interest rates, "may be

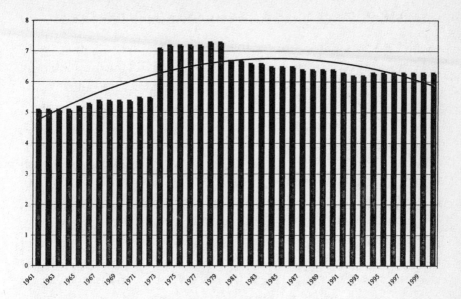

Figure 10.1 Estimates of the Natural Rate of Unemployment, 1961–2000

Source: Stuart E. Weiner, "New Estimates of the Natural Rate of Unemployment," Federal Reserve Board of Kansas City, *Economic Review*, Fourth Quarter 1993.

necessary to help guard against a buildup of pressures that could derail the current prosperity." He remained concerned "that economic growth will run into constraints as the reservoir of unemployed people available to work is drawn down."[2] Nothing unnerved Greenspan quite as much as a shrinkage in the Reserve's army of the unemployed.

Deploying national policy to maintain a large surplus of unemployed workers is certainly an effective way of reducing real wages. However, the adverse effect of the bondholding class on employment has gone well beyond these slow growth policies. These other developments nonetheless help to explain why the *apparent* unemployment rate fell while exerting almost imperceptible pressures on wages and goods prices. At the same time they, too, help to explain why the bondholding class got still richer.

Downsizing: The Path to Recovery From Junk Bond Debt

Besides their connection to the Federal Reserve's slow growth policies, worker layoffs are directly connected to the bondholding class in still another way. The era of mergers by junk bond leveraging came at a high debt servicing cost. As noted, U.S. Steel, a.k.a. USX Corporation, overnight became the nation's twelfth largest industrial company. The mounting servicing cost of "high-yielding" bonds required cost reductions achieved by laying off workers, including middle management. Initially, at least, getting by with less labor boosts profits and stock prices. In the pecking order of villains to the workers, the junk bond dealers are towering, but the bondholding class presently is composed of the movers and shakers. The success of the *bond market strategy* and its encouragement of mergers and layoffs gave the bondholders capital gains in stocks when not making gains in bonds.

The first wave of downsizing is epitomized by RJR Nabisco. It was able to avoid bankruptcy from its junk bond financing only by selling off various parts of its business and laying off workers. Of those laid off, 72 percent eventually did find work but at wages about half of what they had been paid. Lester Thurow, drawing upon a variety of statistical sources, has identified two subsequent waves of downsizing that have eliminated about 2.5 million "good jobs."

The second wave happened, not surprisingly, during the 1990–91 recession. Though workers are always laid off during recessions, this time it was different because the layoffs were *permanent*. Moreover, whereas three blue-collar workers were laid off for each white-collar worker in the 1980–81 near-depression, in the 1990–91 recession the ratio was down to two to one.

The third wave of massive downsizing began *after* the 1990–91 recession, during an expansion, albeit a slow and uncertain one. Announced downsizing was in excess of 500,000 workers in each of the three years—1993, 1994, and 1995. By now, corporations were making the highest profits they had made in more than twenty-five years, helping to fuel the bull markets in bonds and stocks.[3] This wave is epitomized by AT&T's elimination of 40,000 jobs—most of them in relatively high-paying white-collar positions— that welcomed the New Year in 1996. Wall Street analysts applauded AT&T's downsizing and AT&T stock immediately jumped by $2.50 to $67.25.

Thereafter, a *fourth* wave of downsizing began in 1997. Bondholders and shareholders, by now addicted to stunning capital gains, were demanding still more profit improvements. In July, Woolworth and International Paper each euphemistically "shed" at least 9,000 workers, followed by Stanley Works and Fruit of the Loom shedding, not underwear, but nearly 5,000 workers each. The shareholders no longer let companies have very much time to take action. As Whirlpool and Food Lion also announced layoffs, Whirlpool shares immediately spun upward 14 percent, and Food Lion shares roared 4 percent. The self-serving *ideology of the bondholding class* says that ordinary people benefit from such job terminations because rising productivity also elevates wages and "most Americans" own appreciating stock, neither of which is close to the truth.

In 1998, a *fifth* wave of downsizing got underway. In January the unemployment rate was still fairly low, though increasing to 4.7 percent. The rise in unemployment was related to the mass layoffs. This time the alleged villain was the global economy; it had become a jungle out there. The relentless rise in the international value of the dollar and cost-saving restructuring by foreign competitors was forcing U.S. firms to cut their wage bills even more. About a fifth of American workers are exposed to the global tempest; after having cut 142,000 jobs in the last quarter of 1997—the largest batch of job-losses since the recession in the early 1990s—toward the end of 1998, major U.S. corporations announced layoffs at a near-record rate of 574,629, the most since 1993. Boeing Co., the aerospace giant, was one of the major U.S.

casualties of the Asian meltdown, cutting as many as 48,000 jobs by 2000.

Despite a slowing economy by summer 1998, *some* jobs were being created. For example, Kemet electronics, a high-tech company in Shelby, N. C., was laying off 500 workers to move their operations to Mexico around that time. Nancy Blackburn, an unmarried 54-year-old had just been upgraded from a temporary to a permanent $9.80-an-hour Kemet job with full benefits. But her job went south, down Mexico way. Meanwhile, AGI Inc., a printed-materials company "considering" building a new plant near Shelby, was given a new incentive by the Kemet layoffs. There was, however, the downside: more than 1,250 people applied for a mere 80 potential jobs at AGI, offering the health care, vacation, and other benefits usually available only for permanent jobs. Moreover, AGI pays lower wages than Kemet and promises only temporary employment.[4]

An important by-product of downsizing is the temporary worker and the contingent labor force or what might be called "the Wal-Mart labor force." Such workers, often laid off from "permanent" jobs, are compensated less in wages, fringe benefits, and holidays, and are faced with even more insecurity. The male temporary workers earn about half what they would as full-time workers. Most of these, now among the working poor, were *not poor* when they were working full time, but were middle class. Besides, temporary workers are less likely to have fringe benefits, much less jobs which might lead to better opportunities. The reduction in employer-provided health insurance and pension coverage (that would otherwise include financial assets) among employed men in the final decades of the twentieth century has placed still greater stress on families.

Fear suffuses the employment climate, not simply fear of temporary layoffs, but the fear of layoffs becoming permanent and "permanent" work becoming temporary. The bondholders, of course, are immune to these maladies. Besides, to Alan Greenspan's mind, worker insecurity is good because it keeps a lid on wages and inflation.

Bondholders Contribute to Trade Deficits and Still More Downward Pressures on Jobs and Wages

The mounting damage to the working class did not end at the waterfront. The bondholding class has a foreign contingent. Though the United States has long been important to the global economy, only recently, as the bondholding class has gone global, has the global economy become important to the United States. During 1983–96, U.S. interest rates—far above those in Great Britain, Western Europe and Japan—magnetically attracted foreign funds. Foreigners, especially Japanese, were buying a substantial share of the new debt issues. Like the rich in the U.S., wealthy foreigners hold U.S. dollars, not in cash earning zero interest, but in securities. The purchase of dollar-denominated securities by foreigners exerts an upward pressure on the international value of the dollar (the price foreigners pay for the dollar). U.S. Treasury Secretary Rubin also remained committed to a strong dollar policy. By 1997–2000 the collapse of many economies—first in Asia, then Russia, then in Latin America—also made the U.S. a safe haven for rich, foreign bondholders.

A higher-valued U.S. dollar makes American goods and services more expensive to others and foreign goods cheaper for Americans. After a time, a rising dollar discourages foreigners from buying U.S. goods and encourages Americans to buy theirs. The resultant trade deficit was a tolerable $20 billion in 1983, but set a record at $153.4 billion in 1987. Though the deficit was down to $110 billion ten years later, the final predicted figure for 1998 was a new record, $168 billion. Much of the more recent deterioration in the trade balance emanated from Asia's plight, with the Brazilian crisis threatening to pile still more on the deficit. The falling overseas currencies had made imports cheaper and resulted in a flood of steel, cars and other foreign products into the United States. The U.S. had become the buyer of last resort for a collapsing global economy.

When Americans spend more abroad than foreigners spend in the United States, the net contribution of international trade to the growth of the U.S. GDP is *negative*. While U.S. exports earn national income and contribute to employment, U.S. imports generate income for other nations and greater employment abroad. A U.S. trade deficit of $168 billion means $168 billion less GDP. In short, sales of U.S. securities to foreigners, combined later with the Asian and Latin American crises, have contributed to the slowdown in U.S. economic growth.

Beginning with the fragile recovery in 1983, the trade deficit was driven not so much by American producers buying foreign machine tools and capital goods, for most were timid, but by aggressively extravagant, affluent American consumers. Luxury autos, with nameplates like Lexus, Infiniti Q45, BMW, and Mercedes-Benz, became popular with affluent households. The American preference for foreign luxury goods instead of capital goods continued during the nineties: even Donald Trump has been buying paintings by Renoir.

American workers have good reason to agonize about the trade trend. For instance, consider a deficit in merchandise trade in manufactured goods of $168 billion. Since roughly every $54,000 of manufacturing output hires one worker, a $168 billion seepage to foreign markets shrinks the demand for U.S. labor by 3.1 million workers. With the rise of the new leisure class of bondholders and a decline in manufacturing job opportunities attended by downward wage pressures, it is hardly surprising that the economic recoveries from the double-dip downturn of 1979–82 and the recession of 1990–91 were as uneven as the brick streets of Boston. In truth, the benefits were enjoyed only by the upper fifth of families and especially by the richest.

As I said, not all economists agree about the causes of this working class income stagnation. Other elements have doubtless contributed to American trade deficits. (For more on these trade transitions, see Lester Thurow's *The Future of Capitalism* and the provocative books by Ravi Batra.[5]) Whatever the other causes of the external deficits, however, the spread of security holdings to trading allies had the same effect, slowing the growth in GDP. Moreover, the rising trade deficits have put further downward pressures on a working class already adrift from union protection. The bondholding class, though not the sole cause of the ill trade wind that has brought on this increasing job insecurity, have nonetheless added a significant dimension to the malaise. Moreover, the downward pressures on wages have generally benefitted Wall Street—thus far.

A Weakened Asia and Russia Adds to U.S. Financial Volatility and Greenspan's Vulnerability

Nations are increasingly linked, no matter how precariously, by the worldwide proliferation of financial instruments and their unrestrained movements. During 1996, White House international concerns shifted away from the chronic trade deficit with Japan and toward Japan's own economic plight. Following the collapse of the speculative bubbles in Japanese stock and real estate markets during the 1980s, its economy went into a deep recession threatening its banking system. During the twilight of 1996 and the sunrise months of 1997, major White House and Treasury announcements on "balancing the federal budget" were aimed at *strengthening* the dollar to *further expand*, of all things, Japan's trade surplus with the U.S. and bolster its economy. By then, Japan's collapsing banking system was threatening the world financial markets. America's trade gap with Japan comprised nearly a third of the total deficit and increased 15 percent during 1998. Trade deficits, once a private matter between consumers and firms, are now sustained to stabilize other financial systems to save our own.

The global turmoil in foreign exchange, bond, and stock markets shocked the already turbulent U.S. financial markets. Robert Rubin, the U.S. Treasury Secretary, and Alan Greenspan especially were concerned about the vulnerability of U.S. financial markets to Japan's financial plight and the political collapse of Russia. This vulnerability was displayed in the Dow; it fell 4.19 percent on August 27, 1998, eased downward 1.40 percent on the 28th, only to descend 6.37 percent on the 31st. The Dow had plunged 21 percent during that month. Bond prices were exhibiting similar volatility but generally moving up as the Dow moved down despite the threat from Japan's central bank to dump U.S. Treasury securities unless the U.S. intervened in foreign exchange markets to bolster the dollar. Some relief came to the Dow in early September, only to be undone on September 9 and 10, and so it went.

A bond market rally and a 5 percent leap in the Dow on September 8 were linked directly to Alan Greenspan's remarks in a speech in Berkeley, California in which he said Fed policy makers "will need to consider carefully the potential ramifications of ongoing developments, rather than just focusing on the risk of rising [commodities] inflation." His concerns as recently as *only two weeks prior* to this speech were regarding the continuing threat from commodities inflation! Greenspan was clearly worried that everything that had been accomplished for the bondholding class and Wall Street might be undone by crashing financial markets. Having famously failed to talk the stock market down as early as December 1996 with his "irrational exuberance" speech, he was now poised to reduce interest rates to keep the financial asset inflation roaring. Prices in the bond market soared, putting a dream interest rate of 5 percent on the benchmark 30-year bond within reach.

By now even the bondholding class was hoping that Greenspan had put inflation behind him in a world of falling commodity prices. However, he continued to be evasive. In congressional testimony on September 13, 1998, Greenspan denied the prospect of a global interest rate cut coordinated among the major industrial nations (because the Europeans refused to cooperate). Not only did Asian and European stock markets plunge, but Greenspan's statements led to a 206-point slide in the Dow in 18 minutes. Still, the 30-year bellwether Treasury bond gained $4.5625 per $1,000 bond, pulling the yield down to 5.177 percent. The members of the bondholding class who had been holding stocks had long since made a full retreat into the safety and capital gains of a rallying bond market. The 30-year U.S. Treasury bond returned 26.78 percent in the 12 months ending August 31, while Dow stocks returned only 0.67 and the Wilshire 5000, the broadest stock index, returned only 1.22 percent, excluding nearly nonexistent dividends.

Having created the Great Bull Market of the 1990s, Alan Greenspan now faced difficult choices. If, as he believed, the Dow was already overvalued by some 20 percent in December 1996 when he had tried to talk it down, it must have been overvalued by more than 50 percent by midsummer 1998. At first, the Asian meltdown made his life easier. With the economy slowing due to the rising trade deficits, the members of the Sacred College had less and less reason to raise interest rates (though they talked of little else). Greenspan had long feared that the only way to overcome the "irrational exuberance" of his creation, would be to increase the fed funds rate. That action, however, would be dangerous; it could set off the greatest stock market crash in American history. He owed Wall Street better than that.

With the Asian collapse having a domino effect on the rest of the world, Greenspan was now in a quandary. While U.S. workers were getting the first measurable wage increases for many years, he still sensed American inflation coming amidst global depression.

Never before had the balance between raising and lowering interest rates been so precarious. Though being a central banker had become less easy, Greenspan still could rest assured that the bondholding class was resting comfortably in a rising bond market.

While putting together a package to bail out the famously failing hedge fund, Long-Term Capital Management, Greenspan surely realized that the balance had tipped toward interest rate cuts. Otherwise, the bond market rally might come to a nasty ending. In testimony to the Senate Budget Committee on the same day as the bailout, Greenspan mustered all of his rhetorical skills to synthesize his three most recent positions:

> ... in July, I explained that the Federal Open Market Committee was concerned that high—indeed rising—demand for labor could produce cost pressures on our economy that would disrupt the ongoing expansion. I also noted that a high real federal funds rate was a necessary offset to expansionary conditions elsewhere in financial markets. By mid-August the Committee believed that disruptions abroad and more cautious behavior by investors at home meant that the risks to the expansion had become evenly balanced. Since then, deteriorating foreign economies and their spillover to domestic markets have increased the possibility that the slowdown in the growth of the American economy will be more than sufficient to hold inflation in check.[6]

He still did not mention the lowering of the fed funds rate, the key rate that Greenspan had not cut since January 1996. However, Fed watcher Sung Won Sohn of Norwest Corp. concluded, "He told us in unambiguous terms that he will be cutting interest rates next Tuesday [September 29, 1998]. This is the third signal."[7] Two hours later the Dow surged 259 points. As Sohn predicted, Greenspan cut the fed funds rate by a quarter point, followed soon with a second quarter-point cut. Only when wages were sufficiently soft and the threat to the financial markets sufficiently ominous, did Greenspan concede that his fight against inflation in a deflationary world had been won, however precarious and temporary the glorious victory.

Downsizing the Middle Class at the Millennium

Slower growth, job losses and downward pressures on wages are the most visible ill effects of soaring trade deficits. This working class blight continued *during an economic expansion, though a slow one,* and was worsened by the Asian and Latin crises. While slow economic growth has contributed to the slow wage earnings growth, slowly rising full-time employment has failed to benefit most families. Those workers retained full-time were working, but not doing better. Moreover, further deterioration of the trade balance from the global crisis slowed growth and increased the unemployment rate. The growth rate in real GDP dropped to only 1.4 percent during the second quarter of 1998, well below the speed limit set by Alan Greenspan.

Thus, as reflected in U.S. Census Bureau data, during most of the nineties the financial condition of the typical worker continued the long deterioration that began in the late seventies and accelerated during the eighties and most of the nineties. Over that time, real hourly wages either stagnated or fell for most of the bottom 60 percent of the working population. Still, even the brief episode of substantial economic growth during 1996–97 illustrates the good that growth can do for Americans willing to work long hours. By the end of 1997, median household income had risen to $37,005, bringing the figure to just under the median for 1989, though the gain came from the typical family working 4 percent longer than at the start of the decade. That is, by working more during an expansion, the typical family had managed to struggle almost back to where it had been a decade earlier.[8]

Americans define the American Dream as achieving middle class status: it is at least one American middle that is shrinking. This American Nightmare is revealed in a different data source that includes both wage and non-wage income. In 1993 forty-six million tax returns with incomes between $20,000 and $75,000 were filed, an income range often used to define the American middle class; in that year this "middle" represented only 47 percent of wage and salary earners filing income tax returns. Worse, some forty-four million—only two million less than the entire "middle class" or 45 percent of all taxpayers—reported incomes less than $20,000; they are the working poor, an expanding underclass, rapidly approaching half of American taxpayers. The share of American income of the middle fifth of the families declined from 17.5 percent in 1979 to 15.7 percent in 1997.

From 1992 to 1998, while the measured unemployment rate was dropping by more than a third, the real hourly compensation of American workers remained virtually unchanged. Since 1974 the average full-time worker would need to have received $6,000 a year more simply to match the gains in worker productivity. Why, in this environment, would anyone expect that rising wages were threatening to ignite inflation? In truth, the measured unemployment rate counts workers as employed if they hold *any* job—whether it is ten or forty hours a week, temporary, seasonal, or permanent, paying $7 or $70 an hour—or no job, having left many in the labor force hopelessly discouraged. An unemployment rate reflecting the inability to make a decent living and to gain self-sufficiency would be about three times the official unemployment rate.

Whatever the other contributions to the reversal of fortunes, some things nonetheless remain clear. Since the weakening of labor unions during the Reagan years, facilitated by the deepest downturn since the Great Depression, intensified by growing trade deficits, and accelerated by the downsizing begun during the regime of junk bonds and continuing during a period of slow growth engineered by Alan Greenspan on behalf of the bondholding class, ordinary blue-collar and white-collar workers now possess greatly diminished wage bargaining powers and live in fear. The only sustained real income growth has come from *unearned* income—

mostly from interest on bonds and capital gains on securities. Since most American families have small stakes in financial instruments, the multitudes are dependent upon work for income. Unearned income growing at a historically fast pace during a time of stagnant wages explains the decline of the middle class. The history of the final quarter of the twentieth century has provided a recipe not only for a reversal in the trend toward more income equality since the 1930s, but a shift toward unpardonable wealth inequality, our next topic.

NOTES

1. Stuart E. Weiner, "New Estimates of the Natural Rate of Unemployment," *Economic Review, Federal Reserve Bank of Kansas City*, Fourth Quarter 1993, p. 66.
2. Alan Greenspan, Testimony Before the Joint Economic Committee, U.S. Congress, June 10, 1998.
3. See Lester C. Thurow, *The Future of Capitalism* (New York: Morrow, 1995), pp. 26–9 for a more extended discussion of recent experiences. For the data sources, see pp. 334–5.
4. The details of this case in North Carolina are from Michael M. Phillips, "Even During a Boom, Layoffs Persist," *The Wall Street Journal Interactive Edition*, September 8, 1998.
5. See Thurow, *ibid*. Also, see Ravi Batra, *The Pooring of America: Competition & the Myth of Free Trade* (New York: Collier Books, 1993) and Ravi Batra, *The Great American Deception* (New York: John Wiley & Sons, Inc., 1996). Batra contends that free trade has not been beneficial for the United States. As the relative demand for American products has diminished, unemployment has followed, putting downward pressure on wage rates. Doubtless, foreign competition—often unfair competition, compared with the openness of our trading borders—has not been favorable for manufacturing wages. Nevertheless, we might have felt much or at least some of these pressures even without our free-trade policies because of declining unionism in the United States and very low wages in developing countries. As part of the downsizing process, many American firms began to produce in low-wage countries.

6. Alan Greenspan, Chairman of the Federal Reserve System, prepared text of testimony to the Senate Budget Committee, September 23, 1998.

7. Quoted in an Associated Press release from Washington D.C. by Dave Skidmore, "Greenspan Signals a Fed Plan to Cut Interest Rates Next Week," September 24, 1998.

8. For a multitude of details on the behavior of wages and benefits, see Lawrence Mishel, Jared Bernstein, and John Schmitt, *The State of Working America, 1998–99* (Ithaca and London: Cornell University Press, an Economic Policy Institute book, 1999).

———◆≫◆◆≪◆———

ELEVEN

The Bondholders' Non-charitable Contribution to Inequality

Carville's Laws of Economics: 1. Those who say money isn't the problem have plenty of money; 2. Those who say stagnant wages aren't a problem don't have stagnant wages; 3. Those who say wealth stratification isn't a problem are sitting high up in the economic stratosphere.

James Carville, *We're Right, They're Wrong: a Handbook for Spirited Progressives* (New York: Random House, 1996)

Who Got Fat During the "Fat Years?"

A common denominator of both the 1960s and the 1980s is tax reduction. However, a remarkable contrast stamps the two eras of John F. Kennedy/Lyndon B. Johnson and Ronald W. Reagan. Real growth in gross national product during the 1960s amounted to 46 percent, much higher than the 28 percent of the 1980s. Industrial production expanded by 67 percent during the 1960s, but only by 29 percent during the 1980s, as the bondholding class ascended. The unemployment rate never rose above 6.7 percent (1961) during the sixties; it never fell below 7 percent during 1980–86, peaking at 9.6 to 10.7 percent in 1982–83.

A contrast in policy distinguishes the two eras. During the Kennedy–Johnson years, the Federal Reserve followed a monetary policy congenial mainly to broad-based tax cuts, allowing these tax cuts to stimulate the overall economy. By contrast, Dr. Volcker's

monstrous Monetary Experiment merely created bonds for the rich,
while Reagan's lopsided tax cuts gave the rich the additional funds
to buy the bonds, thereby funding the bondholding class.

The fragile Reagan economic recovery of 1982–89 was
nonetheless given a good name by the supply-siders, out of
devotion to their ideas, and by most Republicans, out of a heartfelt
desire to be reelected. They biblically called the post-recession
eighties "the seven fat years." The era was plump for some, the
bondholders enjoying the greatest gains. As noted, however,
workers became worse off, an outcome reflecting a dramatic change
in the structure of American Society. Economists, seldom in accord,
generally agree that the working class took a beating during the
late twentieth century. The sixties' growth had lifted all boats, but
the Reagan expansion hoisted mostly yachts. As has been noted,
in the nineties the main distinction from the eighties was the
length and price of yachts.

Contrary to the *ideology of the bondholding class* emanating from
Wall Street, bull markets in securities do not make workers rich
or necessarily even better off. A great gap exists between token
ownership and amounts owned by the rich. In 1995 only 3 percent
of families owned bonds. In that year about 41 percent of
households owned stock, including stock owned through mutual
funds, savings plans (401k accounts or individual retirement
accounts) and defined-contribution pension plans, or through
direct ownership. Since retired people are more likely to hold
bonds than stocks, the median value of bonds held by families in
the $25,000–$49,900 income range was $29,000 compared with
only $6,900 in direct stockholdings. Even in the upper 5 percent
of the income distribution, the median value of bondholdings was
$58,000 compared with $30,000 in stocks, with half holding more
and half holding less.[1] For the very rich, bonds trumped stocks
by about two to one.

If we look closely at the overall distribution of securities
holdings, the idea that bull markets contribute to wealth equality

seems implausible. Since only 28.8 percent of households have more than a minimal ownership of stock, the wealthiest 1 percent hold 51.4 percent (by value), and the least wealthy 90 percent hold only 11.6 percent, it is obvious that bull markets in stocks have amplified wealth inequalities. Worse, *half* the stock held by American households is owned by the 5 *percent* with the highest incomes, leaving the remains of the day to the bottom 95 percent. Besides, during most of the 1980s–90s, the prices of bonds and stocks rose together, bondholdings being concentrated in even fewer households. Those who owned *financial securities* made capital gains and their net worth soared.

The initial source of great wealth inequalities is usually great income inequalities. Though wealth inequalities are normally much wider than income inequalities, it is difficult to become rich if one is poor in income (disregarding inheritance). In an exploration of the effects of the bondholding class on inequality, we begin, then, with the recent shifts in the American income distribution, tied as it is to the infamous fate of the working class, which was discussed in Chapter 10.

The Infernal Tower of Income: The Upper 5 Percent vs. the Lower 95 Percent

The aforementioned USX Corporation, formerly U.S. Steel, is housed in the 65-story USX Tower in Pittsburgh, containing a microcosm of economic conditions in the United States.

To Tom Usher, the Chairman and CEO earning $1.6 million in 1995, the view of the U.S. economy from his suite of offices at the top looks good, though even he would like to see it growing faster. "The economy is not taking off, which I think it has the potential to do," says Usher, who feared that President Clinton was too content with a slow-growth economy.[2] To Bill Farmer, the shoeshine man on the lower lobby level, 64 stories below Usher, "the economy is kind of bad, and things aren't going to get better."[3] The workers between the top and bottom floors are in the shrinking middle class; they are hoping for better times, doing better or falling further behind.

Irrespective of their jobs, those in the middle do not believe that they have the lifetime job security enjoyed by their parents. They live paycheck to paycheck and worry about retiring, paying for college, and buying a house. John Mankevich and two friends take care of the eleven thousand windows encasing the USX Tower, which, in the middle, offer a realistic view of the economy. The three have union jobs and earn $30,000 to $40,000 a year. Though they do have health benefits and pensions, all three believe that the erosion of union jobs will hurt pay for all workers and Rich Marson can't afford to send his children to college. Tom DeZort says, "every business around is downsizing, the top executives are taking all the money, the work is going out of state and overseas and the working man is hurting."[4] He's right. Even those earning $60,000 see themselves only one paycheck from poverty, and 94 percent of the 131 million working Americans in 1998 earned less than the Social Security wage base maximum of $68,400. The differences among the floors of the USX Tower are similar to those of American society.

In Pittsburgh, several major companies downsized in the eighties, making that city a leading indicator of the effects of downsizing (much of the national corporate downsizing took place during the nineties). Some 35,000 steel jobs were lost in Allegheny County, Pittsburgh's home county, from 1981 to 1994. Still, nearly 30,000 jobs were created in healthcare. In only 13 years, manufacturing jobs were reduced from 23 percent of all jobs in the county to 10.5 percent in 1996. Services went from 25 percent to 36 percent. Unfortunately, most healthcare and other service sector jobs pay much lower wages than those old union jobs in manufacturing.

Not only was this economic restructuring in Pittsburgh similar to that of the entire national economy, inequality within the USX Tower reflects the inequalities in society. Family income, though not *every* family's income, grew more slowly during the 1980s than in the 70s or, for that matter, between World War II and 1973. Even excluding the huge amounts CEOs receive from stock options and other perks, their salaries exploded after the mid-70s. Setting a real wage index for workers and for CEOs at 1.0 for 1976, the two values quickly diverge, falling to 0.896 for workers and rising to 2.5 for executives by 1995.[5] Thereafter, the chasm between worker and CEO compensation widened even more.

In 1996 the average chief executive made 209 times the pay of factory workers. Back in 1980 the CEOs had to settle for only 42 times as much as factory workers. The *average* CEO salary and bonus rose nearly 40 percent during 1996, to $2.3 million. Their total compensation rose 54 percent, to *average* $5.8 million, coming on top of a 30 percent raise the year before. Workers got a paltry raise of 3 percent, enough to keep pace with a mild inflation rate, but too much to keep Alan Greenspan from raising interest rates in March 1997 to curb the "inflationary threat" from "excessive wage pressures." The CEO pay leader at $102 million, Lawrence Coss of Green Tree Financial Corporation, was selling mobile homes to low-income retirees while charging a premium of two or three percentage points above mortgage rates for conventional homes.[6] Meanwhile, Fortune 500 profits rose a record 23 percent.

The dramatic increase in income inequality between the top and bottom floors of society has been well documented. For instance, economists Sheldon Danziger and Peter Gottschalk have used data from the U.S. Bureau of the Census to show how different the social world would have been if relative income growth had continued its pre-1969 trend.[7] Since the Census data *underreport* income from financial assets, however, it substantially understates the true average income of the upper fifth. Despite this understatement, the closer we get to the top of the inverted income mountain, the greater the inequality. From that lofty plateau, we can see that *all of the heightened inequality between 1982*

*and 1989 can be accounted for by the income gains of the richest
5 percent of families.* As a result, the richest 5 percent, the very
rich, receive more income than the bottom 40 percent! The
average income of the top 5 percent has grown from $128,198
in 1982 to $183,044 in 1994. The income growth in 1989–94
was even more unequal than that of the entire 1980s decade. In
1994, for the first time since such records have been kept, the
richest fifth of society received a greater share of national income
than the middle three-fifths, decimating the once comfortable
middle class. The prospects for 95 percent of all families have
changed for the worse.

The bondholding class prefers to view the world only from the
top floor of the USX Tower, from which on a clear day you can
see the New Economy forever. This bondholder's-eye view tells us
that growing inequality has been the result of government welfare
handouts and the disgraceful personal conduct of the poor.
Consider, however, middle-class married-couple families with
children—families representing the Norman Rockwell family, the
country's bedrock culture. They are not on welfare, though they
soon may be. In 1989, the second fifth of these married couples
had an average income of $28,660, only 5 percent above the 1973
average for this fifth.[8] In real dollars, their condition had improved
by only a few cents by the end of 1997, only to be threatened
by a global recession beginning in 1998. Despite social behavior
that would please the most circumspect parish priest, most cautious
Jewish priest, or the most reserved Calvinist, the moral center was
barely holding its own.

Unequal, USA: The Widening Gap in Wealth

But there is more, or perhaps less, because the wealth distribution
is always more unequal than the income distribution. Like yachts
or country estates, bonds and stocks are luxury goods. Though
many during the Great Bull Market of the 1980–90s became

afflicted with a contrary view, the truth is, a rich person can better afford to buy securities than can the typical working stiff. Still, it is consistent with the *ideology of the bondholding class* to contend that shareholdings had become sufficiently commonplace sometime during the 1990s as to now constitute a bulwark of democracy. Russia and Haiti, not to mention Cuba, would soon follow in America's footsteps once Merrill Lynch had proper offices in Moscow, Port au Prince, and Havana.

A contrary view is eminently more convincing. Those earning the greatest incomes can afford not only better cars and clothes, but more bonds and stocks. Furthermore, those already enjoying a greater value in securities, homes, and other wealth most likely will have even more tomorrow. The compounding of interest and dividends, if nothing else, will assure the greater inequality. Shining the spotlight on personal wealth holdings can be as revealing as it is embarrassing. Wealth tells us much more about the rich, their assets being a better measure of the true status associated with accumulation.

We usually measure wealth as net worth (the value of marketable assets such as bonds, stocks, and houses minus the value of liabilities or what we owe such as mortgage balances). Though they number, at most, only 1.1 million families and individuals, the *average* net worth or wealth of the members of the bondholding class is about $7.9 million. They own almost 39 percent of marketable U.S. household wealth.[9] Though their incomes begin at around $190,000, they rise into the multimillions and even billions. They include the Busch family of beer fame and Ted Turner, Vice Chairman of Time Warner. Securities, of course, cannot buy happiness. Turner complains: "Average sex is better than being a billionaire."[10] Of course, he's married to Jane Fonda.

Think not of the bondholding class but of American society as a small village of 5,000 households, large enough to raise a child. Call the village Unequal, for its lopsidedness. Let us begin where most people do—at the bottom. In Unequal, USA, 2,000 families would be living in substandard housing; their average net worth would be only $900 each, held mostly in the equity value of the humble homes in which they live. The next 20 percent or 1,000 families would be living in modest homes; their average net worth would be $45,900, held mostly in homeowner equity. This bottom 60 percent hold *no significant values* in bonds, stocks, mutual funds, or personal trusts.

Now, if we begin our tour of the American village from the top, things look quite different. Somewhat removed from those 3,000 modest homes live the other 2,000 families. Among these, the 1,000 at the top have an average net worth of $858,100. However, like those below, this net worth is not evenly distributed, even though they are among the top fifth of the village's wealth holders.

At the summit is a sliver of 50 households living on large, wooded estates around the perimeter of the village. Their *average* net worth is $7.9 million. They, the 1 percent of Unequal, USA holding nearly 39 percent of the village's marketable wealth, and many of the next 450 families with a *third* of the village's wealth comprise an elite. The a*verage* net worth of these "second-class" 450 families is between $471,700 and $1,115,000.[11]

Whereas the elite 500 enjoy leisure and the super-rich 50 among them have the leisure to enjoy, the remaining 4,500 work and provide surpluses shared unequally with a two-tiered leisure class. Many of the 450 lower upscale families nonetheless are living in exclusive, gated developments called something elegant like Whispering Pines. Whispering Pines has a 24-hour security patrol, fine restaurants and several championship golf courses where residents can play after paying a $70,000 initiation fee. Those with net worth in the $500,000 range would probably have greater net worth without the debt servicing required to maintain the Whispering Pines lifestyle.

The rules governing Unequal, USA are set by this elite of 500 families, though the top 50 have substantially more dollar votes than the others and comprise much of the bondholding class. The policies and attitudes favoring a continuation of the existing degree of inequality are set by these families, often redounding to their personal benefit.

Unequal, USA was not always this unequal. The increasing concentration of marketable wealth during the past two decades reverses a democratizing trend prevailing from the stock market crash of 1929 through the late 1970s. Today, the distance between the rich families and everyone else is greater than at anytime since the bull market of 1922–29. What is more, the inequalities are greater than any other industrialized nation except Russia, and including "class-ridden" England.

Most of the uniquely American gaps in wealth have come from the rising inequality in the income distribution and in the redistribution of financial wealth. Specifically, about two-thirds of the great increase in inequality between 1983 and 1989 can be accounted for by the jump in income inequality. The other third of the increase in inequality seems to be related to the rise in securities prices relative to housing prices. In the more recent era, 1989–95, a modest decline in underlying income inequality has been overwhelmed by obscene inflation in securities prices relative to that in housing.[12]

Generally, the super-rich (upper 1 percent) of Americans, held about a third of the nation's marketable wealth after 1929, dropping to a low of a fifth in 1969, and remaining below 30 percent though the 1970s. Then, fortunes reversed. The share owned by the super-rich soared to 37 percent in 1989 on the way to 38.5 percent in 1995. This dramatic dislocation of wealth to the top reflected the staggering trundling of *financial* wealth upward during the 1980s. The top 1 percent of financial wealth holders—or, in Unequal, USA figures, the 50 super-rich families living on wooded estates—held nearly *47 percent of total financial wealth* by 1989. The share of the bottom 60 percent or lower 3,000 families fell between 1983 and 1989 to only 7 percent. In

Unequal, USA between 1983 and 1989, the 50 top households on the wooded estates received *all* of the total gain in financial wealth, with the other 99 percent *losing* shares of financial wealth.

The financial wealth of the *bottom* 40 percent or lower 2,000 out of 5,000 families *declined absolutely*. The *entire absolute gain* in financial wealth was enjoyed by the *top 1 percent* of households or only 500 families in Unequal, USA.[13] At the tip of the top, the supra-rich (half of 1 percent, or only 25 families in the village) by 1989 owned 40 percent of all assets (bonds, stocks, cash, paintings, jewelry, and so on). Even when expanded to the entire USA of 1989, this tiny sliver of humanity included only about 750,000 souls, including children—comparable in size to the population of San Francisco. The *average* supra-rich household gained $3.9 million in marketable wealth during those "fat years" of 1983 through 1989.

Had the Great Bull Market on Wall Street democratized financial wealth by 1995? Between 1983 and 1995 the average financial wealth (in 1995 dollars) of the super-rich or the village 50 grew by a fifth, and that of next richest 4 percent grew by 6 percent. Financial wealth *declined* for all other groups in the village with the least wealthy families suffering the greatest losses. By 1995, the top 1 percent of households held almost *two-thirds* of the bonds outstanding and *half* of all outstanding stock and trust equity. Despite the ownership, directly or indirectly, of stock shares by 41 percent of households, the richest 10 percent, or only 500 villagers, owned 82 percent of the total value of those stocks. Of course, once we leave the top 50 villagers to their estates, we find few bondholders. The train of the bondholding class left the station at a high acceleration and even if it slows down, the distance between itself and the other villagers is ever-increasing.

The shift in wealth sources from homes to financial assets such as bonds is ominous. Since the early 1980s, the growth rate in tangibles such as real estate worth has slowed from a rate approaching 4 percent during the earlier post-World War II era to about a sixth of that pace. The pattern of growth in net financial worth is virtually the reverse of that for tangibles. Estimates for 1997 have the top 1 percent or super-rich holding stock worth, *on average*, $2.5 million, and the next wealthiest 9 percent holding *average* stock holdings of about $276,000. Their average net worth, including bonds, was nearly $10 million and nearly $1 million, respectively. Since those families in the top 5 percent of the wealthy hold an average of twice the value of stocks in bonds, the improvement was even greater. The estimated share of total stock market gains for 1989–97 was 42.5 percent for the super-rich and only 1.2 percent for the bottom 40 percent of wealth holders. The bottom 40 percent of the net wealth holders held, on average, only $1,600 in stocks. Their average net worth was a mere $3,200.[14] Worse, judging from the panic withdrawals from mutual funds during summer 1998, the smaller players (just about everyone else) lost still more net worth.

The Consequences of 95 Percent Being Worse Off

The boom in financial wealth remains good news for the bondholding class and bad news for ordinary people. Alarmingly, not only has home ownership declined since the mid-seventies, the share of families with private pensions has also been on the downswing. Their real incomes in a squeeze, middle class families have less to put aside in savings and are less able to fund their children's college education. Without college, the future income prospects of those children are clouded and so too the possibilities for the sustained national productivity growth required for a sunny economy. Put bluntly, 95 percent of American families have become not only relatively but *absolutely worse off*.

The concern is not simply financial because the political and social outcomes could be increasingly grim. Those individuals with the highest incomes and the best educations are the most likely to vote. Some 14 percent of the population with a yearly family income of more than $75,000 cast 25 million votes for president (mostly for Bob Dole) in the 1996 elections. Increasingly, the underclass does not vote because it has so little to lose and less and less to gain. In the same election, some 16 percent of the population with a yearly family income of less than $15,000 cast only about 10 million presidential votes (mostly for Clinton). Stagnant incomes and declining college enrollments, leading to even lower voter turnouts, comprise a vicious cycle that threatens democracy.

We begin to question the durability of Wall Street capitalism. If the bondholders have so much wealth, why haven't others in the country prospered? Why have we allowed financial markets to become so volatile? Is using financial market returns as the leading indicator for monetary policy and slow growth in the best interests of the society? Can Wall Street capitalism, based as it is, on *financial* risk-taking that has little bearing on real production, prevail? Since the wealth has percolated up instead of trickled down, to what use—good or bad—has it been put? More important, if we are not growing faster in manufactures, where has the money gone? It has obviously not gone into *real* investment; otherwise, the nation would have greater *real* saving. Has the American economy sprung a leak? We move on to answer these questions at the great risk of offending the few members of the bondholder class.

NOTES

1. These data are from the recent Surveys of Consumer Finances by the Federal Reserve Board. See "Family Finances in the U.S.: Recent Evidence From the Survey of Consumer Finances," *Federal Reserve Bulletin*, Board of Governors of the Federal Reserve System, Washington, D.C., January 1997, pp. 1–24.
2. Mindy Fetterman, "Optimism Prevails on Top Floors, Fades with Descent," *USA Today*, September 20, 1996, p. 10A.

3. *Ibid.* p. 1A.
4. *Ibid.* My descriptions and the identities of all these workers are based on the same article.
5. These two indices were constructed by Ravi Batra in *The Great American Deception* (New York: John Wiley & Sons, 1996), pp. 167–8.
6. These data are from "Executive Pay: Special Report," *Business Week*, April 21, 1997, pp. 58–102. The article contains salaries and a pay-performance analysis for the largest 500 U.S. companies. This report is published annually. Often the worst-performing companies in terms of shareholder return and corporate profit for 1994–96 paid the most to their CEOs in 1996. *Business Week* writes that "stock-option deals have compensation out of control."
7. By 1991 the top fifth had 44.2 percent of total income and *averaged* $95,530. If their share had remained constant, their average income would have been $87,771, or 8 percent *lower*. See Sheldon Danziger and Peter Gottschalk, *America Unequal* (Cambridge and London: Harvard University Press, 1995), p. 51. For considerably more detail on various statistical and demographic shares from U.S. Census data, see especially pages 42–68.
8. Danziger and Gottschalk, *op. cit.*, p. 51.
9. These data, the most recent available (except for estimates for 1997), and those used in the Unequal, USA village, are derived from Edward N. Wolff, "Recent Trends in the Size Distribution of Household Wealth," *Journal of Economic Perspectives*, Volume 12, Number 11, Summer 1998, pp. 131–50. Wolff uses two definitions of wealth. *Financial wealth* includes cash and demand deposits; time and savings deposits, certificates of deposit (CDs), and money market accounts; government bonds, corporate bonds, foreign bonds, and other financial securities; the cash surrender value of life insurance plans; the cash surrender value of pension plans, including IRAs and Keogh plans; and corporate stock, including mutual funds. *Marketable wealth* or net worth includes financial wealth plus the gross value of owner-occupied housing, other real estate owned by the household, net equity in unincorporated businesses, and equity in trust funds. Total liabilities (subtracted to arrive at the net worth figure) are the sum of mortgage debt, consumer debt, and other debt.

10. As quoted by John Fried in *Worth*, April 1997, p. 50.

11. See Wolff, *op. cit.*, Table 3, p. 137.

12. These estimates are from Wolff, *op. cit.*, p. 147.

13. The earlier data are from Edward N. Wolff, *Top Heavy: A Study of the Increasing Inequality of Wealth in America* (New York: The Twentieth Century Fund Press, 1995), p. 7, 1995. Though Wolff taps many sources, much of his historical data are derived from estate tax records. Some of his more recent wealth shares are derived from the net worth reported in Board of Governors of the Federal Reserve System, *Survey of Consumer Finances* Washington, D.C., 1983, 1986, and 1989. These are further updated in Wolff, *op. cit.* from the Fed's 1992 and 1995 surveys.

14. The estimates for 1997 stock shareholdings are from Lawrence Mishel, Jared Bernstein, and John Schmitt, *The State of Working America, 1998-99.* An Economic Policy Institute Book (Ithaca, N.Y.: Cornell University Press, 1998), pp. 269–272.

IV.

PROBLEMS WITH THE BOND
MARKET STRATEGY

TWELVE

———◆———

The "Angels' Share" of Personal Savings

The individual serves the industrial system not by supplying it with savings and the resulting capital; he serves it by consuming its products.
John Kenneth Galbraith, *The New Industrial State* [1967]

A key principle behind the strategy of the bondholding class is that all personal savings magically become real business investment, and this investment makes workers better off. Wall Street has invoked the names of Adam Smith and J.B. Say to support this position. Without this idealized eighteenth-century dogma, the bondholders cannot justify low income taxes and low capital gains taxes for themselves even as they downsize the middle class. Beginning in this chapter, I attempt to explain the problems with this principle and the causes of Wall Street's strategic failure. Doing so requires going beyond conventional views.

In Adam Smith's view, to repeat, individual savings not only generate real investment but the two are always equal. Because of the direction of effects—from savings toward investment—the social purpose of the rich is elevated to uncommon heights. This transmutation of savings assures a natural rate of full employment. The prosperity, even the survival, of capitalism depends greatly on higher incomes and greater savings by the rich: it is a socially convenient myth for the bondholding class.

An equally compressed sketch of John Maynard Keynes' ideas has demand creating its own supply; in this view, maintaining the purchasing power of the middle class is critical to full employment. When incomes of the masses are too skimpy to buy industry's products, business firms have little reason to invest in plant and equipment or in research and development. When private investment is adequate, so too is employment; when inadequate, total demand in the economy is insufficient to employ everyone wanting work. Thus, to a Keynesian, real investment in factories, equipment, tools, inventories, and technical knowledge generates real saving. These grand claims are not as remarkable as their polarity.

Today, both Smith and Keynes cannot be correct. Perhaps they are writing about two different economies or perhaps one is thinking of finance and the other of real output. Perhaps both sets of ideas fail to match contemporary reality. Yet, the art of knowing which policies to deploy depends on a reliable design of the bridges between investment and savings. In this and the next chapter I offer my vision. As I will contend, Keynes comes closer to the truth inasmuch as real investment leads to real saving, but he offers only an incomplete explanation of financial asset inflation and its effect on the real economy.

The "Angels' Share": Solving a Mystery

In today's economics, we correctly measure real saving as the value of *real* investment. A society has not *really* saved unless it has a new factory, equipment or highway to show for it. If personal (household) and business savings do not lead to real investment, in the cloistered world of economists they play no further economic role. Yet, during the 1980s, when money and bonds were thrown, in giant bundles, at rich people, net fixed investment (the *really* real part of investment because it excludes depreciation) *declined* from around 6.7 percent of net national product (GDP minus that depreciation) to less than 5 percent. Most important, the growth rates of capital services in the private business and manufacturing sectors had almost fallen through the factory floor by 1985–88. During the 1980s, the one thing private business did best was depreciate—lose capital to wear, tear, obsolescence, and destruction.[1] In this view, real saving stagnated.

Why—in the Gildered Age when the idolatry of capital had never been greater and personal money savings were surely on the increase—did so many machines commit suicide? Total personal savings *as commonly measured* were nonetheless meager and continued to be anemic during the bullish 1990s. We can, therefore, ask the same question from the savings side. Where did all those exploding personal savings of the rich go, if not into real investment? Did they simply evaporate? As we will see, in the meaning ordinarily used by economists, savings *did* evaporate.

In the vineyards of France, the *angels' share* of cognac is the amount necessarily evaporated to give cognac its celebrated quality. The winemakers think that the amount evaporated seasonally equals all the cognac consumed in France during the year, sufficient to keep many spirits high. In like fashion, most of the personal savings of the bondholding class evaporate; we can call it the *"angels' share"* of savings. Since Wall Street is addicted to these personal savings, the enormous amount evaporated must be sufficient—from the bondholders' perspective—to maintain the celebrated quality of Wall Street capitalism. In truth, Wall Street needs a rapidly expanding *angels' share* of savings for its prosperity.

Even so, where the *angels' share* goes is the great unsolved mystery of Keynesian economics. Put differently, where do personal *and* business savings go when they die (in Keynesian economics)? Once we know the corporeal manifestation of these savings, we at last have a complete understanding of them and what can be done about them—and about the bondholding class.

Taking Proper Measure of Savings and Saving

Getting the new fundamentals straight requires keeping our definitions straight, which means going straight to our definitions. *Savings (the plural)* describes what *individual* households and firms do. Savings for the individual household or firm is different from *saving (the singular)* for the nation.

Individuals' savings accumulate from their spending less than their after-tax income. After paying income and social security taxes, consuming meals, gasoline, electricity, movie tickets, and so on, any dollars left over are savings. The classical economists considered this consumption and savings activity to be a zero-sum game; that is, individuals could save more only by being stingy consumers, buying cheaper cars and living in smaller houses. This belief in the powers of thrift has a wonderfully Calvinistic edge to it and, therefore, considerable moral standing. Nevertheless, in the real world, individuals can increase their savings by simply earning more income. Savings, then, is the difference between our net earnings and what we spend on hamburgers, denims, housing, and so on.

A different view of savings comes from measuring income broadly. If income includes everything that contributes to wealth, then it includes capital gains from stocks and bonds plus wages and salaries. In this broader perspective, savings are the net additions to wealth or net worth. Therefore, if we have income from all sources (including realized capital gains from bonds of $10,000) of $70,000, pay taxes of $15,000, and spend $35,000 on consumption, we have savings of $20,000. If we began the year with wealth or a net worth of $250,000, our net worth at the end of the year will be $270,000, reflecting partly the $10,000 gain in bonds. The boost in net worth is our savings defined broadly.

We can choose to hold our savings in many different forms. "I just put $500 into my savings account," says Mother Jones (the mother, not the magazine). "The retained earnings of Ford Motor Company increased $500 million this month, increasing the firm's savings by 30 percent," writes an editor of *Business Week*. Usually, firms hold these savings in interest or dividend-earning financial assets rather than in cash or checking accounts.

The economist, looking at the overall economy, places the role of saving (the singular) in a different light. In the accounts used to measure GDP, the measured equality of saving and investment applies to *real saving*—"real" meaning a withholding of current income from consumption. Still, when the time comes to close the books, real saving cannot happen without an equal amount of *real investment*. Something tangible like a building or a tractor must be left intact after the smoke of saving has cleared. Such a measure of saving fails to capture the additions to financial wealth or net worth that may result from increases in the value of *existing* financial and tangible assets. And it does not reflect creation of new credit, of which the Fed and the commercial banking system are usually capable.

Green-eye-shaded statisticians at the U.S. Department of Commerce calculate personal savings as any current income remaining after consumption. Such savings is a residual. The statisticians' estimate is very indirect: they do not go from door to door asking personal questions such as, "by how much did your *personal* savings change during the past year?" Instead, the statisticians measure disposable personal income (income after income taxes and government transfer payments) *and* consumption, then subtract consumption from disposable personal income to estimate savings.

In 1996, for example, personal disposable income was $5,589 billion and consumption expenditures were $5,315, leaving estimated personal savings at $274 billion. It's simply arithmetic. By this measure, personal savings as a percentage of disposable personal income had suffered a decline from 7.5 percent in 1981 to 4.9 percent in 1996. In most of the intervening years the savings

230 Wall Street Capitalism

rate was even lower: pundits and economists continue to wring their hands over this declining trend. This measure of savings, however, is much more important to a household than to the national economy. If an individual household saves *too little*, adults in the household may have insufficient funds for retirement, especially if they are long-lived. If a nation saves *too much*, however, unemployment will result from inadequate total private demand in the economy.

What is worse, this measure surely understates personal money savings during the past two decades. Since the Commerce Department uses the narrow definition of savings, it fails to account for changes in net worth, including that created by new credit or by capital gains.[2] If Jenni Jones, Mother Jones' daughter, owns assets, such as securities that appreciate, which she sells at a comfortable profit, are those new savings any less real to Jenni than savings accumulated by thrift? Not all increases in a person's wealth are spent lavishly: spending depends upon one's income bracket and one's tastes, though rising disposable income would normally nourish some increases in *both* consumption and savings. Yet, if Jenni uses capital gains from the sale of her bonds and buys a new car, Commerce records an increase in consumption that *reduces* personal savings. Similarly, would not a depreciation of such assets diminish personal savings?

Such personal money savings do go somewhere and influence the economy, but economists have been unable to track their destination. It is a deep mystery, as if the savings were loaded aboard the Orient Express in Paris but disappear before the train pulls into Constantinople.

Returning to the Federal Reserve System, and considering *its* measure of savings, the plot thickens, as Agatha Christie's eccentric Belgian sleuth Hercule Poirot might say. Mysterious as it may seem, the Fed measures individual savings—indirectly but not covertly—using a flow-of-funds approach. "Flow of funds" means exactly what it says; these funds are identified according to their uses, such as funds for automobile purchases, and by their sources, such as bank loans. It is important to our story that the Fed's measure is a much closer approximation of changes in net worth or wealth (savings). The Fed adds increases in financial assets to net investment in consumer durables (such as a new house purchase), and then subtracts the net increase in debts (such as new credit card charges) to arrive at savings. Now, by this broader measure, savings can decline because people are increasing their borrowing. Even so, the similarity in the two levels of savings— the Commerce Department's and the Fed's—for two decades (1961–81) tells us that they had once been measuring the same thing. However, during 1986, 1987, and 1988 the Fed's measure of personal savings was 30.2, 45.0, and 34.6 percent *higher*, respectively, than that of the Commerce Department's. We have found the missing personal savings.

Just as there are two ways of estimating GDP, there is another way to measure the growing gap between the real economy and the financial casino. GDP is measured two different ways by the Department of Commerce; one estimate is from the product side (consumption, investment, government spending, and net exports), the other from the income side (wages and salaries, profits, depreciation, etc.). Again, capital gains, including those from the financial markets, are not counted as "income" in the national accounts. Though the two ways of estimating GDP should give the same number, there is always some error in measurement leading to differences. The statisticians halve the difference in the two measures—adding half to the lower figure and subtracting half from the higher estimate—to arrive at one reported value for GDP. Generally, it has been said, the product side will be higher than the income side because some income will be hidden through the efforts of business firms and households to evade income taxes. In the past few years, however, the difference between the product measure and the income measure has turned *negative* with the income-based estimate of GDP exceeding the output measure by more than a full percentage point in 1997.

As we have said, capital gains are not part of real output gains either. Increasingly, however, top corporate executives have been paid partly in stock options at no cost to corporations. This practice explains, in great part, why compensation of the highest-paid CEOs has soared into hundreds of millions of dollars in recent times, making CEOs even wealthier members of the bondholding class. Worse, shareholders may receive inaccurate profit reports because, in corporate accounting, the values of stock options are not subtracted from profits. Since the Commerce Department cannot effectively check the official corporate accounts and adjust for the value of newly issued stock paid to executives, the statisticians will overstate actual profits and, more to our point, overstate the income-side measure of GDP.

As it turns out, in fact, the discrepancy between the income and product measures of GDP is highly correlated with the growth in the S&P 500.[3] Since bond prices have mostly risen apace with stock prices, a similar correlation exists with bond appreciation. About half of the gap between income-based GDP and product-based GDP is explained by capital gains in the stock market. Though income-GDP is not supposed to include the effect of capital gains (since such gains add nothing to real output), the green-eye-shaders have inadvertently added such gains to national income. In splitting the difference, of course, the final measure of output-GDP is exaggerated. A true gauge of output would be less than the reported output. Thus, real output growth is even less than the reported rate.

We now can return to our main story having learned that the new bondholding class possesses the bulk of these under-reported personal savings. The more that business and government parcels out payments and dividends as interest, the greater the increases in savings by the financial wealth holders. When 14 cents (net) of every new dollar of government spending goes to bondholders as interest, can anyone doubt that bondholder net worth is rising? The seven cents or so going to the super-rich amount to about $116 billion or an average $106,000 annual risk-free yearly interest income from government bonds per family. When the Dow soars more than a third during a single year, can anyone doubt that the net worth of rich households has risen? Moreover, though a corporation can increase its cash from equities only with new issues (which were rare during the 1980s and 1990s), Warren Buffet's family and other wealthy households can enjoy secondary market appreciation in its equities' holdings without necessarily sharing any of those benefits with business. The net gain of the super-rich will have been about $1 trillion (equaling about an eighth of the national GDP) or roughly an average of half a million dollars per household. Since the bondholding class at the top maintains its financial holdings tightly, can anyone doubt that the wealth distribution becomes more unequal as the bond and stock markets soar?

These wealth holdings are being resold daily so that capital gains are continuously being made. Moreover, the dramatic shift to debt finance during the 1980s assured the explosion in interest income; by 1991, federal government interest payments to bondholders were exhausting *half of all personal income tax revenue*. Those *unearned* income gains essentially add only to the current savings of the bondholding class, and do so without making any contact *whatsoever* with business firms other than brokerage houses. In truth, the middle class was borrowing more in an attempt to maintain its old standard of living.

The final quarter of the twentieth century experienced booming inflation in the value of financial assets, declining or stagnant tangible asset values, soaring debt burdens, and record personal bankruptcies. The prices of securities have been rising compared to the prices of real assets such as the book values of corporations. The lower 95 percent—those living outside gated resort communities and outside wooded estates—who can afford to hold only housing (being, too, a place to live) as the bulk of its wealth, continue to fall behind since the supra rich (top 0.5% of families) alone hold about 47 percent of the total value of corporate stock and only slightly less of the value of bonds.

The Nature of Business Savings

Households are not the sole source of private savings; business firms also are savers. Though we have identified the *angels' share* of personal savings, the solution to the savings mystery is not complete until we account for *business savings*. Business savings are conventionally measured in the GDP accounts as retained earnings of corporations and other firms—those earnings not paid out as dividends to the shareholders. As a percentage of GDP, they fell from around 4.5 percent in the mid-1960s to 2.75 percent in the late 1970s, and to 1 percent during the late 1980s. Alternatively, the Fed's balance sheet measure of corporate savings (which includes stock dividends, and non-dividend cash payments) shows corporate savings actually turning *negative* during the late 1980s.[4] During that decade, corporations were repurchasing their own stock, thereby raising its price, to ward off takeovers during the outbreak of leveraged buyouts—evasive actions that probably explain the negative corporate saving. During 1996–97, for similar reasons, corporations were again buying back great amounts of their own stock.[5] If the change in net worth of businesses is combined with that of households, the annual growth of net worth per adult is a flat-liner during the 1980s. Moreover, from 1982 to 1992 the net worth of the nonfinancial business sector grew at the feeble pace of 0.62 percent per year.

We arrive at a phenomenon, all the more remarkable for having been missed by most economists: *the growth of net worth or wealth in the economy has apparently switched from business firms to selected families.* If magnificent advances in the personal savings (defined broadly) of the bondholding class were being made, the doctrine of Say's Law says that real investment must have been soaring. It wasn't and it isn't. The savings have evaporated, sadly going the way of so much cognac. The *United States* and the world were getting poorer even as its bondholders were getting richer.

Why Household Savings Are Bad for Business

As it turns out, personal household savings present a double-edged sword to businesses. Retained earnings or business savings come from sales revenue. The firm's sales revenue comes from households *spending* their incomes, not from their act of saving! A penny saved by the household is a penny *not* earned by the business firm.

Suppose some households cut consumption by *not* buying new, restyled Oldsmobiles and Buicks. GM's sales will decline and so too its retained earnings or savings. With earnings falling, GM will postpone any expansion plans, reducing its investment in new assembly plants. Auto workers will be laid off, their incomes will fall, and so will their consumption *and* savings. Thus, by a collective failure in consumption nerve, the nation of household savers will have lower incomes and will save less even as business savings decline. Consumption has fallen but incomes have fallen even more.

Going back to the GDP measures, we recall that saving and investment are equal amounts. Now, from the chain of events in the automotive industry, saving and investment will end up equal but lower in amounts. What seems a paradox, a paradox of saving, has been resolved.

In order to better understand real investment, consider the opposite scenario. Suppose households begin to spend more on GM products and reduce their savings. GM sales rise, new workers are hired, even as production begins to strain plant capacity. The intense pressure on plant capacity causes GM management to expand facilities, which increases the employment of construction workers and those working in capital goods industries. In fact, most studies show that rapidly rising demand is the main reason for increases in business investment. Then, incomes and savings rise. That's why investment in new factories and capacity is closely related to retained earnings. In the nation the higher level of real investment will be matched by the higher level of saving (the singular).

During the best growth year of the 1990s (1998) personal savings out of households' incomes was at a rate of only half a percentage point. The extraordinary pace of consumption was sustained in part through borrowing. This consumer behavior was sufficient to offset most of the negative effect of a record trade imbalance on economic growth during the year. Consumers nonetheless cannot sustain such a level of consumption-debt for long.

Consider, again, the difference between what happens when existing financial assets are bought in secondary markets and when new plants are built. Suppose Warren Buffet reduces his consumption by cutting back on his air travel. In turn, he converts his new cash savings into some existing Coca-Cola bonds. The seller of the Coke bonds uses his new cash to increase his air travel by the amount Buffet reduces *his*. Total income, consumption, and saving remain unchanged. Accumulated paper assets are merely others' liabilities or assets acquired at the expense of others. The increases in Buffet's Coke debt holdings are matched by the reduction in the bond holdings of the seller. Price appreciation in Coke bonds will, in turn, swell Buffet's net worth (savings). Still, *national real saving* happens only when the nation acquires real domestic assets—new factories, machinery, industrial tools from R&D, houses, office buildings, warehouses—or net new claims on other nations (foreign investment).

The effects of household savings really are like a two-edged sword. We can witness the effects from the consumer's perspective by considering savings as leftover income after consumer expenditures are made. Not every household reliably spends the same share of an extra dollar in income. For instance, dividing consumer expenditure data into quintiles or fifths, we find *both* spending and savings rising as we move from the lowest fifth toward the highest fifth. (The source of this savings measure, the consumer expenditure survey, *excludes* changes in net worth or wealth as a part of savings. Thus, for example, including changes in net worth would greatly increase the savings shares of the top fifth.) However, as a share of income, savings rise between the lowest and highest fifth. On average, the lowest two-fifths of consumers during the 1980s and the lowest three-fifths during 1987 and 1989 had *negative* average saving rates; these families were drawing upon past savings, borrowing, or relying on welfare to buy necessities. Mostly, these are the expenditures that fuel business sales and become retained earnings of firms. The two highest quintiles did have positive savings, just as the *bond market ideology* claims, but making it only a half truth. In 1989, those with incomes of $50,000 and above saved a third of their incomes.[6] John Maynard Keynes called these reliable tendencies, respectively, the propensities to consume and the propensities to save.

The higher-income households failed to serve fully even their higher savings role. Though the highest two-fifths enjoyed large increases in their savings as shares of their incomes during 1987–91, they flagged in their overall contribution to the overall savings rate. Moreover, despite improvements in savings in some of the lower regions, they too fell behind in their contribution to the national savings rate. The lagging contributions in the middle fifths were the result of the fading American middle class attempting to maintain its living standards through borrowing.[7]

The corporate deployment of securities as a means of raising funds for new investment illustrates how easily we can slip into the supply-side error of thinking that saving "causes" investment. Household savings, for instance, *are* sources of new corporate debt, an indebtedness no doubt incurred solely for real business investment in, as examples, construction of a new Marriot hotel or the purchase of new airplanes by Delta. However, as I have said, these household savings only enter the firm when *new* corporate bonds are issued. Otherwise, households are merely exchanging ownership of corporate (and no doubt government) bonds with each other. Besides, though net corporate bond issues have been substantial in recent years, net new issues of corporate equities were negligible in 1994 and have been *negative* since.

This process, whereby trillions of dollars are required to maintain liquidity in financial markets generating slightly more than a hundred billion or sometimes (recently, in corporate stocks) *negative* amounts of funds, seems highly inefficient. Even the market heralded as the "most efficient"—the U.S. Treasuries market—required an average of 2,702 trades a day and $45.8 *trillion* in secondary market activity in 1994 to yield only $185.3 billion for the Treasury.[8] In short, the value of resales of securities was 247 times the value of funds raised! A labor market working this way would have to hire 247 workers to do the work of *one*. In these highly inefficient markets the value of financial assets is bid upwards and the wealth and income distributions made more lopsided.

While these trillions in securities are being resold, the redistribution of income toward the bondholding class is nonetheless pruning U.S. corporate sales revenue, retained earnings, and the impetus for real investment. The adverse effect on sales revenue is even greater as the preference of luxury goods has shifted toward foreign nations. The mere *existence* of retained earnings, however, is no guarantee that any particular corporation will use the funds to enhance real investment. Some of the later impetus for the Great Bull Market in stocks came from surging *unspent* retained earnings, a by-product of downsizing.

Households such as you and me, *cannot force* corporations to invest. Real investment is a corporate act cloaked in great uncertainty. When real investment does take place, however, it is good for the real economy. Every dollar spent has a multiplier effect; for instance, if the multiplier is 2.5, each dollar spent generates $2.50 in national income, out of which *more saving* takes place. Thus, the more believable parable is the Keynesian one: investment "causes" saving.[9] The low rates of capital investment made by businesses during the last quarter century explain, then, why saving measured the old-fashioned way by the Department of Commerce is in a deep slump.

Once this is understood, Keynes declares: "our argument leads towards the conclusion that in contemporary conditions the growth of wealth, so far from being dependent on the abstinence of the rich, as is commonly supposed, is more likely to be impeded by it." And, he adds, "One of the chief social justifications of great inequality of wealth is, therefore, removed."[10] He realized, of course, that other arguments could be made, but concludes: "For my own part, I believe that there is social and psychological justification for significant inequalities of incomes and wealth, but not for such large disparities as exist to-day."[11] Today those inequalities are obscene. Since extraordinary wealth convergence also increases bond and stock price volatility, and encourages securitization and the proliferation of risky derivatives, we have discovered still other reasons why such large disparities are unjustified and unwise.

Paradoxes Lost

The social myth that personal savings of the rich fuel real investment and growth of capitalism serves to protect and nurture Wall Street and the bondholding class. It is hypocritical to tell the working class that their jobs depend upon the bondholders becoming richer—at best, a twisted truth. Worse, the same workers are told that their jobs will only be safe if American multinationals increase their investment in new plants *in foreign nations*. That is, even when the investments are made *abroad*, they somehow benefit workers at home.

Once we understand the difference between what *savings* do for the family and what *saving* does for the country, an obvious paradox emerges. Though savings are good for the individual family, too many families having too much in the way of savings are bad for the nation. Collective gains in savings reduce consumption and the reason to invest by business firms. Shortfalls in investment in new hotels, capital goods, and new computer technology at home lead to unemployment and falling incomes. From falling incomes families end up saving less than they intended. They, too, are less able to pay for the education of their children, thus diminishing needed investment in human capital. The paradox is resolved.

The deployment of excess savings in the secondary or resale securities markets creates the evaporation or the *angels' share* of personal savings. The rapid expansion of Wall Street capitalism during a quarter century has not only required faster evaporation, but assured it. Moreover, what has been advanced by Wall Street as good for the nation serves instead only the angels and the new leisure class of bondholders. In that same quarter century, personal savings have soared, though for the real economy, they have evaporated. A second paradox, recognized for the first time, is resolved.

NOTES

1. Net fixed investment is derived from the national income and product accounts. Capital services are derived from the Bureau of Labor Statistics capital input series measuring the services derived from the stock of physical assets. The assets included are fixed business equipment, structures, inventories, and land. Financial assets are *excluded* as are owner-occupied residential structures. These data, as well as similar data for other time periods appear in E. Ray Canterbery, "Reaganomics, Saving, and the Casino Effect," in James H. Gapinski (Editor), *The Economics of Saving* (Boston/Dordrecht/London: Kluwer Academic Publishers, 1993), p. 162.

2. Several other problems compound the underestimation of personal savings by the Commerce Department so that theirs is not a good measure of the amount of income households have left over to put into stocks, bonds, or savings accounts. For a detailed analysis of these problems, see Fred L. Block, *The Vampire State: And Other Myths and Fallacies about the U.S. Economy* (New York: The New Press, 1996), pp. 131–4. Block's readable prose also provides a sobering appraisal of America's political fixation on federal budget deficits and the national debt.

3. An estimate of this relation has been made by Dean Baker in "The New Economy Does Not Lurk in the Statistical Discrepancy," *Challenge,* vol. 41, no. 4, July/August 1998, p. 13. In his estimate, Baker finds that 53 percent of the GDP statistical discrepancy is explained by increases in the Standard and Poor's 500 Index.

4. See Canterbery, "Reaganomics, Saving, and the Casino Effect," *op. cit.,* pp. 165–6.

5. Total net amounts raised from corporate equities during 1995, 1996, and the first quarter of 1997 (annual rate) were –$17.7, –$18.5, and –$54.5 billion, respectively. That is, corporations bought back more stock than they issued. In contrast, net borrowing in corporate bonds was $197.0, $146.4, and $189.2, respectively, during the same periods. For the complete data, see *Federal Reserve Bulletin,* August 1997, Tables A37–A40.

6. See Canterbery, *ibid,* pp. 161–3.

7. Different sources provide different specific results, though general patterns remain the same. The periodic consumer expenditure surveys of the Bureau of Labor Statistics, U.S. Department of Labor provide unique insights into spending behavior by households enjoying different levels of income. The savings rates from these surveys will differ from those derived from Federal Reserve data.

8. These data are reported in Michael J. Fleming, "The Round-the-Clock Market for U.S. Treasury Securities," *Economic Policy Review,* Federal Reserve Bank of New York, July 1997, pp. 9–32. In addition to these transactions, the primary dealers on Wall Street also traded $18.3 billion *per day* in U.S. Treasury futures, $5.1 billion in forwards, and $7.8 billion in options.

9. I do not stand alone in saying that investment causes saving. See, as examples, Robert Eisner, *The Misunderstood Economy: What Counts and How to Count It* (Boston: Harvard Business School Press, 1995), pp. 33–41, Albert T. Sommers (with Lucie R. Blau), *The U.S. Economy Demystified*, Revised Edition (Lexington, Mass.: Lexington Books, 1988), pp. 55–9. Sommers, too, explains how net worth as savings can increase through the appreciation of financial assets, but fails to find any cause in the wealth distribution or any adverse effects. Also, Nobelist William Vickery clearly reconnects the causality from investment to saving in a posthumous article when he writes, "Measures to promote individual saving produce exactly the opposite effect," in *Journal of Post Keynesian Economics*, Spring 1997, p. 499. For a recent textbook statement on the paradox of saving whereby attempts by people to save more lead both to a decline in output and to diminished saving, see Olivier Blanchard, *Macroeconomics* (Upper Saddle River, NJ: Prentice Hall, 1997), pp. 54–5. Because of its clear, cogent and readable account of budget deficits and public as well as private investment, I recommend Eisner's book as a companion to *Wall Street Capitalism*.

10. John Maynard Keynes, *The General Theory of Employment, Interest, and Money* (New York: Harcourt, Brace & World, 1965) [1936], p. 373.

11. *Ibid.*, p. 374.

THIRTEEN

———⋙·◆·⋘———

Bond Prices and the Casino Effect

Since Wall Street and the bondholding class have defined savings in their self-interest, we can dismiss their false parable, even as we expand our concerns. If the correct measure of personal savings includes changes in net worth from capital gains, interest and dividends, such unearned income surely plays some role in the future of the nation and of the global economy. A survey of the broader landscape of capitalism puts the net worth view of personal savings into perspective. Not only is unearned income carefully concealed in net worth, its consequences are not widely understood. Its accumulation at the peaks of income and wealth distributions leads to what I have called "the Casino Effect."[1]

At its best, capitalism efficiently deploys the creation, ownership, and financing of capital assets in a way that assures the substantial and smooth growth of production and employment. At its worst, capitalism deploys the creation, ownership, and financing of capital assets in a way that contributes not only to massive wealth inequalities but to hyper-speculation in financial and tangible assets. When it does this, credit and financial markets not only dominate economic decision-making but become notoriously unstable. A financial casino emerges; in it, securities are mostly for resale.

The Casino Effect

Comparative prices are important in the financial casino. Contrary to the wit and wisdom of Alan Greenspan, however, the relative price of gold or the relative prices of commodities generally are, well, relatively unimportant. Critical to this is the price of speculative assets such as secondary market financial instruments compared with the present value of real investment goods—capital goods and plant—the value of which depreciates if not renewed by expanding knowledge and R&D. The pricing of financial derivatives, of course, goes beyond the secondary level to higher degrees of complexity more and more remote from reality.

Unreality is only a financial market away. Consider the two most important of such markets—the bond and stock markets. As noted, the prices of stocks are connected in a roundabout or circular way to bond prices. As the great gathering of wealth chases bonds, bond values soar and so too the values of stocks. Imagine tossing different-sized ingots of gold bullion into a smooth-surfaced lake; the larger the volume of bullion, the greater the circle made from the ripples. The ripples relate both to the value of bonds and stocks. Hopefully, I will not be accused of making a circular argument.

If, for instance, Michael R. Bloomberg, developer of a computerized data service for Treasury bond traders, had bought $1,000,000 in long-term zero coupon Treasury bonds in January 1989 and sold them five years later, his proceeds would have been $3,100,000! During the past twenty years the correspondence between 10-year bond prices and the Dow has been around .40; that is, if the trader selling these bonds to Bloomberg had used the proceeds to randomly select and purchase blue chip stocks, he would have enjoyed appreciation in at least 40 percent of the stocks.

Since members of the bondholding class are also shareholders, the abrupt shifting of funds back and forth between the two financial assets has, as noted, added to volatility in the financial markets. Again, toss that gold bullion into a smooth-surfaced lake; now, the greater the volume of bullion, the faster the ripples roll and the greater the circles made. Sometimes the circles pulsate. The great sucking sound you hear when the bullion is suddenly hoisted from the placid lake is the sound of securities prices going south.

The bullion metaphor illustrates how increases in real wealth in the upper reaches of the wealth distribution multiply the values of existing financial instruments. In the real estate collapse of the late 1980s and the subsequent failure of the S&Ls, however, a large gap developed between real estate prices as they deflated and the values of mortgages behind the real estate, since they continued to be valued at the former real estate prices. This widening gap was an early warning of what was about to happen. A similar gap can develop between bond and stock prices. As noted earlier, shortly before the 1987 stock market crash, bond prices were falling as stock prices continued their climb. Beginning in mid-1997, the same kind of gap began to emerge as the bull market in stocks seemed to ignore all signs of mortality and individual rationality.

Now we arrive at the Casino Effect. Not only do speculative asset prices move in lockstep as greater and greater wealth becomes more and more tightly gripped in fewer and fewer hands, over time the prices can begin to explode or grow exponentially. Securities prices can go the way of tulip prices in seventeenth century Holland. The velocities at which wealth is trundled into its bond or stock incarnations accelerate. Their speeding prices make the Jaguar XK8 look slow. These velocities in association with exponentially rising prices constitute the Casino Effect. Of course, if things begin to go wrong, as they did with stock markets in early October 1987 and with bond prices during 1994, velocity can fall, liquidity can dry up, and prices can *fall* at exponential rates.

Wall Street Feels its Pain

Historically, speculative episodes such as those leading to the Panic of 1907, the stock market crash of 1929, and the Great Depression, have been preceded by dramatic movements toward greater wealth inequality. The events of the late twentieth century are unexceptional in this regard. That is a pity. In the prosperous decades preceding financial turbulence, ordinary Americans not only consider the rich benign, but they often emulate them. That gross inequalities can lead to financial and economic disasters afflicting most Americans is discomforting. We resist rules and regulations that might limit what the rich can do with their wealth, fearing that those rules will be enforced the very year of our great windfall.

When everything does go sour in financial markets, nonetheless, Wall Street is often blamed by the working class. The financial holdings of the middle class are meager and those of the poor nonexistent, but pensions are proportionately important to those of modest means. Just as the President of the United States does not like to be blamed for economic recessions, Wall Street does not like to be saddled with financial cataclysms. The remedies, however, are never palatable to Wall Street even though, if they were effective, the Street would never have to be subjected to the great derision it finds painfully ineluctable.

Though it is human nature for most capitalists to condemn the rules keeping capitalism viable, the capitalistic system has always been remarkably flexible despite the efforts of its most devout friends. It has reinvented itself a great many times; it may be time to end its Wall Street incarnation before democracy loses its struggle against money. In this regard, almost everyone, excepting people like Alan Greenspan and bankers, sees the advantage of restoring commercial banking's historical regulation.

The Necessity of Well-regulated Commercial Banks

Commerce does not have to depend entirely on volatile bond, stock and commercial paper markets for finance. Once, commercial banks played a powerful and critical role in funding American capitalism. Today, despite the rapid growth in commercial paper, junk bonds, and securitization, private commercial banks such as Citigroup continue to finance real investment. If, economy wide, the external funding needs of business exceed the household savings made available to finance investment, most of the shortfall would have to be met by some combination of an increase in the money supply, a decrease in households' money holdings, or by an increase in the rate at which money is turned over (its velocity).

Private banks often ride to the rescue, led by what fanciful pundits have called the loan arranger, to provide finance and thereby increase the money supply. Again, the initiative comes from the nonfinancial business firm; Microsoft will not borrow money if it doesn't need it or if it is retrenching rather than expanding. Since business debt has to be serviced through scheduled payments on principal and interest, cash flows (and debt servicing commitments) influence the course of investment and thus of production and the need to hire workers.

The regulated financial system is at the core of this debt creation and repayment process. Money is created as banks make loans, mostly to businesses, in response to the expectation of profits. This supply of money is destroyed as profits are realized and loans are repaid to the banks. In this way, the monetary system's stability depends on profit flows to borrowers sufficient to pay back loans and to service debt. At the same time, the interest payments on debt comprise a portion of the unit cost of production even as profits are assured for the bankers. Interest payments continue to eat away at manufacturers' net worth.

Interest Rates: Two Traditional Views

Interest rates and banks go hand-in-hand like love and marriage. Banks only lend for interest. Just as the way we think about concentrations of wealth influences public policy, so too does the way we think about interest rates. Just as Adam Smith and John Maynard Keynes did not agree on differences between saving and savings, these influential thinkers had different ways of explaining the interest rate.

The classicals propose that the interest rate in the loanable funds market assures an equality between investment and saving, sustaining Say's Law. The amounts of loanable funds demanded by firms are the same as the amounts of real investment. The supply of loanable funds comes from penny-pinching savers who buy newly issued corporate bonds. The government also taps this loanable funds market by issuing new bonds. The interest rate adjusts to the level necessary for making equal the amounts of corporate and government bonds demanded and supplied. Thus, in the world of Adam Smith, the bond market and its mirror image, the classical loanable funds market, are strictly *primary markets* or markets for new issues.

Keynes never missed a chance to turn the classicals on their heads, perhaps in his hope that blood rushing to their brains would arouse clearer thought. For Keynes, the interest rate in a money market is based on the notion of liquidity (and opportunity costs or the foregone interest on bonds from holding money). That is, people hold money for day-to-day transactions, not only in goods and services, but also for buying and selling bonds. The money supply comes from the central bank. The interest rate, then, is fixed at the point where the amount of money demanded for liquidity equals the amount supplied by, for example, the Fed. Since we can neither buy nor sell money, it is the exchange of money for bonds that *really* decides the interest rate. In Keynes's explanation of the interest rate, apparently only *secondary markets* matter because Keynes opposes the classical idea that "the" interest rate sets real saving equal to real investment. Besides, the preference for liquidity can only be satisfied in secondary markets. Back in the days of the buy-and-hold-forever strategy of the widows of Chevy Chase, the primary market ruled; today, however, the secondary markets are in control.

How the Reserve and the Bondholding Class *Really* Set Interest Rates

Again, Smith and Keynes cannot both be correct and—possibly— both are wrong. As I said before, the fed funds rate—that initial, key interest rate—is set by the Sacred College of Bonds and Money. In setting that rate, the Reserve also determines short-term Treasury bill rates. Finally, the bondholders add an inflationary premium and a risk premium to the 52-week T-bill rate to arrive at a longer-term bond rate. However, whether it is T-bills or T-bonds we are talking about, their interest rates are set in the *secondary* markets, *not* the primary markets. When the U.S. Treasury considers a new issue of 10-year bonds, it sets the price of those bonds according to the interest rate or yield to maturity then prevailing in the secondary market for bonds maturing in ten years. The same pattern rules for new issues of corporate bonds.

The relatively new dominance of the *secondary bond market* takes on heightened significance. Today, the prices of bonds (and hence their yields to maturity), are decided by the new bondholding class. More exactly, since the bond players look to the Reserve for guidance, bond prices are based on *expectations* regarding what the Fed might do. When the prices of bonds are high, the prices of stocks look appealing, so transfers are then made into (usually) the secondary stock market. Only a small minority of traders determines these asset prices and their inflation while people like Alan Greenspan and Wall Street worry mostly about *expected* inflation in goods prices.

Ironically, none of these Wall Street centered activities have a
direct connection to the corporate investment decision, since the
dominant events happen in the secondary or resale markets. The
cat-and-mouse game between the bondholding class and the head
of the Reserve, not real saving and investment, sets the price of
bonds and thus long-term interest rates. As noted earlier, the
Federal Reserve ends the game with higher interest rates to
slow or to end expansions. Moreover, its high interest rate bias
virtually guarantees a rate of economic growth most notable for
its slowness.

This situation is downright perverse. Surging financial wealth is
wonderful to behold for the rich and, doubtless less so, for the
rest of us as vicarious consumers of opulence. Still, the vast bulk
of this soaring net worth of the bondholding class has no place
to go except back into the *secondary* securities markets. The
bondholders, of course, buy the new issues when they happen, but
91–99 percent of their buying and selling value takes place in used
or, as car dealers would say, "previously-owned" securities. At the
end of 1992, a year in which the value of new issues required
to fund the federal deficit was $283 billion, total *daily* trading
volume in U.S. government bonds averaged $400–550 billion.
During the 1990s the corporate bond market was about three-
quarters the size of the U.S. Treasury market. Much of the growth
in the market was the result of the growth in securitization, not
the growth in debt-funded real investment in factories, etc. Rather,
securitization served mostly to fund the great consumer credit
boom of households having stagnant real incomes.[2] Trading
activity is as feverish in U.S. Treasuries as it is cool in corporate
bonds; yearly volume in corporates amounts to a few days trading
in Treasuries. Ironically, the "safest" securities have become the
fastest traded!

Still, those engraved pieces of paper pile up in the financial
casino. In this manner, the compounding of personal savings serves

mostly to bid securities prices higher, even as income is diverted away from real investment. Inflated financial values or speculative bubbles are not to be confused with real economic activity.

Where does the money go? Regrettably, it becomes the *angels' share* of savings. These kinds of savings seep out of the real economy, or perhaps put more aptly, they are never available to be utilized in the first place. The initial, substantial amounts are not only derailed from the spending stream but are negatively multiplied in their effects on GDP. While the bond debt from all corporations grew from 13 percent of GDP in 1980 to only 18 percent in 1995, new bond issues by *strictly financial firms* soared from 3.3 percent of GDP to 14.8 percent. That is, most of the growth in corporate debt was related to the aforementioned securitization within the finance industry.[3] When incomes are received but not spent—even rentier incomes—they reduce the pace of economic growth and the overall size of the GDP pie. Ironically, at this level of inequality, as the bondholders take larger and larger slices out of a shrinking pie, the real pie shrinks even more.

As we know, the supra-surplus savings of the bondholders are not the only source of seepage from the economy. When the head of the Reserve uses monetary policy in his efforts to slay the imaginary demon of inflation, he initially heightens inflation and then, with enough tightness, eventually reduces real output and employment. The slowdown in credit growth (reflected also as a slowdown in the growth rate of the money supply) diverts funds from both consumption and potential real investment. In Smithian economics, a slowing of the money supply would alter only the overall price level, without retarding production. Not so in Keynesian economics where rising interest rates would ration credit and diminish real investment. In *neither* explanation does rising interest rates initially ignite more inflation.

Seepage From the American Economy

Over the course of several chapters we have identified four sources of seepage from the American economy, seepage that lowers the real rate of economic growth and employment. First, the Federal Reserve System withdraws credit from the economy in the belief—mistaken as it is—that the only way to slow inflation is to create, if not sloth, an outright business recession. Such reduced credit now and then withdraws funds from the private economy. Second, international trade deficits are funded by net borrowing from abroad, generating net real investment in foreign countries. The excesses of U.S. imports over U.S. exports directly subtract from GDP and its real growth. Third, the exploding personal savings from interest payments and capital gains, comprising the *angels' share*, evaporate without benefitting the lower 95 percent. Fourth, the bondholding class, in addition to pushing the Reserve toward a generally tighter money policy, diverts savings into a financial casino, serving mostly to inflate the prices of financial assets to the detriment of the real economy. Can these seepages be measured—at least, roughly?

Independently of my writing, Treval C. Powers has provided some remarkable estimates of impediments to economic growth.[4] What Powers calls "leakage," I call "seepage," to distinguish our terms. They are not identical twins but, perhaps, similar siblings. In Powers' perspective, some Americans are enjoying positive savings while others are borrowing (engaging in negative saving). So far, so good. In the aggregate, however, any part of this *total income* received—whether it is from blue-collar employment or from interest payments—and not spent, is "leakage" or noninvestable savings. He, too, defers to the Greeks and calls this *alpha leakage* (he carefully avoids the use of *beta*).

The greatest share of alpha leakage is what I have called the *angels' share*, an evaporation fueling Wall Street and the bondholding class. With the growth rate in potential output at 13.1 percent per year during the Eisenhower era (1953–61), alpha leakage was

7.6 percent and the rate of economic growth could have been 5.5 percent, assuming no other leakages. Other sources of leakage exist, but Powers found that when the rate of leakage was zero, the growth rate of national output equaled the rate of growth of national productivity (rate of growth of output per capita) plus the rate of growth of the population, a slight variation of what economists often call the potential output growth rate.

What Powers next suggests intersects with the idea that the propensities to consume diminish at higher income levels. Regardless of the source of the income, some people receive more money than they know how to spend. Though conspicuous consumption prevails among the members of the bondholding class, either their imaginations have finite limits when it comes to sumptuous or extravagant expenditures or they run out of time before they run out of money. Excessive savings turn out to be the curse of the bondholding class since the failure to spend all income *in the aggregate* leaves economic growth well below its potential. As noted before, if real investment is inadequate, *total real saving* in the economy will fall.

A source independent of Powers confirms this result. Let us return to the BLS consumer expenditure surveys discussed in Chapter 12. Again comparing expenditure and savings patterns from the two periods, 1981–83 and 1987–91, eras commanded by the bondholding class, the average *overall savings rate* fell from 13.7 percent in the earlier period to 9.9 percent in the latter. It would be easy to jump to the conclusion that the bondholders must have had disincentives to save during 1987–91 (capital gains taxes too high, oppressive income taxes, egregious discrimination against rich people, and so on). Not so. Higher savings by the rich did not make up for the severely reduced savings of the remaining 80 percent of households. The bottom three-fifths found it necessary to increase their dissaving (negative saving) in order to maintain living standards as they faced the reality of stagnating real incomes. The highest fifth increased their share of total income on average from 44.4 percent in 1981–83 to 46.9 percent in 1987–91 (the only fifth to enjoy an increase), and managed to increase modestly their contribution to the national saving rate from 13.9 percent to 14.4 percent, even while reducing their own savings rate slightly. The failure of the top fifth *to spend enough* within the U.S. to keep the economy moving at a faster pace contributed to a lower *national* personal savings rate and less total real saving and investment! The lower income groups continued to borrow to buy goods throughout the 1990s.

Powers measures our first source of seepage, the withdrawal of credit from the economy by the Federal Reserve System through tight money policies. This leakage, also undeniably Greek to some people, he calls *rho* (continuing to avoid *beta*). For instance, the Eisenhower-era economy was reined in by the Reserve and perhaps also by tightened budgetary policies. Powers estimates this *rho leakage* to have been 3.2 percent since the realized growth rate was 2.3 percent (5.5 − 2.3 = 3.2). During the Kennedy–Johnson Administration, the average economic growth rate was 5.6 percent, a rate suggesting that the economy was allowed to grow unrestrained by the Federal Reserve during those five years.[5]

Nonetheless, the effects of tight monetary policy changed dramatically in the early 1950s. Prior to this, during the era preceding the Great Depression, 1898–29, and the post-World War II years, 1947–52, production lost as a result of pernicious monetary policy was regained in the rapid recoveries. However, since 1952 any loss of economic growth due to tight money policies was *permanent*. As Powers puts it, "From 1953 to 1990, the loss of growth time due to monetary restraint and the leakage amounted to more than 14 years. This is a loss of 38 percent of 37 years of growth time."[6] That's a great amount of lost time *and* lost output.

During the early Reagan years, of course, tight money policy would have ensured *a high rate of rho leakage*. However, that which was borrowed from the new bondholding class was spent by the government (mostly by the Pentagon), greatly *reducing the overall alpha leakage*. As I have said, the shift from paying for government by borrowing rather than by progressive taxation has shifted the wealth distribution toward the tip of the top—to those who can afford to buy government securities. The bondholding class should not fret about their children's future being mortgaged by the size of the federal debt. Their children, the inheritors of the bondholders' wealth, will probably *hold* mortgages, as a great part of their assets. Meanwhile, as the federal budget runs those celebrated surpluses, federal expenditures will no longer partly offset alpha seepage, much less counterbalance seepage from the *angels' share* of savings.

It is the final, yet widely unrecognized irony of federal deficits and federal debt. The more the federal government depends on deficit finance rewarded by interest payments and the less it relies on progressive taxation, the more the rich benefit. Yet, of all the people, those who come to the defense of the "struggling" bondholders inveigh against federal deficits and the national debt with vitriol normally reserved for foreign enemies.

Prospects

The United States, nonetheless, remains wedded to an awkward over-reliance on tight monetary policy as the sole deterrent against inflation, effective only as it succeeds in creating slow growth, recession or depression. Even with the faint scent of a vigorous economic upturn in the air, the Sacred College historically has put the brakes on the rate of growth in credit and the money supply. Worse, the Clinton White House, taken hostage by Alan Greenspan and the Treasury, reduced still further the fiscal options for faster economic growth, giving the Reserve still more control over our economic fate. Sustained economic expansion appears impossible in the presence of the Reserve and in the absence of new policies in the government's arsenal. These issues, too, come within our sights in the closing chapters.

NOTES

1. The Casino Effect was first identified in Canterbery, "Reaganomics, Saving, and the Casino Effect," *op. cit.*, 153–75.
2. The secondary market also dominates the stock exchanges. Between 1981 and 1996, for example, U.S. nonfinancial corporations retired $700 billion more in equities than they issued. Even those individual corporations issuing stock to generate funds made very little real investment. Truth is, most of the funds for factory expansion and renewal came from internally raised funds—that is, from profits dependent on sales, including those sales made possible through the magic of consumer credit.
3. Again, a similar lack of connection between funds and real investment is found in the stock markets. The yearly total value of new issues of stocks are equaled in a week or less of trades on the New York Stock Exchange.
4. Treval C. Powers, *Leakage: The Bleeding of the American Economy* (New Canaan, Connecticut: Benchmark Publications, 1996).
5. Further confirmation for Fed cooperation during the Kennedy–Johnson years is provided by E. Ray Canterbery, *Economics on a New Frontier* (Belmont, CA: Wadsworth, 1968).
6. Powers, *op. cit.*, p. 194.

V.

WHAT TO DO: SOME IMMODEST PROPOSALS

FOURTEEN

———◆•◆———

Lifting the Impenetrable Veil of Money

The FOMC continues to see the distribution of inflation risks skewed to the upside and must remain especially alert to the possible emergence of imbalances in financial and product markets that ultimately could endanger the maintenance of the low-inflation environment.
Alan Greenspan, before the Committee on Banking, Housing, and Urban Affairs, U.S. Senate, February 26, 1997.

For the Vatican to keep the idea of repentance secret from believers in purgatory would be difficult to defend, but possible. Can the practice of central banking, whereby earthly unemployment is created, be so mystical as to be beyond the grasp of the public? Can the Reserve's head continue to hide behind the impenetrable veil of money? Let's try to solve some of the Reserve's mysteries. It is less esoteric than Alan Greenspan, as one example, would have us believe. Besides, like those heading for purgatory, we have a need to know. Taking on the bondholding class requires penetrating the secrets of the Sacred College of Bonds and Money.

The Fed's Trading Desk and the Bond Dealers

We begin by returning to the alliance of investment bankers and the New York Fed, within which monetary policy takes place. The close association between the Federal Reserve Bank of New York and the dealers it designates has developed because the Bank's trading desk manages open market operations for the entire system. Is it possible to understand what they do?

Sandy Krieger, at the time of writing the Fed's open market manager, directs the analysts and traders who buy and sell securities. To anticipate what might happen in the federal funds market, hers and her staff's workday begins with a review of developments from the previous day. Her staff engages in early morning conferences with primary dealers in the New York money market. They do this, they say, to "get a feel for the market." They share information about prices, yields, quantities, and qualities of debt instruments traded the day before, and the opinions of money market dealers. Krieger and her staff do with T-bills what it would be illegal for the U.S. Securities and Exchange Commission to do with common stock trades.

Krieger then consults the directives from the FOMC, the Sacred College, and sometimes conducts telephone conferences with the Board of Governors (members or staff) and occasionally with all members of the FOMC, and the regional Reserve banks. Greenspan and the Sacred College may, for example, say, "An action to buy seems appropriate this morning." Krieger then may consult with the Treasury by phone to check on any Treasury transactions that may be affecting the money supply. She then decides, "We'll go into the market at 11:00 a.m. and buy $5 billion."

The trading desk is on the newly built ninth floor of the New York Fed. Sandy walks into the room where several security traders are seated at several rows of desks with computers. The trading desk's computers are linked with federal bond dealers by the Trading Room Automated Processing System (TRAPS). All open market operations are performed through this system. A minute or so later, a message is electronically transmitted simultaneously to all the primary dealers, indicating the type and maturity of the operation. The Fed traders give the dealers several minutes to respond with their offers, allowing them time to reconnoiter some of their customers—the private commercial banks, insurance and finance companies. Sometimes the dealers sell holdings of clients.

Dealers inform the Federal Reserve traders of any offers (the prices and quantities of securities). After the offers are assembled and displayed on a computer screen for evaluation, the trading desk selects all offers, beginning with the most attractively priced, up to the $5 billion to be purchased. Minutes later the Fed traders then notify each dealer, through TRAPS, of those offers that have been accepted. This actual trading process is usually completed within a few minutes. Meanwhile, the dealers have sold billions of dollars of securities.

The $5 billion in U.S. Treasury notes purchased by the trading desk, with delivery and payment on the same day, will increase the money supply by some multiple of this amount. The Federal Reserve credits the accounts of the sellers of the securities, thereby adding to the reserves of the private banking system. Those reserves, a part of "high-powered money," are multiplied as reserves and deposits cascade through the banking system. The swelling money supply exerts downward pressure on the fed funds rate.

The Critical Role of the Private Dealers

Three things are notable about these transactions and the conduct of monetary policy. First, the actions of the New York trading desk are easy to understand; they are not mystical. Anyone who has bargained with a street vendor in Mexico City can understand the process, the only difference being the Fed's use of computers. Second, we can understand fully the importance of the selected security dealers and brokers to the Reserve.

Without the dealers, forming a national market for securities would be difficult. Put differently, arriving at one price for a particular security with a particular maturity date would be difficult. The traders at the New York Reserve can "make the market" by buying and selling through only three or four dealers. Otherwise they would have to deal with the thousands of individuals, banks, and other institutions, each perhaps offering different prices. If the dealers turned off their computers, panic at the Fed soon would follow; it would be like your spouse turning you down for a date.

All of which brings us to the third important thing. Understandably, the New York Fed traders and the private dealers have some common interests. Together, they make the money and bond markets of the United States go round. By extension, the Sacred College is beholden to the private dealers: without them, the College could not conduct monetary policy, as presently structured. If, on a particular day, the private dealers cannot find any buyers for securities, T-bill prices would go through the floor and interest rates through the ceiling. Then, the stock market would crash; the bond market might close. Present arrangements intricately connect the fate of the bondholding class and Wall Street to the Federal Reserve System. They are the Siamese triplets of the securities business. Is this so difficult to understand?

The Bankers' COLA and How Monetary Policy *Really* Works

Nor are the basic outlines of the effects of this monetary policy process all that demanding. In its attempt to slow down real or imaginary inflation, the Reserve usually shrinks the nation's supply of money (primarily commercial bank deposits) and, therefore, the available funds for loans made by the banks. The New York trading desk can reduce checking deposits by *selling* government securities in the open market, since this reduces the bank reserves on which the banks base those deposits. (When checks are written on private bank accounts to pay for the securities, bank deposits and bank reserves are reduced by the same amounts, then multiplied in a downward spiral.)

These Fed transactions have at least two effects on economic activity: (1) a "liquidity" or bank credit effect, which influences general spending patterns; and (2) an interest rate effect, in which higher interest rates impinge directly on businesses' ability to service debt. However, the immediate effect of higher interest rates is to increase the cost of buying durables (household appliances and autos) and houses; sufficiently high interest rates will crush the construction industry.

Earlier, I discussed these consequences for monetary policy during Volcker's monstrous Experiment of 1981–82. We can assure ourselves that the experience was not unique. During the inflation of 1974, following the first oil crisis, the Reserve threw the housing industry into its worst depression in several decades, and the entire construction industry plunged into a deep slump. Widespread layoffs and a large rise in the unemployment rate reflected the shocking deterioration in economic activity. At the time, the drop in real GDP was the sharpest since World War II, only to be superseded by the 1981–82 recession, the deepest since the Great Depression.

Neither Fed Governors nor the legions of Fed economists tell us that "tight money" and rising interest rates are *initially inflationary*. This is the Reserve's dirty little secret, or perhaps merely its delusion. Although the interest rate directly decided by open market operations is the fed funds rate, all other short-term rates soon follow this key rate. For example, the prime rate (the rate charged by private banks for loans to their largest, least risky customers such as General Electric and General Motors) is the fed funds rate plus a mark-up. Other loan rates, in turn, are the prime rate marked-up still higher.

Suppose we obtain a five-year car loan from Union Trust. Private bankers such as Union Trust, of course, seldom altruistic, expect to be repaid the money's purchasing power, not just the original nominal dollars lent. So it comes to pass, if Union Trust lends for five years and expects an average yearly 3 percent inflation rate, it will also mark up the interest on the five-year loan by three percentage points. Economist-writer George Brockway has called this mark-up the "bankers' COLA," or cost-of-living adjustment.[1]

Long-term interest rates are only slightly less simple. The 10 or 30-year bond rate has an inflationary premium built in (when many expect inflation), plus a premium in respect of the risk of holding a bond so long (which is now of only slight relevance, since long-term bonds are generally not held more than a few days). Brockway's bankers' COLA is greater on long-term loans. That is, the private bankers' index their returns on loans to inflation, using the CPI as the cost-of-living index.[2] Greenspan, as chair, was vocal in denouncing the indexation of wages, social security benefits, income taxes, and welfare payments. By early 1995, in fact, he was a cheerleader for chopping 1.1 percentage points off the yearly CPI to reduce government benefits and to increase federal revenues, gaining a balanced federal budget sooner. Greenspan, however, favored the bankers' COLA.

Brockway suggests that the bankers' COLA "is more than forty times the Social Security COLA.... It is roughly triple the deficit for fiscal year 1994; it is almost four times the entire cost of Medicare; it is almost double the cost of the Department of Defense." In still another comparison: "It is greater than giving every working man and woman in the land, from part-time office boy to corporate CEO, a 15 percent raise—and there'd still be almost enough left over to pay the unemployed $4,200 each and every one."[3]

More important, if indexation of wages and government benefits feed the wage-price spiral, so too does the bankers' COLA. The interest payments by consumers had risen from around 10 percent in 1977 to nearly 20 percent of incomes by the early 1990s. As Brockway suggests, *"the bankers' COLA will always increase inflation because the outstanding domestic indebtedness is greater than the GDP.... If (as is frequently, if not generally, the case) the bankers' COLA is greater than the inflation rate, the cost of the bankers' COLA is exponentially greater than the cost of inflation"* [Italics in original].[4] Without the bankers' COLA, inflation would not have existed during the 1990s!

The bankers' COLA further unravels the apparent paradox of tight money policy: rising interest rates accelerate the inflation they are intended to cure. Worse, not only did Greenspan fail to complain about the bankers' COLA, though it invites invidious comparison with all the other types of indexation he opposed, his policies helped to guarantee it. Since sometime in 1993 when the Reserve abandoned M2 as an indicator of monetary policy, Greenspan's avowed goal, among others, has been to conduct monetary policy in a manner to maintain a particular real interest rate. Since the *real* interest rate is 4.5 percent or so, every increase in the inflation rate of 1 percentage point leads the Fed to raise the targeted nominal interest rate by 1 percentage point. That is, if this year's inflation rate is 3 percent, the Fed targets the bankers' nominal interest rate at 7.5 percent (4.5 + 3.0). Put differently, the Reserve's policy *guarantees* the bankers' COLA so that interest rates go up as the rate of inflation goes up.

The Close Association of the Fed Funds Rate and Inflation: An Apparent Paradox

The Reserve's anti-inflation "remedy" is similar to a medical doctor prescribing pain killers that cause throbbing headaches. Not surprisingly, the association between the fed funds rate and percent changes in the CPI is extremely high. Figure 14.1 shows the tight connection. In the figure the interest rate is lagged one quarter-year behind the inflation rate, suggesting that the causality is from the interest rate to the inflation.

The tango of interest rates and inflation is sufficiently coordinated to be embarrassing to the Reserve. After concluding that "the Federal Reserve implements monetary policy by targeting a federal funds rate ... it deems compatible with sustained, non-inflationary economic growth," one of the many Reserve Bank publications

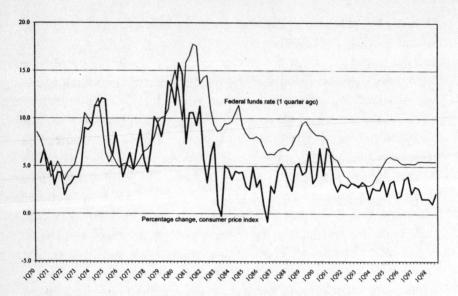

Figure 14.1 Inflation Closely Tracks the Federal Funds Rate

Source: Board of Governors of the Federal Reserve System

goes on to marvel at the tightness of "the relationship between inflation and the funds rate." Then, it hurriedly makes a disconcerting admission: "However, the fact that the two series [federal funds rate and CPI inflation] tend to move in the same direction seems to contradict the notion that increases in the federal funds rate are an effective means of lowering inflationary pressures."[5] Though such frankness is rare, the Fed's economists go on to resolve the "contradiction" by compounding it.

Perhaps the Reserve is not responsible for the rate increase: the fed funds rate went up because of a rising demand for loans from excessively exuberant consumers and producers investing in new plant, equipment, tools, and inventories. Well, not really; this "explanation" fails to square with another salient observation by the same authors: "the federal funds rate generally moves in the opposite direction of GDP growth."[6] In other words, the fed funds rate rises sharply just before economic recessions and usually peaks before the middle of the trough. The Sacred College keeps the petro pedal on the fed funds rate until it is absolutely sure that "inflation" has been run down—that is, after sufficient data reveals an ongoing recession.

This same Reserve Bank (Cleveland) keeps returning to this issue, as if it is merely a paradox waiting to yield the orthodox Reserve conclusion. "The mechanism by which such actions [hikes in the fed funds rate] are supposed to fight inflation is straightforward: increases in the funds rate lead to slower monetary growth. Slower monetary growth, at least over a sustained period, should in turn provide lower inflation." But wait, more is to come. "However," the economists quickly add, "one of the strongest correlations in economics is the positive relationship between inflation and the fed funds rate." They state the "paradox" with crystalline clarity: "Thus, we are left to contend with the paradox that ultimately lower inflation must be associated with *lower* [italics in original], not higher, interest rates."[7]

We must admire the tenacity of these economists. They attempt again to resolve the paradox in language that is as opaque as their statement of the paradox is clear. The fed funds rate, they say, contains both a real rate and "an inflation premium." Usually, the higher the inflation premium, the higher will be the nominal rates. Still, they do not explain how an overnight lending rate can embody expected inflation during a period when most businesses are closed and which is so short that the inflation expected is compressed into twelve or fourteen hours.

Never mind these small matters, the resolution cometh. "The core of the paradox, as economist Irving Fisher pointed out long ago, is the role of inflation expectations." How do expectations play out this role? "Persistently high interest rates may signal to the public that the central bank itself anticipates continuing inflation. This may pose a significant impediment to the Federal Reserve's ability to signal its commitment to price stability."[8]

Translation: the Reserve raises interest rates before the public (or anyone with any sense) perceives an "inflationary threat." The public response: "Inflation must be around the corner because the Fed is raising interest rates!" The public increases its purchases of big-ticket items before interest rates go even higher, thus putting upward pressure on prices. The Reserve must then raise interest rates even higher to fight the inflation that it is causing—a significant impediment indeed!

How the Reserve Causes Inflation in Housing

Since one of the critical transmission belts of monetary policy is the housing industry, it is hardly surprising that higher interest rates are initially inflationary. Housing represents more than 40 percent of the CPI, and two-thirds of this comprises rental or attributed rental cost (on houses otherwise not "for rent").[9] Rising rental costs lead to "inflation" measured by the CPI, leading the Reserve to tighten monetary policy. Those who might have been considering the purchase of a house postpone the purchase because of high interest rates, choosing meanwhile to rent. This behavior increases the demand for rentals, raising the rate of inflation of rentals and of imputed rentals, further increasing inflation as measured by the CPI. Then, the bankers' COLA kicks in: a vicious cycle of interest rate hikes, depressed real estate markets but rising rents follow. If landlords pass higher interest rates along to renters, inflation gets another kick. When that inflation elevates the bankers' COLA, rising interest rates add to the cost of consumer and producer durables. Conservative bankers may get no kick from champagne, but they get a big kick from their COLA!

These behaviors help to explain the frustration of the Reserve when it is trying to fight inflation. The Reserve takes actions that raise interest rates and inflation accelerates. Then, the Reserve must raise interest rates again, and again, and again, until slumps in construction and production are underway. According to still other

Reserve Bank economists, housing activity accounts for 53 percent
of the declines in GDP in recessions since 1959 (but only
22 percent of the expansions).[10] After the fall, the monetary
authorities can declare, "we have fought gallantly and won the war
against inflation!" They neglect to mention the share of inflation
that they created.

Since rising interest rates have such a dampening effect on
construction and other kinds of production, unsurprisingly, slow
economic growth is closely related to a rising fed funds rate. No
matter how lagged or averaged, more than 40 percent of the rate
of economic growth during the past few decades can be "explained"
by the behavior of the fed funds rate. This powerful alliance is
dramatically illustrated in Figure 14.2. When the fed funds rate
zigs, the rate of economic growth zags. The pattern of real GNP
is virtually a mirror image of the path of the fed funds rate.

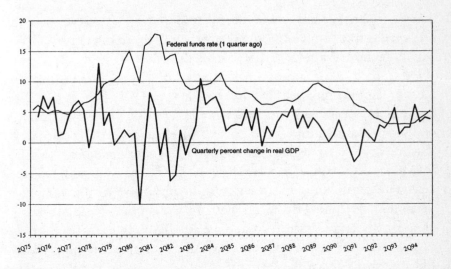

Figure 14.2 Quarterly Change in Real GDP Tends to Move in the Opposite
Direction to the Federal Funds Rate

Source: Board of Governors of the Federal Reserve System

Again, is this enigmatic, defying understanding? Many economists, especially those at the Reserve, will counter that monetary policy is the only policy available to fight all that dreadful inflation always lurking behind every improving economic indicator. Who will protect the widows of Chevy Chase, if not the Fed? These same economists have spun theories to support such claims and have failed to consider less damaging ways of coping with inflation— that is, when it does happen. I will return, in short order, to the alternatives. The nation should be able to slow inflation without first accelerating it and, then, should be able to stabilize prices without unemploying people. Unsurprisingly, from time to time Congress has become disenchanted with the Fed's stiff-necked refusal to take the public into its confidence even while it rubs elbows with bankers and brokers of all pinstripes.

Pursuing the Idea of Reform at the Federal Reserve

Several reform plans have been proposed. The most radical proposal comes from Milton Friedman and the monetarists. They would require that the Fed increase the money supply by a set amount each year (from 3 to 5 percent, depending on which money supply measure is used). This rule is based on the presumption that the Federal Reserve always does the wrong thing or that to err is human, and to live by rules divine. Yet the idea that economic knowledge is so poor—or the members of the FOMC so automatically incompetent—that a rule should replace deliberate decisions is an anachronistic repudiation of the scientific revolution. Despite Friedman's faith in the automatic adjustments of the competitive market system, giant business exercises such a strong influence on so much of the American economy that those adjustments are hardly guaranteed. The monetarist rule would probably continue to condemn us to long periods in the economic doldrums rather than lead to the millennium of a growing economy.

A more modest proposal has been to put the Fed directly under the authority of the President of the United States, who the public generally holds responsible for mistakes in monetary policy anyway. Doing this, however, would militate against one of the real accomplishments of the Fed as it is now set up; by operating outside the vast federal bureaucracy, it has developed effective machinery for carrying out monetary policy. The Fed is a model of administration in the excellent handling of its service functions; even its mistakes are carried out efficiently. Making it merely another executive department would probably cause it to be unduly constrained by the complicated federal rules and vague regulations that often shackle other agencies.

Another proposal has been to make sure that various groups—unions, academicians, small businesspeople, consumer advocates—are adequately represented on the boards of the Federal Reserve banks. These positions are mostly honorific, however, since the Board of Governors in Washington supervises the banks themselves and the banks depend upon the Board for funding. A part-time board has neither the time nor the expert knowledge to quarrel intelligently with the policies of the Governors.

Any move to make the Cardinals of money more responsive to social pressures rests on the belief that their Sacred College does not have divine rights concerning the money supply, credit and interest rates. From this view, we should give no institution in a democracy solitary jurisdiction over the tripartite functions of determining, achieving, and enforcing such an important part of the public's business.

Making the Federal Reserve Responsive to the Needs of Ordinary People

Prudent judgment moderated by political reality recommends that the Federal Reserve System should somehow be made more responsible to the body politic without taking away the Fed's operating efficiency. Reforms that could accomplish this would generally enhance congressional and White House authority.

First, we should give the Joint Economic Committee of Congress authority to set up a watchdog committee, the Congressional Monetary Committee (CMC), comprising academic and technical experts who would evaluate monetary policy on a continuous basis within the framework of the Humphrey–Hawkins Act. The responsibilities of the CMC would be comparable to the federal tax analysis now provided by the bipartisan Joint Tax Committee of Congress and the federal budget analysis of the bipartisan Congressional Budget Office. The findings of this new subcommittee, which could include dissident former Federal Reserve economists (out of concern for the full employment of economists), should be published monthly, with a more lengthy year-end report issued. Such a subcommittee could counter protestations from Wall Street and the bondholders.

To add force to the recommendations of the CMC, we should give the Joint Economic Committee itself direct authority to appoint two of the seven Governors. The new power of Congress could be balanced by allowing and *requiring* the President to appoint a board chair with a term that corresponds to his own. Only a few men, thirteen to be exact, have chaired the Federal Reserve Board since its establishment in 1914 and only seven since authority was centralized in the Board in 1935. Once there, the chair, now serving a Wall Street constituency, is almost impossible to dislodge. The President should have the authority and be required to appoint his own chair.

Another reform would change the internal workings of the Federal Open Market Committee: the practice of placing five regional Reserve Bank presidents on this Sacred College, four of whom are on a rotating basis, would be ended. These individuals are generally career Fed employees and are, in any event, often subservient to the Board. This action would, of course, remove from the FOMC the president of the New York Fed, currently a permanent member of the committee, who, with the exception of the chair, generally has had most to say about monetary policy. Such reform would also weaken the close ties of the Fed to its financial constituency, especially to investment bankers on Wall Street.

The Monetary Mystery Solved

Let there be no mistake regarding the purpose of these reforms. Their effect would be to shake the foundations of the Sacred College of Bonds and Money. They would remove the Federal Reserve from the cloisters of monetary management and make it a broader social institution, subject to appropriate pressures from the public at large, rather than permitting it to cater to the policy preferences of its laity on Wall Street. The high-handed inference that only an exclusive club of inbred alumni can understand monetary policy is at best a self-fulfilling myth coming from the Reserve's own cult of mysticism.

The public may not yet fully understand the monetary policy alternatives. Nevertheless, after we remove the impenetrable veil, public knowledge will grow. As the Fed becomes less of a mystery, we will inevitably raise its standards of economic policy and its sense of public responsibility. If money is a public good, we should manage it for the good of the public. In a democracy, the public should have some say regarding what is good, helping to define the proper role of money and even interest. Next, we consider what can be done about both money and interest.

NOTES

1. See George P. Brockway, *The End of Economic Man,* Third Edition (New York, London: W.W. Norton, 1995), pp. 211–6 and, by the same author, *Economists Can be Bad for your Health* (New York, London: W.W. Norton, 1995), pp. 132–6.

2. Dismissal of the bankers' COLA as a minor blip on the big screen of the economy may seem easy, but it would be wrong. Brockway estimates the COLA in 1993 to have been between 4.50 and 4.83 percent, or, in dollars "between $501.9 billion and $591.3 billion, and of course, it was very much higher in 1994 and 1995." See Brockway, *The End of Economic Man, op. cit.*, p. 213. Brockway estimates the real prime rate from its average during a period of rate stability (1961–65) as 4.5 percent; therefore, any percentage points above a prime rate of 4.5 percent would be the bankers' COLA. The average interest paid on $12.2 billion of debt in the U.S. was 8.6 percent so the bankers' COLA was 4.1 percent and in dollars, $501.9 billion.

3. *Ibid.*

4. *Ibid.* p. 214.

5. "Monetary Policy," *Economic Trends*, Federal Reserve Bank of Cleveland (November 1994), p. 2.

6. *Ibid.*

7. Federal Reserve Bank of Cleveland, *Economic Trends*, February 1995, pp. 4–5.

8. *Ibid.* p. 5.

9. These estimates were made by Dimitri B. Papadimitriou and L. Randall Wray, "The Consumer Price Index as a Target of Monetary Policy," *Challenge: The Magazine of Economic Affairs*, September–October 1996, pp. 22–3. The argument in the balance of this paragraph closely follows their analysis.

10. Andrew J. Filardo, "The Outlook for Housing: The Role of Demographic and Cyclical Factors," *Economic Review*, Federal Reserve Bank of Kansas City 81, No. 3 (Third Quarter 1996), pp. 39–61.

FIFTEEN

＝◇＝

Interest and Principal Without Bondage

Too much wealth in too few hands has not only led to financial fragility at home, but the effects have reached out to touch the entire world. The financial collapse in Japan—feared by Robert Rubin, Alan Greenspan, and thus Bill Clinton—could spread to delicate U.S. financial markets. Since the global system now depends upon the U.S. as importer of last resort as well as lender of first and last resort, a deep economic recession in the United States could put at risk not only the U.S. financial system but that of the whole world. The global economic system is endangered.

Income and wealth inequalities are not new to Americans; what is new, in the experience of this generation, is the magnitude of the inequalities. As budget surpluses at the expense of the underclass dash its hopes and as stagnant wages, job insecurity, and slashes in school budgets nullify the expectations of the declining middle class, democracy itself becomes endangered. No civil society can endure immense inequalities that perpetuate the unearned privileges of a small leisure class of bondholders. Democracy loses its efficiency and even its meaning when dollar votes dominate over one person, one vote.

The bondholding class constitutes a clear and present danger; it contains individuals and families who have the financial power under Wall Street capitalism to control the national agenda and political outcomes. As noted, its political strength reaches into the

275

White House. By the end of his second term, we could understand what Bill Clinton meant by "New Democrat." The titular head of the Democratic Party, the President of the United States, placed the interests of the bondholding class above those of the working class, poor or not. The myths perpetuating this new leisure class had clouded Bill Clinton's judgment. Unless we change minds in the White House and on Capitol Hill, only a popular political revolt together with a new agenda can mitigate the inequalities and the speculative excesses that otherwise threaten what has always been a precarious balance between capitalism and democracy.

Breaking the Chains of The Bond Market

We have seen how, during the early 1980s, the agendas of Wall Street and Washington began to coalesce. Wall Street's agenda has been promoted by myths, the most persistent being the necessity of great inequalities that, it insists, guarantee a faster growth of savings and investment. At the same time, however, Wall Street has abandoned the goal of rapid economic growth in favor of sloth, all the better to serve the interests of the Good News Bears.

The first step in any reform is to break out, to soar above the myths. Hopefully, the preceding chapters have contributed to the unmasking of the bondholding class, the Federal Reserve, and the Treasury—*their* conventional wisdom, *their* agenda. In this chapter, I go several steps further, to propose even more specific policy remedies regarding financial markets. These recommendations will seem reasonable, even desirable, to those who have broken free of the ideological chains of The Bond Market. Admittedly, the proposals are "radical," but in the correct sense of the term, for I aim them at the root causes of our social and economic problems.

The supra-rich cannot be trusted to argue against its own interests any more than the Pope in the real Vatican Palace can be trusted to break his covenant with the Holy Trinity. Welfare benefits "caused" the deficits, and the federal debt has mortgaged everyone's children: this is the "moral ground" for flagellation of the poor and the working class. It nonetheless diverts attention from some inconvenient facts. Such deceit not only hides the bondholders' high unearned incomes, but is all the more effective in concealing the initial source of the bondholders' wealth impetus, whereby the accumulation of the federal debt itself redounds to the bondholders' collective benefit. This alchemy nonetheless has made invisible the new leisure class.

Again, diversion and concealment are crucial. Otherwise, higher capital gains taxes and a truly progressive income tax might replace higher social security taxes and diminished welfare programs as the means to federal budget surpluses. To state the truth, if the choice is between balancing the federal budget on the backs of the bondholders or not at all, the bondholders will decide that those budget deficits are not the evil incarnate that once served their interests so well.

Still, we would be unduly pessimistic to presume that the bondholders will fail to perceive the threat that a system-wide failure poses to themselves. Had the rich on the maiden voyage of the Titanic fully understood the dire consequences of the shipbuilder's hubris, they would have embraced national guidelines for the number of onboard lifeboats, if not international shipbuilding standards.

Short-Term Debt and Increasing the Issues of Discount Bonds

As I have said, the main problem with the national debt is not its size compared with the GDP but the huge interest payments to bondholders required to service it. First on our reform agenda would be the reduction of the interest burden or servicing cost of the debt. If interest payments had been zero, the budget in 1996 would already have been running a surplus!

Robert Rubin, as the U.S. Secretary of the Treasury, was acutely aware of the interest burden of the debt. The Treasury took two measures aimed at reducing interest payments. First, it began to issue zero-coupon bonds. Like U.S. Treasury bills, these bonds are discount bonds; their rates of return are based on the difference between their discounted purchase prices compared with their higher face values. The U.S. Treasury makes *no* interest payments on zero-coupon bonds. What is surprising is that the Treasury issued so few, especially since it had aggressively pursued the issuance of Treasury bills requiring no interest payments if "rolled over" into new T-bills.

Since the new bondholding class buys and sells bonds for capital gains, scant reason to issue bonds with guaranteed interest payments exists. Whereas a structure of purely short-term debt might make foreigners nervous because the Treasury would have to rely on the investment bankers to continue to "roll over" the debt as it quickly matures, a more aggressive shift away from interest-bearing debt and toward long-term discount bonds could greatly reduce interest payments without having to rely on short-term debt. Besides, much of Asia and Latin America now recognizes, more than ever, that U.S. Treasuries are a safe haven for their funds.

The Hidden Value of the Treasury's COLA Bonds

The U.S. Treasury had a second idea for reducing interest payments. In January 1997 it began to issue 10-year bonds indexed to the rate of inflation. This indexation is the newest COLA, or cost of living adjustment, coming out of D.C. The rate of inflation increases the initial prices of the COLA bonds, leaving the real or inflation-adjusted price constant. Though the buyer will pay taxes on any annual inflation-related increments, they will not pay out the adjustments for inflation until maturity ten years down the engraved-paper road. For instance, if inflation increases 3 percent during the year, a $1,000 note (the minimum denomination) would be adjusted upward to $1,030, potentially increasing tax liabilities by $30. The coupon rate next year will be applied to the higher price, so that interest lost to inflation, too, is partially redeemed.

The real reason behind these new bonds may be a well-kept secret. With this guarantee, buyers will be willing to buy bonds that have a *lower* nominal yield, knowing that the Treasury protects them from the ravages of inflation. Since it makes all interest payments in nominal dollars (not inflation-adjusted dollars), the interest payments on the low-interest bonds will be below the interest payments on coupon bonds of the same maturity. The COLA bond buyer, however, will come out ahead of the other bond buyers only if inflation is substantial and of an unexpected amount.

After the bidding of auction participants had ended on the first 10-year indexed-notes issue of $7 billion, the interest coupon rate settled at $3\frac{3}{8}$ percent. In comparison, the coupon interest rate on the government's previous auction of 10-year notes, which were not inflation-indexed, was much higher at $6\frac{1}{2}$ percent. COLA bonds will reduce interest payments from the Treasury if inflation remains tranquil. If inflation begins to soar, the payments of interest in inflation-adjusted values will not increase, though payments in actual or nominal dollars will. The effect on the federal budget of rapid inflation is essentially a draw. Rising tax revenue will offset rising interest payments since tax payments rise with inflation.

Though we cannot be sure that the COLA bonds will be sufficiently popular to displace a large share of non-indexed bonds, in principle (and in the public's interest) we can urge the aggressive marketing of such bonds by the U.S. Treasury. Buyers oversubscribed the first issue at bids five times the values of bonds sold, with most of the participants being Wall Street traders and institutional investors such as pension funds rather than individuals. However, the sales sizzle turned to fizzle by early spring 1997. Still, the bonds have spawned imitators—the Tennessee Valley Authority and the Federal Home Loan Banks have issued inflation-indexed notes, while Fannie Mae and Freddie Mac were considering selling similar bonds.

A Financial Transactions Tax on Speculators

More can, and needs to be done. Few doubt the potential behavioral changes awaiting targeted tax changes. For instance, Republican politicians and even some New Democrats have supported capital gains tax cuts for stimulating national saving. Except for capital gains on housing, however, those who gain by far the most from such tax cuts are the bondholders. Though tax cuts on capital gains from financial capital do add to the savings of the rich, as noted, they have adversely affected *national* saving. Even a pinch of fear that capital gains taxes will impoverish the bondholders is excessive. Still, fear must have driven the White House and Congress to lower the maximum tax on financial and other capital gains from 28 percent to 20 percent in 1997.

Long-term capital gains—taking place over several years—within an industrial firm have long been considered the flywheel of capitalism. Rare is the economist who suggests that long-term capital gains are undesirable. I am with the majority on the blessings of strong *long-term* capital gains. Quick capital gains on secondary financial instruments are of a different character; generally, the purpose of such sudden sales is to make money out of money, something accomplished in a time too brief and too indirect to produce goods or services. If we prefer lasting to fleeting capitalism, we would discourage speculative gains.

Nobelist James Tobin has recommended a small transactions tax on foreign exchange and stocks to dampen speculation in such markets. I endorse the Tobin tax but suggest it be substantially greater than half a percent. A transactions tax also recommends itself for other kinds of domestic financial transfers. The purpose would not be to punish manufacturers for earning profits or stockholders for unearned dividends. Profitable manufacturers hire workers and make real investments. They deserve our applause and our support during a time when such enterprise is under siege.

The 30-year bond, for example, was not designed to change hands daily. It and 10-year bonds were intended to provide funds for long-term, real investment. Mortgages for financing housing is another example that comes easily to mind. Even equities were originally considered "long-term capital investments" both because perpetual corporations used them to provide finance for new factories and because households held them such a long time.

A properly designed financial transactions tax would discourage speculation in securities. I recommend a transactions tax, not as a levy on productivity, which it isn't, but as a penalty for pure speculation. It is intended to punish people for the misuse of money and wealth. Such a tax, sufficient to sting but not so great as to eliminate all gains, would be directed at the new leisure class of bondholders, who have increased financial market volatility and made speculation more lucrative, moving from bonds into stocks and back again.

Any person or institution buying and selling General Motors or any other stock in less than a year has either been imprudent in its purchasing decision or is speculating. A transactions tax, graduated from a high percentage near term and vaporizing at the end of a two-year holding period, would discourage short-term speculation in the stock markets. The design of the tax itself should be subject to long-term study.

Still, as a starting point for discussion, I would recommend a transactions tax of 12 percent on the value of the spot sale (or purchase, in the case of a short position) for all stocks held for less than thirty days. Thereafter, the transactions tax would be reduced by a half percentage point for each month that the shares are continually held. The tax would be introduced gradually but would eventually be applied to all stock holdings. The same tax would be applied to financial derivatives based upon stocks.

The purpose of a transactions tax penalty is not to discourage the buying and selling of securities. If speculators can gain more than 12 percent (after other fees) during the first holding month, they will still make a profit, though a smaller one. Moreover, the government will have additional revenue going toward deficit reduction (and reduced interest) or toward particular programs.

Because most mature in less than a year, U.S. Treasury bills are not a speculative threat. However, U.S. Treasury bonds and corporate bonds are intended to be long-term investments. Federal, state, and municipal bonds have a variety of maturities. The same 12 percent transactions tax could be levied on bonds maturing in one year and held for less than thirty days with a downward-sliding penalty equaling a full percentage point less every thirty days thereafter. If the bonds are held to maturity, no transactions tax would apply. For bonds maturing in two years, the 12 percent transactions tax would be phased out by a half percentage point every thirty days. The same kind of structure would apply to the transactions tax on bonds maturing in three or four years. Further, a tax good enough for standard financial instruments should be applied, perhaps with even greater enthusiasm, to financial derivatives based upon bonds.

After four years, we are looking at truly significant holding periods, and we do not wish to discourage individuals and institutions from buying such long-term bonds. The 12 percent transactions tax would be phased out at zero after holding a bond for five years, whatever its final maturity date. Thus, a bond maturing in ten years or thirty years would be subject to no transactions tax if sold at the end of five years. A transactions tax structured to encourage the buying of longer-term bonds would have a surprising benefit. By encouraging the purchase of longer-term bonds, that part of the bond market would be deepened and would enjoy greater liquidity, making it less subject to sudden collapse.

The Clinton administration did exhibit an awareness of the importance of longer holding periods for financial investments. The 1997 capital gains tax law lowers the top rate from 20 to 18 percent for assets purchased after the year 2000 and held at least five years. Immediately effective, those with incomes less than $41,200 (joint filers) enjoy a capital gains tax rate of only 10 percent for 18-month assets and 8 percent for five-year holdings. Unfortunately, households at this income level do not hold sufficient values of securities to merit taxation.

Still, some will say that a transactions tax on financial debt instruments and equities will take some excitement out of the markets. They justifiably indict such a tax. However, the gaming tables and slot machines will still be open for business in Las Vegas, Reno, New Orleans, Atlantic City, and even Biloxi. Leisure-class speculators lusting after fast gains or losses can enjoy them in the same manner as the working class.

Interest-free Loans for Infrastructure

Policies or institutional changes to reduce interest rates, especially long-term interest rates, would greatly benefit the real economy. As noted, though the Federal Reserve prematurely uses higher interest rates to fight imaginary inflation, the initial effect is to inflate costs of production and consumption. That is, as every businessperson knows, high interest rates are initially *inflationary*, not deflationary! Eventually, when the rising cost of production leads to a reduction in the pace of inflation and the unemployment of wage earners, the Reserve greatly slows economic growth or creates an outright recession. If the period of slow growth or recession grinds on long enough and if it slows full-time employment, disinflation or even deflation takes place. Tight money policy is a roundabout and thereby a very costly way to engage inflationary fires.

What I next propose—to counter partly the adverse effects of high interest rates—is not an original idea. Tax-supported bodies— state and local governments—should be able to borrow money, *interest-free*, directly from the U.S. Treasury for capital projects and for paying off existing debt. Such a loan—*not* a grant—would be for capital projects only, *not* day-to-day expenses. For example, public schools could borrow to build new classrooms but not to pay teachers. Moreover, such investments are in need of stimulation. Though public investment had averaged 3.0 percent of GDP from 1955 through 1980, it averaged only 2.3 percent from 1981 through 1997, even less in recent years. State and local governments typically account for 85 percent of such investment.

Other benefits would soon flow from interest-free loans for infrastructures. Research has shown that public capital investment stimulates private investment, suggesting that Clinton's initial focus on public infrastructures was sound. A study shows that *private* business fixed investment from the late 1960s through the late 1980s would have been 0.6 of a percentage point higher as a share of the GDP had the nation devoted an additional 1.0 percentage point of GDP to *public* investment.[1] Lower interest rates alone would make private investment projects more attractive and they would stimulate real investment. Of course, to the extent that a transactions tax subdued financial speculation, real returns in industry would begin to supersede the paper profits from paper.

Furthermore, public investment has very high rates of return because it stimulates economic growth and employment as better highways, schools, airports, and cleaner water boost the output and sales of private industry. According to a recent study using state-level data, an increase in the ratio of public to private capital stock from a current 0.45 to 0.50 would increase output growth by 0.8 percent per year and employment by 0.3 percent per year (peaking at 0.5 percent after 15 years). Moreover, the positive effects are sustained for centuries. At the end of two centuries output climbs by some 27 percent and employment by nearly 21 percent.[2] Even if the effect on economic growth were only half as large as the research suggests, the nation's wealth and income would now be about a fifth higher if the 1955–80 pace of public investment had been maintained. Virtually every nook and cranny of the private economy benefit from improved roads, airports, and schools.

The advantages of using interest-free loans for funding public infrastructures are many. The U.S. Treasury would get the money not from the federal budget but from Congress which would create the money [as authorized in the U.S. Constitution: Article 1, Section 8, Clause 5]. The action by the Congress and the Treasury would increase the money supply—which is otherwise an exclusive privilege reserved today for private commercial banks and the Federal Reserve. Not only would such loans reduce interest costs, they could be used to reduce taxes on both income and property, even while serving, to an enhanced degree, the necessary and legitimate needs of communities and the nation. Money supply additions from such loans (if not neutralized by securities sales by the Federal Reserve) would be subtracted by an equal amount when the loans are repaid to the Treasury.

Vital infrastructures—bridges, roads, airports, schools, court houses, and so on—could be built without adding to deficits. (Alternatively, existing loans could be exchanged for interest-free debt and taxes could be reduced.) Since the interest cost on state, county, city and schools *doubles* the cost of a project funded by interest-bearing bonds of more than twenty years maturity and *triples* the cost of one of more than thirty years, the public presently pays taxes for two or three schools while getting *only one*. Not only would the payrolls of private contractors be enhanced, employment would rise even as construction costs and inflation cooled. The presence of zero-interest loans would exert downward pressures on average private loan rates for automobiles, appliances, and houses. If this is such a win-win idea, we might ask, why hasn't it been done?

The answer will surprise many. Such interest-free loans for public infrastructures have been deployed *several times*, even in this country! It was done by the colonies, by the founding fathers. Later, during the prolonged depression of 1837–43, Congress enacted a special national bankruptcy law in 1841 to provide relief to debtors; the Treasury Department, faced with rising budgetary deficits, also issued non-interest-bearing government notes. Abraham Lincoln issued similar interest-free notes (mixed with periodic rallies for interest-bearing bonds) during the Civil War. More recently, the Federal Reserve cooperated with the Treasury during World War II to yield virtually the same effect, when the federal government borrowed money at less than 1 percent interest.

When proposed by President Lincoln, a Republican, he said, "the privilege of creating and issuing money is not only the supreme prerogative of Government, but is the Government's greatest creative opportunity. By the adoption of these principles, the taxpayers will be saved immense sums of interest." After all, the money supply *is* a public good. As one of humans' greatest inventions, it was not supposed to serve primarily the purposes of the bondholding class. Though the bondholders would have us believe that the money supply was invented to threaten the value of its bonds (and hence, indirectly, of its shares of stock), money was originally invented as a means to improve the production and sale of real commodities—grains, timber, textiles, and so on.

New Zealand introduced a modified version of interest-free loans. During the Depression of the 1930s, the central bank of New Zealand issued money to plant trees and build roads and housing, enabling the country to be the first to recover economically (and go on for thirty years of prosperity). Until 1981 its central bank gave loans at 1 percent interest to the Dairy Board, helping to establish the dairy industry. The Federal Reserve did the opposite during the Great Depression, calling in discount loans from a failing private banking system.

The longest and most resolute use of interest-free public funding of infrastructures has been in the island state of Guernsey, in the English Channel. In 1816 Guernsey's sea walls were crumbling, its muddy roads only four-and-a-half feet wide, and its debt, £19,000. Out of an annual income of £3,000, £2,400 was used to pay interest on the debt. Unemployment was very high.

The government created and lent £6,000 of interest-free state notes. It continued to issue more notes over time until, by 1837, £50,000 had been issued interest-free for sea walls, roads, a marketplace, a church, and a college. By 1958, more than £500,000 had been issued. Contrary to what monetarists would tell us, no inflation followed these issues.

By 1990, the island had 60,000 permanent residents with the equivalent of $13 million in interest-free notes in circulation. Guernsey has no public debt, its unemployment rate is zero, the average family owns 3.3 cars, and the price of gasoline is $2 a gallon compared with $5 in England. Income tax is a flat 20 percent, and a surplus of government funds earns interest. Even with such interest-free public infrastructure funding, Guernsey has a small but humble bondholding class. The state of Guernsey has become a "cash cow."

A not-for-profit organization of taxpayers, Sovereignty, in Freeport, Illinois has recently renewed and proposed the idea of interest-free public debt. Not only has the group drafted a bill for Congress, its proposal has been endorsed by at least 64 cities, including St. Louis, Missouri, Cleveland, Ohio, Independence, Missouri, and Lansing, Michigan, plus the Southwest (Chicago) Conference of Local Governments, the St. Louis County Municipal League, and many school districts, townships and counties. The idea has widespread, even popular grass roots support.[3]

The idea of interest-free loans seems to be catching on. S. Jay Levy and Walter M. Cadette of The Jerome Levy Economics

Institute propose the establishment of a Federal Bank for Infrastructure Modernization (FBIM), which would buy and hold approximately $50 billion annually of zero-interest mortgage loans to state and local governments for capital investment in projects recommended by Congress and the President.[4] The "deposits" created as liabilities of the FBIM would be held as assets by the Federal Reserve System.[5] The $50 billion annual investment would return public capital spending only to the standards of the 1955–80 period. They suggest a maximum mortgage of 30 years, the period of repayment depending on the type of project, with the principal repaid in annual installments.

As started earlier, the authority to provide interest-free loans for infrastructures is available to Congress. It is the same authority that allows the Federal Reserve and the commercial banking system to create bank credit in the same manner. One negative aspect of the proposed bill is that it would not alter the present powers of the Federal Reserve.

If Congress created the money for interest-free loans to tax-supported bodies, the Sacred College of Bonds and Money would have several options. First, if the College did not want the money supply to increase by the amount of the new loans, it could sell government securities of an equal amount from its huge portfolio, reducing the reserves of the banking system, thereby negating potential expansion of the money supply. Second, the Fed could raise banks' reserve requirements by the amount of the interest-free loans and then allow banks to create the same amount of money they otherwise would. The new, higher reserve requirements would make the banking system safer. Third, the Fed could deploy both policies in mixed amounts.

Doubtless, the multitude of conventional economists at the Federal Reserve would scream, "The inflations are coming! The inflations are coming!" though the multitude of supporters of the proposal from cities and local communities do not share that fear. Latin American countries such as Brazil and Mexico have had inflation stemming from the printing of money, but the notes printed by their central banks and treasuries are used for consumption more than for investment and require no repayment. Moreover, Latin America does not have broad and deep government securities markets like the United States. Their central banks do not have the leverage over the money supply enjoyed by the Sacred College of Bonds and Money. And, the Federal Reserve would—if nothing were to change—retain whatever control it now has over the money supply.

The Use of Interest-free Bonds as a New Weapon Against the Business Cycle

Just as with golf swings, timing is vital with most reforms. The Treasury could introduce interest-free loans during economic recessions or periods of slow economic growth. In fact, interest-free bonds could become a flexible, new fiscal policy. The size of deficits and the national debt since the early 1980s has decimated the traditional use of fiscal policy as a means of countering the business cycle. In turn, the absence of fiscal policy has placed too great a burden on monetary policy as the sole available policy for combating recessions and inflations. Though counter-cyclical timing of new issues of interest-free bonds could resurrect fiscal policy, its effectiveness, like the success of low interest rates during the financing of World War II, would require the cooperation of the Federal Reserve. With the central bank's cooperation (or reform measures to guarantee its support), the timing of new issues of such bonds during recessions could increase employment without adding to the federal budget deficit or to the national debt.

The lending of funds to state and local governments has enormous public appeal. The amounts lent could be based on the populations of the tax-based creatures. It would be a short, though perhaps more controversial, step for Congress to issue interest-free bonds for financing national infrastructures, much as earlier

Congresses have done. But, if such loans are good enough for wartime killing, why not use them to sustain the domestic peace, if not democracy?

Conservatives ceaselessly demand that the federal government should behave more like a business firm. If the government kept its books in the manner of business firms—one budget for current revenues and expenses, another for investment—interest-free bonds could partly fund the investment side of the budget. Becoming more businesslike at the Office of Management and Budget also would add still more flexibility to the use of the new fiscal policy by the White House and Congress.

Tax Progressivity and the Business Cycle

Though monetary reforms are critical, true tax reform is an essential counterpart in the restoration of economic well-being for ordinary citizens, made even more urgent by the so-called 1997 Taxpayer Relief Act. According to the Citizens for Tax Justice, almost half of that "tax relief" will ultimately go to the richest 5 percent of Americans (receiving more than 75 percent of its benefits), the lower 95 percent, as ever, getting the residual. Worse, the one-percenters will pay at least $16,000 less in taxes while the benefits for middle income families will be less than $200. The bipartisan Joint Committee on Taxation estimates the total cost at $95 billion from 1997 through 2002. Hopefully, readers by now will have been convinced of the economic waste in giving the bondholding class more chips to play with in the financial casino.

We have seen how deficit finance as a substitute for progressive tax finance gives windfall gains to the bondholding class while hurting everyone else. The bondholders have reaped most of the benefits from budget deficits and a rising national debt tied to regressive taxation. The political rhetoric of a balanced budget for its own sake is a clever diversion, by which the real problem of the widening division between the leisure class and the working class can be ignored. If the nation needs a debate on budgets, no shortage of critical issues exists. As a starter, the tax burden of the working class has steadily increased with each increase in social security tax payments. Not only has the income tax system become ever more regressive (with higher rates applying to lower incomes), it has become an inadequate source of general revenue. The federal government has transferred ever greater fiscal burdens to state and local governments that have always relied on regressive taxes.

The federal government needs tax revenue for many reasons. The more successful a financial transactions tax in slowing speculation, the less government revenue it will yield. In that regard, the transactions tax is like a tariff on imports. Still, the tariff was once the main source of tax revenue for the federal government. The transactions tax, too, would likely become an important new revenue source. If, however, we want a federal investment budget and we want to keep the current revenue and expenses budget roughly balanced over the course of the business cycle, the nation needs an enhanced tax base, only part of which could come from a faster economic growth pace. Besides, as I have said, an over-reliance on deficit finance pushes income and wealth toward the top of the pyramid.

In addition to a new tax base, the country also needs a means of fighting inflation other than the Fed's twin sledgehammers—tight money and high (inflationary) interest rates—designed as they are to beat the economy into submission. It is bad enough that the costs of construction and durables are pushed skyward by rising interest rates, it is still worse that employment and lower incomes for workers must be exchanged for "price stability." It is a Faustian bargain. Though inflation has not been a problem for more than a decade, even relative price stability and the prospect for worldwide deflation did not prevent Alan Greenspan from continuing to fight the ghost of inflations past.

If we ignore social security deductions for workers and capital gains taxes lower than taxes on earned income, federal income taxes are modestly progressive in structure since the average tax burden rises with income. However, state and local taxes are highly regressive, a problem made worse by the shifting of federal responsibilities to the states and municipalities initiated by the Reagan administration and continuing unabated to this day. Since those with the highest incomes receive the greatest benefits from a stable, democratic government and from the free enterprise system, it is poetic justice that those who benefit most from government's nurture and preservation of wealth should pay the highest tax rates.

Of course, many contend that all taxation is a burden. Let there be no mistake about it, it is, but such antagonists (or anarchists) sometimes miss the point. Unless the federal government enforces contracts and deters crime against property, develops and maintains a national system of communications and transportation, guarantees a nationwide system of education that provides a skilled labor force for industry, stabilizes the economy, regulates trade and finance, and protects factories from foreign enemies, then individuals and businesses will not be able to utilize fully their capacities for earning incomes. Taxation is a burden that individuals agree to share to maintain the necessary infrastructures for corporate enterprise and a free society. No political theorist ever said that government enterprise was a free lunch or that it should be. A plane cargo without an airport, a truckload of personal computers halted by a collapsed bridge, a factory bombed by the enemy, or an information industry dependent upon illiterates are all useless.

Since any details regarding tax reform go beyond the scope of this book, I am content to outline the many advantages from making federal taxes more progressive.[6] First, wealthy households receive the greatest benefits from the private economy as well as from public infrastructures. Second, historically lopsided income and wealth distributions have always led to speculative excesses, a rise in the *angels' share* of savings, financial crises, and, more often than not, economic depressions. Tax revenue from savings that would otherwise evaporate could be redeployed as capital infrastructure to speed real economic growth. Third, a truly progressive tax provides a built-in fiscal stabilizer for the economy. When the economy is growing rapidly, rising tax revenues can prevent the growth from being overly exuberant. When the economy is tilting toward recession, households fall into lower tax brackets reducing the government's revenue but providing a natural stimulus for the economy.

Many have suggested that the taxes of the rich comprise so small a share of total income taxes that they do not bear the cost of collection. If so, it must be because the rich are greatly undertaxed relative to the near-rich. In 1992, the imposition of a 30 percent marginal tax plus a 50 percent surtax on the taxes owed by the top 1 percent of taxpayers would have raised about $225 billion in tax revenue, enough to cover all welfare, unemployment compensation, health and education costs that year. Yet, the *effective* average tax rate on the super-rich would have been only about 33 percent!

In the next few pages, as I close with an Epilogue, I will comment on recent developments. In these comments the urgent need for enacting financial market reforms will become clear, if it isn't already.

NOTES

1. See David A. Aschauer, "Is Public Expenditure Productive?" *Journal of Monetary Economics*, March 1989, pp. 177–200 and David A. Aschauer, "Dynamic Output and Employment Effects of Public Capital," Working Paper No. 191, The Jerome Levy Economics Institute, Annandale-on-Hudson, N.Y. For a summary of some of the early research on this topic, see Sharon J. Erenburg, "The Real Effects of Public Investment on Private Investment: A Rational Expectations Model," *Applied Economics*, June 1993, pp. 831–7.

2. See David A. Aschauer, "Output and Employment Effects of Public Capital," Working Paper No. 191, The Jerome Levy Economics Institute of Bard College, April 1997.

3. More information can be obtained directly by writing to Ken Bohnsack, Chairman, Sovereignty, 1154 West Logan Street, Freeport, Illinois 61032 or calling him at (815) 232–8737.

4. S. Jay Levy and Walter M. Cadette, *Overcoming America's Infrastructure Deficit*, Public Policy Brief No. 40 (Annandale-on-Hudson, N.Y.: The Jerome Levy Economics Institute, 1998).

5. The FBIM's balance sheet would have the zero-interest state and local government mortgages on its asset side and the similarly zero-interest "deposits" of the Federal Reserve on the liability side.

6. Elsewhere, I, and others, have presented detailed plans for tax reform and other policies consistent with dealing with the bondholding class. A survey of the plans appear in E. Ray Canterbery, *The Making of Economics*, Third Edition (Belmont, CA: Wadsworth, 1987), Chapter 17. An initial proposal appears in an article by the same author in "Tax Reform and Incomes Policy: A VATIP Proposal," *Journal of Post Keynesian Economics* 5 (Spring 1983): 430–9. A later, more detailed version of the plan appears in E. Ray Canterbery, Eric W. Cook, and Bernard A. Schmitt, "The Flat Tax, Negative Tax, and VAT: Gaining Progressivity and Revenue," *Cato Journal* (Fall 1985): 521–36 (based upon a paper given at the Conference on the Flat Tax Proposals, Florida State University, March 14, 1985). Embedded in these reforms is a new kind of incomes policy that would use tax incentives to limit wage and profits inflation, making it unnecessary to use monetary policy to cause recession and slow growth to limit inflation.

SIXTEEN

⟨⟩⟨⟩⟨⟩

Epilogue: The Final Insult

With a third of American households invested in Wall Street, and mushrooming millionaires made there, Wall Street is more important than ever.

Roger Altman[1]

We end as we began. Wall Street knew that the impeachment and trial of President William Jefferson Clinton would not damage the financial markets. Despite all that the White House had done for Wall Street, what Wall Street appreciated most was what *Time*, an increasingly conservative news magazine, called "The Committee to Save the World." *Time* had the three marketeers on its cover (February 14, 1999)—Alan Greenspan, up front and looking as smug as he had at Clinton's first State of the Union address, the then-Treasury Secretary Robert Rubin, smiling over Greenspan's suitably right shoulder, and Lawrence Summers, Rubin's carefully groomed successor, peering seriously over the left shoulder. For the historical moment, it was Wall Street's final insult.

Wall Street had made compellingly clear who it considered to be important. Of primary importance was Alan Greenspan, who would remain head of the Federal Reserve no matter what happened to Clinton. Having purged that great demon, goods inflation, or so it was thought, Greenspan was again busily inflating bonds and stocks. The devil, of course, is often in the details. Wall

Street still was marveling at Greenspan's interest rate cutting performance. When the markets merely shrugged as the Fed trimmed just a quarter percentage point off the fed funds rate, Greenspan immediately realized his error and followed up two weeks later with another quarter-percentage cut, without even calling a meeting of the Sacred College. Markets rallied instantly: bonds and stocks leapt. On November 17, 1998, David Wessel, a Staff Reporter of the *Wall Street Journal*, gushed about how Greenspan "knew the move would grab attention: it was the first time since 1994 that the central bank had changed interest rates between scheduled policy-committee meetings." Greenspan cut interest rates three times over the seven weeks between September 29 and Wessel's article.

This time, the Reserve said, it wanted to reassure financial markets that it was prepared to do what was needed to avoid a global economic meltdown. The Reserve was acting as the global economy's central bank. Japan and Russia, mired in depression, were suffering political paralysis. Europe was preoccupied with monetary union and an economic slowdown. Indonesia, Malaysia, Singapore, Thailand, and Brazil were into severe contractions. A giant hedge fund had just been bailed out by the Reserve. Greenspan, not Clinton, was in position to protect the bondholding class.

Odd as it may seem, nonetheless, global financial meltdown was only an *indirect* trigger for Greenspan. If Greenspan really was saving the world, he was only solving a problem to which he may have contributed. At a time when the Fed and the Treasury imagined inflation everywhere and were reducing liquidity, they simply missed the global deflation in commodities. Besides, Greenspan's central concern was keeping Wall Street delusionally happy. The Fed chair saw an unusual gap between the yields on two different issues of 30-year Treasury bonds—one sold in August 1997, the other in August 1998—as a gauge of intense "investor anxiety." Moreover, there was a widening yield gap between ultra-safe Treasuries and corporate bonds. The widening gaps meant that liquidity in the bond market, especially for risky issues such as junk bonds, could dry up. That is, Greenspan's main concern was that buyers of bonds were no longer willing to take great risks! To the great relief of the Street, money was flowing back into corporate junk bonds from the high, safe ground of Treasuries after the cuts in the fed funds rate. Alan Greenspan's status as the Pope of Wall Street was assured.

Two other officials' names were often mentioned in the same breath as Greenspan's—his soulmate, then Treasury Secretary Robert Rubin, and Larry Summers. The cosmic, and only, fear in the removal of Clinton centered on the distinct possibility that Rubin and Summers would follow Clinton out the door. It would be the only reason Wall Street might have to worry about Clinton's fate. Rubin had earned his wings as Wall Street's angel with a strong international dollar policy that had kept inflation low and had provided a cushion for the Federal Reserve to lower interest rates. A strong dollar, of course, made U.S. exports more expensive overseas and has contributed to historically massive trade deficits and downward pressures on American wages and full-time jobs. As noted, lower wages and interest rates, in turn, were good for both bonds and stocks.

Among those reporting on the importance of being Rubin was Bill Barnhart for the *Chicago Tribune* (December 10, 1998). Barnhart quotes David Hale, chief global economist for the Zurich Group. If Rubin resigned, "that would be a major event," Hale is quoted as saying. "There would be an immediate sell-off in the dollar." As Tim Geithner, the Under Secretary for International Affairs, told *Time* the day after Valentine's Day, 1999, Rubin has remade the Treasury into an organization that is "more like an investment bank." Thus ended any doubt, minor though it may have been, that the takeover of public policy by the investment bankers and the Federal Reserve was complete. This, however, was not the final insult to ordinary people.

Larry Summers, invariably called the Kissinger of economics, had to prove himself to Wall Street. Back in the early 1980s, Summers had proposed a transactions tax on short-term financial trading, not greatly different from the one proposed in this book. (At the time, Rubin was doing short-term trading for a very good living.) Wall Street did not like the idea. Moreover, Summers is a stranger to humility. Rubin realized that he would have to be Summers' Professor Higgins so that he, Rubin, could be replaced without spooking the financial markets. As a result, the replacement of Rubin by Summers was the smoothest, most orchestrated shift in power in American cabinet history. Rubin's departure and Summers' succession would be simultaneous. The financial markets were given a full trading day to digest the news. To allay market anxieties, Alan Greenspan reassured Wall Street that he had not only a close friendship with Summers but a close working relationship. "He is a person of extraordinary talent and judgment," said Mr. Greenspan. Although Vice President Gore sent signals that Summers would be a strong *candidate* for the Treasury post in his administration, there is no assurance of his permanence. President Clinton, however, was careful to explain why the transition would keep the global financial system stable and intact. Though bond and stock prices took a sharp dip after the announcement of Rubin's imminent departure, they rallied the same day, as Rubin expected, with the realization that Greenspan, a friendship, and Wall Street's *bond market strategy* remained intact.

Alan Greenspan's expressed goal in Little Rock (before Clinton had stepped into the White House) was the achievement of a bull market in financial markets through a balanced federal budget and a zero inflation rate. Armed with the *bond market strategy*, Greenspan had created hyperinflation in financial assets and contributed to a near-zero U.S. consumer inflation rate. With the three quick cuts in the fed funds rate ending in November 1998, wild movements in bond and stock prices resumed, and speculation in newly-minted Internet stocks created a bubble within a bubble.

Still, even officials inside the Reserve began to worry about the great financial bubble amidst a global economy in decline. Would Greenspan have to act?

Early in 1999, someone at the Ayn Rand Institute must have reminded Greenspan what he had always believed—that free market outcomes are always right. In defense of the Internet stocks, Greenspan told the Senate Budget Committee on January 28, "the size of that potential market is so huge that you have these pie-in-the-sky type of potentials for a lot of different vehicles." Mr. Greenspan attributed the rise of Internet stocks to what he called "the lottery principle," under which people are willing to spend seemingly irrational sums of money in the hope they will hit the jackpot. He went on blithely:

> But there is at root here something far more fundamental. And indeed, it does reflect something good about the way our securities markets work; namely, that they do endeavor to ferret out the better opportunities and put capital into various different types of endeavors, prior to earnings actually materializing. That's good for our system. And that in fact— with all of its hype and craziness—is something that ... probably is more plus than minus.

"Craziness?" Amazon.com, Yahoo! eBay, and America Online took giant leaps upward that same day. Around mid-March, 1999, Yahoo!, the online directory service, had gone to $175 from a year earlier price of $16. America Online went from the same price to $105. Meanwhile, the Dow broke 10,000. By now, the Reserve's chair had, in quick succession, set off two rallies *inside* a speculative bubble of his own creation. Once fretting about "irrational exuberance," Greenspan now saw "craziness" in the financial markets as not only rational, but "good." People placing bets on companies with no earnings is what capitalism is all about! Willie Nelson wrote the song, Patsy Cline famously recorded it, but it was Alan Greenspan romancing the financial markets. He had certified the financial casino.

Through more indirect actions, Greenspan at the Fed and Rubin–Summers at the Treasury can take credit for some other results. Both institutions have insisted on two things for the global economy; first, there must not be any regulations in any country that would impede the free flow of financial capital; second, anything that goes wrong in an emerging nation must be corrected by their tightening their belts, eliminating budget deficits, reducing their money supplies, and creating unemployment. That is, what often constitutes good policy for the United States is even better for developing nations.

Thus, when free-flowing financial capital fled East Asia, those nations had to devalue their currencies—an act that immediately reduced their price levels and employment. Similar events followed in Russia. Next came Brazil, the lynchpin for Latin America. As unemployment tripled in Thailand, the middle class was wiped out in two months. In Indonesia, suburban housewives had to take jobs as domestics in other countries. After deflation leapt to Korea, its currency collapsed and unemployment rose to 21 percent. The deflation and depression in Russia were so bad that the Russians were selling nuclear power plants for a couple hundred thousand dollars. Even the financial locomotives of Western Europe—Germany and France—wheezed and strained. German unemployment approached its highest levels since 1946, and German banks prepared for a new round of catastrophic losses from Russian defaults.

While the Federal Reserve was fretting over a commodities inflation that never was and never came, the global economy slumped into a deflation afflicting about 85 percent of the world's households. Moreover, U.S. Treasury and Federal Reserve policies were behind the unregulated financial capital flows leading to devaluations around the world. Worse, Treasury dominance of the International Monetary Fund guarantees that the only way out for such countries is *more* deflation, *more* unemployment. In reaction to severe criticism, the IMF has agreed to reform itself, in part, by involving the private sector in forestalling and resolving crises. Its "reform" measures read like a script written by Alan Greenspan; of course, his and Rubin's fingerprints are all over these measures.

Meanwhile, as official Washington, D.C. was looking the other way, commodity deflation walked on cat paws into the United States. Falling agricultural commodity prices afflicted farmers. The price of corn had fallen from a high of about $5.00 a bushel to $2.25 in early 1999. Slumping demand in Japan and elsewhere has put downward pressure on metal prices. For example, copper demand has been declining at an annual pace of 34 percent. In early 1999, copper was selling for 65 cents a pound compared with $1.30 a year before. Crude oil prices were headed for all-time lows. Because of the competitive pressures radiating from Japan, Korea, and Russia, steel prices were plunging. The wholesale price of automobiles suffered its steepest decline since records have been kept.

What did the Federal Reserve have to say about the global collapse of currencies and the aftermath? Alan Greenspan spoke at a meeting of the Securities Industry Association in Boca Raton, Florida on November 5, 1998:

> Dramatic advances in computer and telecommunications technologies in recent years have enabled a broad unbundling of risks through innovative financial engineering.... The consequence doubtless has been a far more efficient financial system. [*Clearly, then, whatever happened was for the best. In fact, markets have never worked so well.*] Market discipline today is clearly far more draconian and less forgiving than twenty or thirty years ago.... [Restricting short-term capital flows] will invariably also restrict direct investment that requires short-term capital to facilitate it. [*Shame on failing nations who*] cannot enjoy the advantages of a sophisticated international financial system without the internal discipline that enables such economies to adjust without crisis to changing circumstances.

That is, if nations are to accept the American gift of unregulated free-flowing financial capital, they must be willing to adopt policies that will disemploy many of their citizens. All central bankers and governments should extend to their own citizens the same courtesies that Greenspan had extended to American workers. This may not be the final insult, but it is revealing.

The ironies continue, and F. Scott Fitzgerald's novels again come to mind.

One week, Greenspan was singing the praises of a New Economy whereby productivity was growing so fast that commodity inflation had been subdued. The next week, he warned that a pre-emptive strike might have to be taken against inflation because wage pressures had risen to a dangerous level. With stock prices so precariously high, the Fed became increasingly cautious in its policy announcements. On St. Patrick's Day, David Jones, a Fed watcher of Wall Street brokerage Aubrey G. Lanston, warned: "If the Fed raised rates by a quarter percentage point, it could prick the stock market bubble and send the world economy into a free fall."[2] In May, a month of zero inflation in consumer goods, Greenspan changed central bank tactics: early warnings were given so that bondholders would push bond prices down and long-term interest rates up. Exercising a newly adopted disclosure policy for the first time, the Fed made a statement that it was so "concerned about the potential for a buildup of inflationary imbalances" that it was leaning toward raising rates in the coming months. Eventually, because of these "free market forces," the Reserve would have to raise the fed funds rate, aligning this key rate with "market-determined" higher rates. If a financial crash comes, it will not be set off by Greenspan's raising interest rates. His record with Wall Street will remain, as it were, unimpeachable. The Fed's own quandary continues.

Meanwhile, despite the historic financial gains for the rich, median family income in 1997 was still only $285 higher than it was in 1989. Jobs had become less secure and are even less likely to provide health and pension benefits. Wherever the typical American family had been able to hold its ground, it had been through a large increase in the hours worked by family members. In stark contrast, between 1989 and 1997 (projected), the wealth share of the top 1 percent of households grew from 37.4 percent of the national total to 39.1 percent, while the wealth share held by the middle class fell from 4.8 percent to 4.4 percent. Because of the rise in debt, the value of middle class wealth holdings actually *fell* between 1989 and 1997. Since in 1995 fewer than a third of all households had stock holdings greater than $5,000, and 90 percent of the value of all stock was held by the top 10 percent of wealth holders, projections suggest that 85.8 percent of the increase in stock values between 1989 and 1997 went to the richest 10 percent. The gains for those holding bonds was even more lopsided.[3]

Our story of the great inequalities created by the bondholding class would be incomplete without revealing the Federal Reserve's recent views on inequality. The Federal Reserve Bank of Kansas City, recognizing an important policy issue, sponsored a symposium on income inequality, at Jackson Hole, Wyoming. Sessions were held in the shadow of the magnificent Grand Tetons, August 27–29, 1998, at the pinnacle of the season. Fed chairman Greenspan, in opening remarks, stated that a central bank's goal regarding distributional issues is to pursue a disciplined stable-price policy. Such a policy "will offer the best underpinnings for identifying opportunities to channel growing knowledge, innovation, and capital investment into the creation of wealth that, in turn, will lift living standards as broadly as possible." Mervyn King, the Deputy Governor of the Bank of England, summed up central-banker mentality as he emphasized that central banks should be viewed as "limited purpose" organizations with a goal of pursuing price stability.

Later, in mid-1999, Greenspan contradicted himself, telling Harvard's graduating class that the gains from the long bull market in stocks "regrettably ... have not been as widely spread across households." Though he doesn't seem to know why this has happened, he is quite sure that the Federal Reserve had nothing to do with it and can do nothing about it. Some 40 students walked out in protest, apparently unconvinced of the Fed's innocence. For them, this was the final insult.

This final insult is to one's common sense. We have revealed the process whereby the Federal Reserve not only helped to create but continues to sustain the bondholding class and truly obscene inequalities in income and wealth. Of course, it has had plenty of help from the White House and the U.S. Treasury. The marshaling of policies that benefit a small, wealthy elite in the narrow interests of Wall Street is not only undemocratic, but unsustainable. Its gigantic speculative bubble surely will burst.

* * *

Still, there are reasons to believe that Wall Street capitalism will not end soon. On the same day that Alan Greenspan was certifying craziness as a highly sophisticated construct of rationality, Ianthe Jeanne Dugan published her article (cited in the epigraph to this chapter) about Wall Street and Al Gore, the Dauphin of the New Democrats. When Gore walked into Manhattan's posh Four Seasons Hotel for a luncheon in his honor, sixty Wall Street executives stood up and cheered. They included Henry Paulson, the conservative co-chief executive of Goldman Sachs & Co., and J.P. Morgan & Co. chief Douglas "Sandy" Warner, a staunch Republican supporter.

Dugan quotes Steven Rattner, chief executive of the large investment bank Lazard Freres & Co.: "The Vice President is not as well known in the Wall Street community as the President, but as people have gotten to know him, they have been impressed." Rattner apparently has taken on the role once played by Treasury Secretary and former Goldman Sachs co-chairman Robert Rubin, and expects to be Gore's Treasury Secretary. Dugan also quotes Jon Corzine, co-chief executive of Goldman Sachs and a major Democratic soft-money donor: "The Vice President has tried to understand how the global economy works from the eyes of someone sitting in Wall Street."

Gore's supporters believe that Wall Street is not only the window to million-dollar salaries and some of the globe's richest political donors, but also to the hearts of a citizenry irrationally infatuated with stocks. The way political campaigns are financed may sustain the Wall Street–Washington, D.C. marriage through tough financial times. When the Russian debt default threatened to destabilize world financial markets, Dugan reports how the Vice President invited a Wall Street "Who's Who" to the White House. The list of powerful financial executives included global investor George Soros, Lionel Pincus of E.M. Warburg, Pincus & Co., Bankers Trust chief executive Frank Newman, Lehman Brothers Inc. chief executive Richard Fuld, American International Group chief executive Hank Greenberg, Stan Schuman of Allen & Co., and David Shaw, a former Columbia University computer science professor who runs a major investment pool in New York. Like that famous 1969 conference at the Arizona Biltmore at which Wall Street promoted monetarism, the meeting at the White House did not include any blue-collar workers or labor union leaders.

It is not so much history ending, as history repeating itself.

NOTES

1. Formerly Deputy Secretary of the U.S. Treasury, Altman is now a New York investment banker. He is quoted by the Ianthe Jeanne Dugan in "Al Gore's Wooing Wall Street," *The Washington Post Weekly Edition*, January 18, 1999.
2. Quoted by Rich Miller, "Active Dow Gives Fed No Easy Choices," *USA Today*, March 17, 1999.

3. These data and much more can be found in the most recent report on the state of working America; it remains the best source on the economic well-being of the average American. See Lawrence Mishel, Jared Bernstein, and John Schmitt, *The State of Working America 1998–99* (Ithaca, N.Y.: Cornell University Press, 1998).

Index

Index

"too large to fail," 169
regulation of, 246
role of, 247
Barnhart, Bill, 297
Barrons', 141
Barstansky, Peter, 184
Bartlett, Bruce, 120n
  *"Reaganomics": Supply Side
    Economics in Action*, 105
Bartley, Robert, 104
Batra, Ravi, 201, 207n, 221n
Blanchard, Olivier, 242n
Blau, Lucie R., 242n
Block, Fred L., 241n
Born, Brooksley, 186
Bowles, Erskine, 138
Branden, Barbara, 142n
Beardstown Ladies Investment
    Club, 41
Bear, Stearns & Co., 57
Beck, Rachel, 31n
Beckner, Steven K., 142n
Belski, Brian, 20
Bentsen, Lloyd, 129–31, 134
Bergman, Ingrid, 39
Bernstein, Jared, 31n, 208n, 222n,
    306n
  *The State of Working
    America*, 31n, 208n, 222n,
    306n
Beta, 165
Black Thursday, 170
Blinder, Alan, 129, 137
Bloomberg, Michael R., 244
Boesky, Ivan, 139
Bohnsack, Ken, 294n
Bonds
  the bellwether Treasury, 39,
    203
  class holdings and, 22

COLA bonds, 278–80
coupon, 34, 38
and financial fragility, 7
as a fixed-income security, 41
growth of financial industry
    debt from new, 251
historical role of, 154
holding period for, 7
importance of capital gains, 154
inflation and prices of, 155–6
long-term, 40, 281
the market and, 18
maturities of, 39
price determination of, 249–51
price volatility of, 7, 41–2,
    149–55, 165, 167, 202–4
speculative derivatives and, 7
stocks and prices of, 160–1
volatility of yields of, 150–3
yields of, 151
zero-coupon bonds, 278
see also securitization
Bondholding class, the, 23
  and bond prices, 249–50
  benefits from budget deficits
    and national debt, 290–1
  and diminishing propensities
    to consume, 253
  and economic seepage, 252–3
  and the financial-economic
    history of the final quarter of
    the twentieth century, 68
  social purpose of, 34
  standard deviations and prices
    of, 150–1
  as claimants of the *angels'
    share* of savings, 232–4, 238
  bailout of Long-Term Capital
    Management Fund and, 187
  conditions for its ascent, 102

Bowie, David, 178
Brockway, George, *x*
 Bankers' COLA (cost of living
  adjustment), 263–5, 268,
  273–4*n*
 The End of Economic Man, *x*
Brown, William, 59
Bruck, Connie, 122*n*
Budget Reconciliation Act of
 1997, 138, 141
Buffet, Warren, 23, 35, 183, 233,
 236
Bullish markets,
 definition of, 150
 see also Goldilocks economy
Bureau of Labor Statistics (BLS)
  consumer expenditure
  surveys, 253–4
 see also saving(s)

Cadette, Walter M., 287, 294*n*
Campeau Corporation, 175
Canterbery, Ray E., 84*n*, 120*n*,
 189*n*, 240–1*n*, 256*n*, 294*n*
Capital asset pricing model, 109–10
Capital gains
 contributions to net
  worth, 231–3
 derivatives and, 168
 exclusion from the measured
  savings, 230–2
 importance to bondholding
  class, 278
 long-term benefits, 280
 national savings and, 280
 real output versus, 232
 see also saving(s)
Capital gains taxes
 agenda of bondholders
  and, 277

excessive fear of, 280
and New Democrats, 280
in Republican party
 literature, 37
Capitalism, 2
 benefits and detractions of, 243
 and democracy, 276
 flexibility of, 246
 see also Casino Effect; financial
  casino; Wall Street
Carroll, Lewis
 *Alice's Adventures in
  Wonderland*, 17
Carter, Jimmy, 89
 and the Credit Control Act of
  1969, 95
 deregulation and, 176
 and Volcker's
  appointment, 89
Carville, James, 8, 209
 *We're Right, They're Wrong: a
  Handbook for Spirited
  Progressives*, 209
Casino Effect, the, *xi*, 243–5
 wealth and, 245
Caskie, Max, *xi*
*Challenge: The Magazine of Economic
  Affairs*, *ix*
Chase Manhatten Government
 Securities, Inc., 56
Chevy Chase Country Club, the
 Widows of, 33, 37
Citicorp (Citigroup), 176–7
 merger, 183–4
Citron, Robert, 190–1*n*
Clark, Lindley H. Jr., 81
Class of '43, 124–5
 see also The Collective
Classical economics
 on interest rates, 248

as a rentier, 61
reform of, 270–3
reporting of the money
supply, 81–2
and rho leakage, 254
treatment of inflation, 78, 291
Wall Street and, 87–9
on wealth inequalities, 303–4
see also Greenspan, Alan;
expectations; fed funds rate;
financial reform measures;
inflation; Long-Term Capital
Management Fund; NAIRU
Fed Watchers, The, 59–60
Fetterman, Mindy, 220n
Filardo, Andrew J., 274n
Financial assets
capital gains from
and lower tax rates, 67; and
the "rich", 210–11, 215–19
financial casino and, 178, 231
and inequality, 21
market liquidity and, 173–4
as a measure of economic
well-being, 17, 193
the paradox of saving and, 235
prices of, 19, 20
volatility of, 201–3
secondary markets and the
savings illusion, 235–8, 240
see also financial casino
Financial casino, the
certified by Alan Greenspan, 299
comparative prices in, 244
and the domination of
markets, 243
and economic seepage, 252
gap between real economy
and, 231
Internet bubble and, 298–9

speculative asset prices and, 245,
298–9
and tax policy, 290
see also financial assets;
financial markets strategy
Financial markets strategy, 131
see also bond market strategy
Financial reform measures
COLA bonds, 278–80
for the Federal Open Market
Committee (FOMC), 272–3
for the Federal Reserve
System, 270–3
financial transactions tax on
speculators, 280–3
interest-free loans for
infrastructure, 283–90
federal investment budget
and, 289; the Guernsey
experiment with, 287;
history of, 286–7; The
Jerome Levy Economics
Institute's proposal for, 287;
President Lincoln's creation
of, 286; as new fiscal policy,
298; New Zealand's
experience with, 286–7;
Sovereignty's proposal for, 287
progressive taxation, 290–3
the Tobin Tax, 280
zero-coupon bonds, 77–8
Financial transactions tax, 280–3,
291
see also financial reform
measures; Tobin Tax
Fisher, Irving, 82, 166n
on inflation expectations, 267
Fitzgerald, F. Scott, 28, 302
The Great Gatsby, 33, 164
Fleming, Michael J., 241n, 167n

Great Crash of 1929, the, 4, 170,
  172, 183, 246
Great Depression, The, 4, 206,
  246, 286
Great Gatsby, The (Fitzgerald), 33,
  164
Great Monetarist Experiment,
  the, 93–100, 263
  see also monetarism
Greenspan, Alan, *x*, 1–3, 8, 142*n*,
  166*n*, 207*n*
  antitrust enforcement,
    Microsoft and, 126
  Ayn Rand and, 124–5
  the *bond market strategy*
    and, 120, 161, 298
  as chief economic advisor in the
    Ford administration, 125
  the Clinton Adminstration
    agenda and, 123–4, 127–34
  "Committee to Save the
    World" member, 295
  derivatives and, 169, 179–89
    deregulation of, 187–9,
    301–2; *see also* derivatives
  embraces the bond market
    ideology, 129
  expectations created by, 169,
    296, 298–9
  on indexation and the bankers'
    COLA, 264–5
  the federal budget deficit and,
    128, 135
  during global financial meltdown,
    295–6
  Greenspanspeak and, 63, 204
  and inflation policies, 26–8,
    53, 193–5, 202–4, 213
  influence of, 47–8, 62, 295

  irrational exuberance and, 28,
    161, 170, 202–3
  legacy of, 140
  Lincoln Savings & Loan
    collapse and, 175–6
  monetarism and, 79–80
  Nixon's presidential campaign
    and, 125
  Pope of Wall Street, the,
    25–6, 48, 194, 297
  pre-emptive monetary action
    and, 156–7
  radical ideology of, 124–6
  rescue of Long-Term Capital
    Management Fund and,
    182–7
  see also Long-Term Capital
    Management Fund
    and the Reserve's army of
    the unemployed, 195
  Testimony in 1992, 27
  Testimony before the Senate
    Committee on Banking,
    Housing, and Urban
    Affairs, 259
  Wall Street connections, 90
  see also Federal Reserve
    System; Federal Open Market
    Committee; Sacred College
    of Bonds and Money
Greider, William, 101*n*, 121*n*
Gross Domestic Product (GDP), 10
  measurement of by the Commerce
    Department, 231–2, 235
  correlation with the growth of
    the S&P 500, 232
Group of Eight industrialized
  countries (G8), 62
Guernsey, 287
Gyohten, Toyoo, 101*n*

Interest-free loans
 ability of the Federal Reserve to mitigate, 288
 authority to create, 285, 288
 history of, 286–7
 as a tool for fiscal policy, 289–90
 as a way to fund public investment, 284–6
 as a way to increase the money supply, 285
 see also financial reform measures
International Business Machines Corporation (IBM)
 "bond fire" sale, the, 94
 see also bond market, collapse of
International Monetary Fund (IMF), 93, 188
 reform of, 300–1
Investment
 net fixed investment, 226
 real investment
  cash flows and, 247; definition of, 226; driven by consumer demand, 235–7; as a measure of real saving, 226, 229, 235, 239; and the multiplier effect, 238–9; and Say's law, 234–5
Investment banking
 consolidation, 57
 Russian currency crisis and, 55
Invisible Hand, the
 definition of, 72
Irving Securities, Inc., 57

Jazz Age, the, 6, 17, 164, 173
Jerome Levy Institute, 287–8

Joint Economic Committee, the, 272
Johnson Lyndon B., 209
Jones, David, 302
Jones, Homer, 82–3, 92
 see also the Friedman–Jones principles
Jorion, Philippe, 191*n*
J.P. Morgan & Co., 54, 182–3, 304
Junk bonds, 87
 downsizing and recovery from, 196
 takeovers and, 168
 stock market crash and, 174–5
 see also Milkin, Michael

Keating, Charles, 175
Kellner, Irvin, 59
Kemp, Jack, 140
Kemp–Roth bill, 107
 see also Economic Recovery Act of 1981
Kennedy, John F, 37, 209
 steel price action, 48
 leakage and growth rates during era of, 254
Keynes, John Maynard, 84*n*, 242*n*
 on demand driven economics, 73–4
 effective demand and, 74, 226
 on full employment, 74
 General Theory of Employment, Interest, and Money, 74
 on government intervention, 72, 74
 on interest rates and investment, 251
 on the propensities to consume and to save, 237

on saving and investment,
73–4, 226–7, 239
view of secondary markets,
248–9
Keynesian Policy, 90, 93
and the fed funds rate, 91–3
King, Mervyn, 303
Kohlberg Kravis Roberts, & Co.
(KKR), 114–15
Korn, S., 166*n*
Krieger, Sandy
managing Federal Reserve
open market operations, 260–1
Kristol, Irving, 105
Krueger, A.B., 167*n*

Laffer, Arthur B.
and Reaganomics, 104
Laffer Curve, the, 104
Laissez faire, 4
and the invisible hand, 72
definition of, 72
in practice, 69
Lamont, Thomas W., 170
Lanston, Aubrey G., 302
Latin American financial crisis,
171–2, 185, 199–200
Lauren, Ralph, 19
Lazard Frères & Co., 137–8, 304
Lehman Brothers Inc., 305
Levitt, Arthur, 186
Leisure class, the, 5
Lerner, Abba, *viii*
Leveraged buyouts (LBOs), 113
Levy, S. Jay, 287–8, 294*n*
Limbaugh, Rush, 102
The Way Things Ought to Be, 102
Liquidity, 11
Litner, John, 109
Locked in the Cabinet (Reich), 123

Long-Term Capital Management
Fund, 29, 174
bailout by Fed, 181–187, 204
see also Federal Reserve System;
Federal Reserve Bank of New
York; Greenspan, Alan

Madness of crowds, the, 170, 173
Malabre, Alfred L. Jr., 79–81, 83,
84–5*n*, 120*n*
Malkiel, Burton G., 153, 166*n*
Mankevich, John, 212
Marathon Oil Company, 115
Marson, Rich, 212
Mayer, Martin, 190*n*
McDonough, William, 183, 181
see also Long-Term Capital
Management Fund; New York
Federal Reserve Bank
McGee, Suzanne, 165*n*
McJoynt, Patricia S., 190*n*
"Masters of the Universe", the 182
Media, the
and supply-side economics, 103–5
Meriwether, John, 182
see also Long-Term Capital
Management Fund; New York
Federal Reserve Bank
Merrill Lynch, 54, 150, 182–3, 215
Merrill Lynch Government Securities,
Inc., 57
Merton, Robert, 182
see also Long-Term Capital
Management Fund
Meyer, Laurence H., 137
Microsoft
antitrust suit, 126
Middle class, the
in the USX Tower, 212, 214
Milkin Institute, The, 142

and secondary financial
markets, 235–8, 240
various definitions of, 228–32
Savings & Loan bailout, 188
Say, J.B., 225
Say's law, 73, 106, 133, 234–5
Schmitt, Bernard A., 294n
Schmitt, John, 208n, 222n, 306n
　The State of Working America,
　　31n, 208n, 222n, 306n
Schroeder, Michael, 191n
Schuman, Stan, 305
Secondary market, the, 39–41, 44,
　148–9, 154
　domination in determining
　　bond prices, 249–50
　and the Keynesian view on
　　interest rates, 248
　and liquidity, 249
　and securitization, 250–1
　speculative nature of, 41, 44
Securities and Exchange Commission,
　the (SEC), 174, 186
Seepage from the economy
　sources of, 252–4
　see also Powers, Treval C.;
　　alpha leakage; rho leakage
"Seven fat years" the, 210
Sinatra, Frank, 162
Sharpe, William, 109
Shaw, David, 305
Skidmore, Dave, 143n, 208n
Sloan, Alan, 1
Smirlock, M., 166n
Smith, Adam, 84n, 99
　classical economics and, 72
　and ideology, 68–9
　the invisible hand and, 72
　laissez-faire and, 72

on money supply and the
　price level, 251
philosophy of in contrast with
　1980s, 74–5
primary financial markets and,
　248–9
on savings and investment,
　72–3, 225
Smith Barney, 54
　see also Salomon Smith Barney
　　Holdings
Solow, Robert, *viii–ix, xi*
Soros, George, 305
Speculation
　asset prices and, 245
　bubble, 4
　　in Internet stocks, 11,
　　298–9
　derivatives, 184–6
　reform tax on, 280–3
　see also Casino effect;
　　derivatives; financial assets;
　　stock market crashes and
　　mini-crashes; Tobin Tax
Sohn, Sung Won, 204
Sommers, Albert T., 242n
Sovereignty, 287
Spinello, John, 150
Sprinkel, Beryl, 80
Stagflation, 96
Stewart, James B., 122n
Stewart, Rod, 178
Stockman, David, 107
Stock market, the
　crashes and mini-crashes in U.S.,
　　18, 19, 170–3, 175, 202
　in Japan, 201
　record levels in U.S., 28
　see also systemic market failure